THE SOUTHERN PACIFICS

BULLEID'S RADICAL DESIGN

THE
SOUTHERN
PACIFICS

BULLEID'S RADICAL DESIGN

ROGER J. MANNION

SUTTON PUBLISHING

First published in 1998 by
Sutton Publishing Limited
Phoenix Mill · Thrupp · Stroud · Gloucestershire GL5 2BU

Reprinted 1999

A catalogue record for this book is available from the British Library

ISBN 0 7509 1734 2

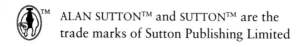
Typeset in 10/13pt Sabon.
Typesetting and origination by
Sutton Publishing Limited.
Printed in Great Britain by
Butler & Tanner, Frome, Somerset.

CONTENTS

The inspiration behind the 'Merchant Navy' and Light Pacifics, Oliver Vaughan Snell Bulleid.

National Railway Museum, York

PREFACE AND ACKNOWLEDGEMENTS

The Bulleid Pacifics were always an enigma, displaying what, on the face of it, would seem to be obvious engineering problems that any half-decent engineer should have foreseen. But is this really the case? With the benefit of hindsight it is very easy to make criticisms and condemn out of hand a truly radical design, but we are fortunate enough to have the aid of computational sciences, fluid dynamics and the instant virtual representation of problems, with attendant solutions, without the difficulties of metal cutting and complicated design work on a drawing board. Today who can use a slide rule, or would even recognize one?

The fact is that Bulleid faced a number of additional pressures which may have influenced his designs, not least a world war that could have seen the end of Great Britain as we know it. Against this background Bulleid attempted to provide a locomotive that would create fewer problems of maintenance and make driving less awesome. No doubt it could be argued that he was unwise to attempt such a radical change at that time, but then Bulleid was always the innovator. If nothing else, the locomotives proved to be a catalyst for future designs and were a step ahead of the basic Stephenson locomotive concepts which had been in existence since the beginning of the railways.

I have tried to view the decisions that were made from a slightly different angle and with additional information that may have not been previously available, I hope with some success. I first saw an unrebuilt Bulleid Pacific during the last years of Southern steam. I can remember being totally surprised by the different shape and the funny wheels, but some minutes later when the electric train I was travelling on was overtaken at considerable speed by this strange machine I started to appreciate and like this particular class of locomotive. Saying that, I have never been completely sure how I feel about it – my heart wants to admire it, but the engineer in me demands to criticize the seeming errors of judgement in the design. The Bulleid Pacific will always be a contradiction but one with such power and panache!

As with any project of this nature a number of people have helped, given succour and contributed with kindness and enthusiasm. I would like to thank Phil Atkins and Ed Bartholomew at the National Railway Museum for help with the technical and photographic research; Hugh Davis and Colin Stacey for assistance with the picture research; and Hugh Madgin for the data on the preserved scene.

Finally, thanks are due to Tricia for her support and also to the boys in our lives, Matthew and Tristram, neither of whom wants to be an engine driver when they grow up! As always any errors in the text are mine and not the responsibility of the contributors.

The last word I believe should go to a very young enthusiast at a recent steam gala who, on seeing a Bulleid Pacific under steam for the first time ever, shouted with total pleasure and happiness, 'It is awesome!' If the Bulleid design can still do this today there cannot be too much wrong.

Roger Mannion
February 1998

An impressive departure as 'Battle of Britain' No. 34083 *605 Squadron* leaves Victoria in 1957 with the sanders in operation.

Norman Simmons, Hugh Davies Collection

A 'MERCHANT NAVY'
IN ESSEX

The weather is cold and the November sky is grey and dismal as we approach the car park for the Colne Valley Railway at Castle Hedingham. The damp and the cold immediately strike as we make our way along the footpath to the Down platform of what was the old Colne Valley & Halstead Railway (swallowed up in 1924 by the LNER, which was itself taken over by British Railways in 1948).

The platform furniture and the buildings are very much Victorian, albeit refurbished, and in the cold and gloom we can almost see the passengers of that

No. 35010 *Blue Star* awaiting to be rebuilt and steamed again at the Colne Valley Railway in December 1997.

long-gone era waiting for the trains to take them on some further adventure in their lives. The combination of the weather and time of year creates a powerful atmosphere: one of sadness but also of hope for the future. The platform track is full of quiet and empty carriages, some Pullman sets awaiting maintenance and a teak-sided Gresley coach, all seeming out of place at a small country station.

At the end of the platform buildings we turn right towards what used to be the station yard. In front on the first length of siding is what we have come to see, a very large Pacific, without a tender and painted overall in black. A Bulleid 'Merchant Navy' class, No. 35010 *Blue Star*, a rebuilt member of the class, stands on the overgrown siding in a very forlorn and unhappy condition. The locomotive almost looks embarrassed, as if this once-proud engine feels shame at its current condition and should be hidden away under cover to protect itself from prying eyes.

Closer views show that while there is a lot to be done to bring this leviathan of power and style back to life some of the old pride still exists. We can almost feel that the station and the waiting coaches at the platform edge are urging the locomotive to come to life, that the coaches are waiting to be hauled and formed up behind this powerful locomotive.

As we turn away, having admired the lines of this superb design of Pacific, it becomes apparent to us all that one day this locomotive will once again come alive, and in so doing will, as in the past, give many people a great deal of happiness; in turn the locomotive itself will no longer feel embarrassed but will be proud of not only the past but also the future.

CHAPTER ONE

A NEW BEGINNING

Early June 1934 brought a surprise to the commuters of King's Cross, as Sir Nigel Gresley's P2 class 2–8–2 locomotive arrived for trials and test runs on the route to Peterborough. Apart from the sheer size, which was awesome, the shape and style of the locomotive were completely different from those that had gone before.

The P2, No. 2001 *Cock o' the North*, was a highly innovative design and was the forerunner of many new designs on the London & North Eastern Railway (LNER). The locomotive had three cylinders, as did all of Gresley's large locomotives, and as a departure from his previous designs was fitted with Lentz poppet-valves actuated by rotary cam gear. The cam boxes for the valve gear were fitted on the outside of both mainframes and driven by worm gear actuated by return cranks fitted to crankpins on the second coupled axle.

The smokebox was fitted with twin blastpipes directed into a Kylchap double chimney, which, while improving the boiler's ability to steam, invariably created the need for a complete review of the outline for the locomotive. Consequently, detailed work was carried out at the City and Guilds College of Engineering to produce the correct shape for the smokebox, and the size and design of smoke deflector plates. The results were a highly original shape to the front of the engine. The smokebox was fitted with a sloping top starting some three-quarters of the way above running-board level and stretching to behind the double chimney. Smoke deflectors were also fitted, which, while forming part of the boiler cladding at the rear and taking some of the shape of the boiler, extended forward of the smokebox at the sides and curved in at the top to form a wedge-shaped opening; this narrowed at the rear of the double chimney. The result was highly effective smoke and steam dispersal. A further innovation was the wedge-shaped cab front, which Gresley imported from France; this not only increased the view from the footplate but also helped to disperse any lingering smoke or steam.

Bulleid had been closely involved with the design of the P2 and had been a party to most of the innovative ideas put forward by Gresley. There is little doubt that he had a strong influence on the locomotive designs of the LNER. It was Bulleid who spent three weeks in France with Gresley while No. 2001 was tested at the locomotive testing plant at Vitry-sur-Seine. In 1947, in discussions about the P2 class, Bulleid was to say that *Cock o' the North* 'was not an extravagant engine at all but was in fact extremely efficient on the French testing plant and compared favourably with the French engines in her coal consumption per

'Merchant Navy' No. 35008 *Orient Line* at Salisbury shed, when it was an Exmouth Junction locomotive. Alongside is N class 2–6–0 No. 31846.

Norman Simmons, Hugh Davies Collection

drawbar-horsepower-hour. When tested on the open road between Orleans and Tours she developed a very high horsepower, of the order of 2,800, and again showed herself to be an efficient engine from the point of view of coal consumed per d.h.p-hr.' Bulleid added that 'in service she was an extravagant engine. The fundamental reason . . . was that she was not properly used, . . . with the result that she showed a heavy coal consumption, most of the coal being burnt through misuse rather than working trains.'

So it was, against this background of engineering innovation, that Bulleid formally became the Chief Mechanical Engineer (CME) for the Southern Railway (SR) on 1 October 1937. Bulleid's latter time at the LNER had been as assistant to the CME, working very closely with Sir Nigel Gresley. The Gresley–Bulleid combination made a strong team and produced some superb designs. How much of Gresley's success can be put down to Bulleid's sparkling ideas is uncertain but Gresley's firm control over Bulleid's highly original ideas produced a very innovative and successful partnership. During his tenure at the Southern Bulleid was without this restraint and became the lord of all he surveyed – with some sensational results.

The SR's previous CME, R.E.L. Maunsell, had been in less than perfect health for a number of years and on 28 May 1937 an official announcement was made about his impending retirement. This coincided with the retirement of the General Manager of the SR, Sir Herbert Walker. Walker and the Board were very concerned about making the right choice for the new CME and while he did not know it Bulleid had been shortlisted. The fact that he was finally considered to be the ideal candidate for the job had much to do with the advocacy of Gilbert Szlumper, Assistant General Manager and the son of the builder of Waterloo station. Bulleid received a letter from Walker to present himself at Waterloo for a meeting and there Walker told him that as no appointment had been made to replace Maunsell he wanted Bulleid to apply. Bulleid was advised to consult his own General Manager, Sir Ralph Wedgwood, who then told him 'it is a mere formality, the job is yours'. Bulleid was totally surprised as he had considered that having been Gresley's assistant for so long the job was more or less permanent, and no doubt it was also in his thoughts that he might eventually take over when Gresley retired.

On 9 June 1937 Maunsell took Bulleid on a tour of inspection around the works with the directors, thus showing the staff the new heir apparent. On 20 September Bulleid installed himself at Waterloo, giving sufficient time for Maunsell, who formally retired at the end of October, to show Bulleid the ropes. With the retirement of Maunsell, Walker also left and Szlumper was appointed in his place. Szlumper while appreciating Walker's views on the continuing needs for electrification of the SR, also understood and ultimately supported Bulleid's views on the need for urgent steam traction improvements. So the stage was set for the highly significant and radical changes in steam locomotion which were to have such an important impact on the future of the SR and also to a certain extent the nationalized British Railways locomotive design.

Oliver Vaughan Snell Bulleid was born at Invercargill in New Zealand on 19 September 1882. His father, William, was a successful importing agent and founder of the firm Price & Bulleid. During a business visit to England in 1878, William met his future wife, Marianne Vaughan Pugh, an old friend from his youth, at a music soirée in London. They were married within a month and returned to New Zealand in the autumn of that year. The marriage was happy and contented, and young Oliver was to inherit his father's sense of adventure, independence and financial talent.

The extent of this inheritance was illustrated during the five-year-old's first visit to the Invercargill Races, the major social event of the year. Prior to the family's departure the young Bulleid disappeared and after much effort and consternation the family left without him. When they arrived at the course Mrs Bulleid noticed her son busy washing glasses at the back of the refreshment room, thereby making pocket money for himself! 'I discreetly looked the other way, said not another word and steered your father in another direction,' she recounted afterwards. 'Washing up was not the work for young gentlemen.'

William Bulleid died suddenly in 1889 at the age of forty-three and it left Oliver's mother devastated. Less than a year later the family returned to Mrs Bulleid's home town of Llanfyllin, Montgomeryshire. At that time the Pugh family still lived in one of the larger houses of the town. They were held in high esteem for it was Oliver's great-great grandfather, John Pugh, who had brought the railway to the town as a branch line to Llanymynech, part of the Oswestry & Newtown Railway, on 17 July 1863. (The railway was absorbed by the Cambrian Railways in 1864 and ultimately became part of the Great Western Railway (GWR).)

During Oliver's time at the family home he was marked out as a brilliant scholar and he was constantly seeking more knowledge. Private tuition in Latin, bookkeeping, commerce and geography still did not satisfy his thirst for knowledge. Llanfyllin at that time had a number of skilled craftsmen and Oliver enjoyed spending time with them, listening, watching and learning. He would help David the cobbler with the thread, Jack the gas to keep up the pressure, Tom the blacksmith with his ironwork and would ask David the joiner to make him yet another top. Oliver was noted as being happy with his own company, brave and curious and always stressing his independence. He was seen as a dreamer who combined a deep reserve with unusual charm and graceful manners.

In 1892, due to the machinations of his mother's older sister Janet Sandeman, a very dominant woman, Bulleid was sent to Spa College, a preparatory school in Stirlingshire, where he endured the harsh discipline and Spartan conditions with stoicism. At the end of his final year at Spa his aunt again made plans for the young Oliver, insisting that he continue his education at Accrington Technical School while staying with her family. Again Oliver was forced to hide his true feelings with a degree of stoicism. The move ensured his success, but one wonders at what cost.

During his time at the technical college Bulleid learned English, Latin, geography, French, history, applied maths, pure maths, art, chemistry and physics, and was at or near the top of his class in all these subjects. In 1899 he passed the London Matriculation in the First Division and at seventeen left Accrington Technical School.

While he lived with his aunt and uncle he became a competent musician, taught by his aunt, and also gained further exposure to the world of engineering. His uncle had a well-equipped workshop complete with a number of sophisticated tools, including a lathe. It was here that Bulleid, with the help of his cousin Vaughan, built a number of operational model guns; one of them, with a bore of .303, began to throw lead shells across the local reservoir, landing in a private garden beyond. At that point his uncle was constrained to force the boys to cease!

Following Bulleid's departure from the technical school the family again took a hand in his future, deciding that he should make his way in the legal profession in New Zealand with one of his father's friends from Devon. It was also agreed that Bulleid should travel with his mother to Tilbury via Doncaster and stay with another member of the family, Revd Edgar Lee, Vicar of Christ Church.

By this time Bulleid, while attracted to engineering, was still undecided about his future and was remarkably open to suggestions from his family. He was a non-smoker and teetotaller, with no discernible vices, a young man who had inherited his father's sense of adventure and independence coupled with impeccable manners. In addition he had his own attributes of a quick brain, a love of craftsmanship, individualism and inventiveness, and sensitivity to the

'Battle of Britain' No. 34049 *Anti-Aircraft Command* passing Farnborough with a West of England express. Note the superb lower quadrant signals.

Bob Barnard, Hugh Davies Collection

feelings of others. At the same time he was self-reliant, introspective and did not often show his true feelings. He would talk freely but his laughter was not heartfelt, and while he rarely lost his temper his expression was always enigmatic. He viewed his world from on high and while he always welcomed visitors to his world would rarely come down to other worlds. He was a young man who was deeply affected by having lost his father and been torn from his mother.

Revd Edgar Lee was a High Anglican, approaching Catholicism, a musician of talent and dominant in his relationships. He was to be a catalyst in Bulleid's own conversion to Rome. Among his parishioners at Christ Church and a firm friend was the Locomotive Superintendent of the Great Northern Railway's Doncaster Works, Henry Alfred Ivatt. The thought that Bulleid should be committed to spending his life in New Zealand filled Revd Lee with outrage and as a result he suggested to Ivatt that maybe he could take on Bulleid as a premium apprentice at Doncaster.

Most railway apprenticeships were reserved for sons of skilled craftsmen employed at the works but a restricted number of outsiders were accepted for a premium of £50. These young men were expected to work like ordinary apprentices and learn the skills of each of the shops. Bulleid was at a disadvantage being, at eighteen, some two years older than the normal starting age. However, he attended an interview with Ivatt on 13 November 1900. Both were impressed with the other, Bulleid seeing Ivatt as someone with an outstanding presence, who could be trusted and admired. The Register of Apprentices at Doncaster recorded that 'Mr Ivatt consents to this youth starting at Easter, 1901, and to serve for four years from that date'. Thus it was that the future CME of the SR commenced his engineering career.

Bulleid's background had given him the drive to be successful and by January 1907 he had become the assistant to the Locomotive Works Manager. Over the next year he made a significant impression at the works, driven no doubt by personal ambition but perhaps also by his desire to marry Marjorie Ivatt, the daughter of Henry Ivatt. In this he faced strong opposition, it has to be said, from both families. However, Bulleid accepted an offer of employment as Chief Draughtsman and Assistant Works Manager at the Freinville Works of the French Westinghouse Company near Paris. With a salary of £218 per year – enough, it was considered, to keep a middle-class wife in tolerable comfort – parental objections were overruled and the couple were married at Christ Church in November 1908.

In the following years Bulleid remained in Europe, becoming Mechanical and Electrical Engineer for the Board of Trade at the Brussels and Turin trade exhibitions. Finally, in 1911 he returned to Doncaster to rejoin the Great Northern Railway (GNR) where Nigel Gresley had become Locomotive Carriage and Wagon Superintendent. Gresley took on Bulleid as his personal assistant, thus starting a partnership which spanned more than a quarter of a century, including when Gresley became CME of the LNER. This period had a significant effect on Bulleid and was a major influence on his future designs for the SR.

In 1937, at the time of Bulleid's appointment as CME, the SR was still carrying out significant electrification of both the suburban and longer-distance services. Consequently, steam traction had taken a definite second place. Concurrent with this was the increase in loadings, as the country started to move out of the Depression years, particularly the boat-trains to the south and express services to the West of England. The current steam locomotive stock was becoming worn and unable to deal with the expansion in loadings and services, but at the same time there were severe financial constraints on the building or purchase of new steam traction. Major investment was instead being directed towards electrification. Thus Bulleid was faced with a serious motive power problem.

The difficulties for Bulleid were both historical and the result of the size of the SR, it being the smallest of the four grouped companies. By 1937 the SR was predominantly a passenger carrier, in particular providing suburban services out of and into the major conurbations of London and the South. It was also the most financially successful of the four railway companies, paying a dividend to its shareholders of nearly 5 per cent. Southampton was built up as the major passenger port of the country and electric services were expanded into the countryside of Kent, Surrey, Sussex and Hampshire, allowing the workers of London to move further away from the centre of congestion. In 1936 the number of electric train miles exceeded those of steam train miles. The SR gained a reputation for reliability, frequency, comfort and presentation.

When Bulleid arrived at Waterloo his first step was to review and write a report on the locomotive stock of the SR. By so doing he hoped to convince John Elliot,

'Battle of Britain' No. 34067 *Tangmere* with an Up train consisting of Hastings stock approaching Hildenborough in 1957.

Norman Simmons, Hugh Davies Collection

the Assistant General Manager, of the need for a new building programme. The then present stock of locomotives was aged to say the least and at the same time the SR was reaching the geographical limits of economical electrification. Consequently, if the provision of the heavier and longer-distance services was not to falter or break down altogether then something had to be done. Bulleid commented in the report: 'If you replace half a cavalry regiment with tanks this does not make the horses any younger.'

In the short term Bulleid was able to make some improvements to existing stock, through experience gained from personal footplate runs. These led to the improved front end and exhaust for Maunsell's 'Lord Nelson' class, as well as for some of the 'Schools' and 'King Arthur' class locomotives. But in the longer term a new building programme was the only answer.

Bulleid's charm, persistence and powers of persuasion enabled him to gain agreement for a modernization of the steam locomotive fleet. His first designs were for a fast mixed traffic locomotive with a 4–8–2 wheel arrangement, designed to have good acceleration, good route availability, a speed capacity to meet 75 m.p.h. timings and to be suitable for both goods and passenger traffic. This concept was modified and a 2–8–2 design was substituted. The civil engineer, George Ellson, was less than impressed and put forward serious objections until the pony truck was changed to a Helmholtz arrangement. To be fair to Ellson, his objections were based on the emotions generated by a tragic accident when a 'River' class tank engine was derailed at speed. Bulleid did eventually win agreement to produce a pair of 2–8–2 locomotives, but he believed that they would have difficulty in being accepted and consequently produced a new proposal for a 4–6–2 Pacific. This was a much more acceptable alternative. The new design became the 'Merchant Navy' class, a class which was to have a considerable impact on the SR.

The design of the Bulleid Pacifics was radical to say the least. Much of the design could be considered controversial but when examined more closely some areas were based on sound engineering decisions. Typical of this were the Bulleid Firth Brown (BFB) wheels, clasp brakes and steel firebox. Other parts of the design need closer examination and consideration for what, on the face of it, could be seen as fairly fundamental errors of judgement.

A great deal has been written about the Bulleid Pacifics and in particular the airsmoothed casing and chain-driven valve gear. While these aspects of the Pacifics are discussed in more detail later, it should be remembered that there were significant pressures on designers to improve availability and cut costs. Furthermore, in view of the knowledge at the time, were Bulleid's designs really that radical?

To put the chain-driven valve gear in context, it is worth noting that in 1940 Gresley had proposed a revised layout for the conjugated valve gear on his A4s. This was based on his original design but with an oil-tight housing containing the valve gear immersed in an oil bath. It is believed that Bulleid's original arrangement used gears immersed in an oil bath and driven by a propeller shaft somewhat similar to the successful Lentz poppet-valves fitted to the LNER P2 No. 2001, but this had to be changed owing to wartime restrictions on supplies.

The airsmoothed casing has always been stated as being designed to allow the locomotive to pass through the carriage-cleaning plant. However, at the time of the design's conception the chairman of the SR, Mr R. Holland-Martin, known behind his back as RHM, envied the publicity gained from both the LNER and the London Midland & Scottish Railway (LMS) because of the streamlined services. RHM was something of an eccentric, with a habit of losing papers, driving an ancient, open two-seater car – badly and very fast, and always having pockets full of what he called gadgets, which intrigued him. All these certainly made him a less than orthodox company chairman. Perhaps airsmoothed was a synonym for streamlined to encourage a positive response from the Board of Trade inspectors when wartime approval was sought to build the locomotives. The inspectors were likely to have a very jaundiced view of any unnecessary extras which would divert important wartime supplies from front-line requirements, nonetheless it was mandatory to have their permission before going ahead with the project. In any case Holland-Martin was certainly very interested in gaining some of the publicity for his company and, rightly, streamlining was considered a suitable vehicle for this.

Against this background maybe the designs were not so radical or erroneous in concept. It is also possible that Bulleid was a victim of the times, when lesser designs had to be substituted for the original ideas owing to wartime shortages. Perhaps also his upbringing, which encouraged him to be self-reliant and less than comfortable with opening himself to others, had an effect on the way his

'West Country' No. 34106 *Lydford* with a Waterloo to Weymouth train at Southampton Central on 16 May 1954.

M.H. Walshaw, Hugh Davies Collection

locomotives developed. From this distance in time it is difficult to see into Bulleid's mind but surely any designer transfers some of their personality into their work; if this were the case with the Southern Pacifics then Bulleid was a very special designer. He was to say about other engineering designs that they were, 'a good idea later seen to have been carried out imperfectly owing to a lack of mechanical know-how at the time', though 'an idea deserving development'. Perhaps this should be the epitaph for the Bulleid Pacifics?

CHAPTER TWO

PACIFICS ON THE SOUTHERN

The SR was the smallest of the railway companies at the Grouping and at the same time did not have a constituent company of the ilk of the Great Northern or Midland Railway. All in all the SR was an understated and genteel railway being predominantly a passenger carrier, with commuters and holidaymakers providing the main traffic.

The constituent companies of the SR at the Grouping were the London & South Western Railway (LSWR); the London, Brighton & South Coast Railway (LBSCR); the South Eastern & Chatham Railway, which was itself the managing committee for the London, Chatham & Dover Railway (LCDR); the South Eastern Railway (SER); the small group of railways on the Isle of Wight and a few other tiny companies.

The LSWR conveyed passengers in stylish comfort to Plymouth, Exeter, Weymouth, Bournemouth, Southampton and the Isle of Wight. In addition it was able to collect a rich clientele from the Wimbledon, Richmond, Surbiton, Kingston, Ascot and Farnham areas. As the south of England's major racecourses were also part of the LSWR's routes, further income was generated from Ascot, Sandown and Hurst Park. The railway was practical and welcoming, with staff wearing red ties and guards sporting roses in their buttonholes. It was never one to produce speed records but was able to hold its head up with the major northern companies.

The LBSCR was predominantly a suburban railway, with a maximum run of 86.5 miles from London Bridge to Portsmouth. The London terminal was at Victoria with a City terminal at London Bridge. The trains were tidy and economical but largely unheated and ran to points all over south London. The company also had control over a number of seaside resorts including Hastings, Bexhill, Eastbourne, Littlehampton, Bognor and Southsea, plus the service from Newhaven to Dieppe. The LBSCR spent much time and energy playing off its neighbours and was always spoiling for a fight. This attitude gave very little benefit to the passengers.

The other companies in the south-eastern corner of England also indulged in internecine fighting on and off for a number of years, so much so that most, if not all, of the towns in Kent and East Sussex had two, sometimes three, railway stations. This was directly due to the ambitions of both Edward Watkins of the SER and James Forbes of the LCDR. Battle after battle was fought and lost by both sides and the situation brought comfort to nobody, except possibly the music halls. The companies were able to keep going because of the rich boat-train traffic from Dover and Folkestone as well as the suburban networks and seaside resorts of Margate, Ramsgate and Hastings.

A clean 'Merchant Navy', No. 35017 *Belgian Marine*, with the 'Bournemouth Belle', passing Raynes Park during 1957.

Norman Simmons, Hugh Davies Collection

The grouping together of these diverse companies produced some interesting characteristics compared with the other big three railway companies. Not untypical was the completely different method of train identification using a complex system of headcode discs; these included up to six different positions and were carried at one to three locations, depending on the route. To further complicate the scheme the same code was used for a number of different routes, as long as they did not conflict. The seemingly perverse procedures of the constituent railways of the Southern were to bring particular difficulties to the CME, including the significant differences of loading gauge and weight allowances. The one good engineering aspect to emerge was the seeds of electrification, which were sown across the whole system by the inclusion of electric traction from the grouped companies. At the Grouping the SR inherited 24.5 miles of AC traction with overhead cables from the LBSCR and 57 miles of DC traction using a third rail from the LSWR. Both these companies had been forced into the use of electric traction because of severe competition from the London County Council's electric trams in the early 1900s, which had taken traffic away from the railways. They found that as steam traction gave way to electric, the passenger receipts started to return to previous levels.

The electrical engineer of the SR, Herbert Jones, took detailed advice from the USA regarding the most appropriate electrical traction system and the LSWR system was agreed upon. With hindsight it probably was not the best technical solution in the longer term for the SR, but by 1930 over 800 miles of suburban line had been electrified. On New Year's Day 1933 the line to Brighton was completed and in 1935 electrification reached Sevenoaks, Eastbourne, Bexhill and

Hastings. Shortly prior to Bulleid's arrival at the SR, Portsmouth was joined to London by electrified lines and one fast and two slow trains ran to the capital every hour. In addition, at the annual meeting of the company in 1937 the chairman announced a five-year plan in which over £5 million would be spent on further electrification schemes.

Against this background of changing and modernizing motive power it is a wonder that the SR considered Bulleid at all for the job of CME. His own background was completely different from that of the railway for which he was about to work. Apart from his time at Westinghouse and as the Mechanical and Electrical Engineer for the Board of Trade, Bulleid had spent his formative years with the GNR and latterly with the LNER, either directly at Doncaster Works or as the personal assistant to Gresley.

The Bulleid–Gresley partnership produced some highly innovative designs in coaching stock and wagon stock locomotives, culminating in the ultimate success of Gresley's time as CME: the A4s. Bulleid added his own special contribution to these locomotives when Gresley looked at the smokebox during the design stages and said to Bulleid that something ought to be done about the streamlining of the cylinders and running board. Bulleid went away and produced the aerofoil side valances, thus adding his own personal touch to the A4s.

During the First World War Bulleid had been involved with railway transportation in France and over that period he suffered the loss of probably his closest friend, his cousin Vaughan Sandeman, and it was possibly this loss that finally pushed Bulleid to become a member of the Catholic Church.

From 1919 until February 1923, when Gresley became CME of the LNER, Bulleid was Carriage and Wagon Superintendent at Doncaster. As such he followed Edward Thompson, who had returned to York to work with Sir Vincent Raven, one of whose daughters Thompson had married. Bulleid produced a number of innovations including the quintuple, articulated coaching sets, electric cooking equipment for restaurant cars and twin articulated sleeping cars. The respect that Bulleid held for Gresley was much heightened by his time at Doncaster. He said later: 'The carriage men were so loyal to Mr Gresley that had any change been suggested which they thought he would not like, I believe they would have refused to do it.'

Bulleid acquired extensive experience during his time with Gresley. Not only was he working within an organization which positively thrived on engineering excellence, he was also working for a man who was constantly enquiring into new areas and seemed to collect ideas like a sponge absorbing water. This could sometimes be highly irritating as Gresley never lost his attention to detail. On a journey from Glasgow to Euston in an LMS sleeping car Gresley drew Bulleid's attention to a coat-hanger which did not allow for a man's habit of taking his jacket off before his trousers. Bulleid tried to conveniently forget the conversation until, after a number of increasingly sharp reminders, he felt obliged to put forward a new design. He succeeded in designing a hanger which had the horizontal support for trousers above the curved section for jackets. This became the standard design for the LNER and was fitted to all the company's sleeping cars.

As well as being involved in the design of the A4, P2 and the booster engines for the P1 Mikados, Bulleid was an enthusiast for welded carriage underframes. An experiment was carried out, witnessed by Gresley, at the smith's shop in York. A carriage step board bracket, with the foot cropped off, was welded to a piece of scrapped carriage sole bar, a striker was then instructed to try to knock the bracket off with a large hammer. To Bulleid's intense relief the bracket held, even though it was bent right over. The result was that an experimental carriage underframe was designed. This was followed by a welded wagon; many other wagons followed, as did welded coaches. In addition three all-welded boilers were obtained from Babcock & Wilcox in 1933 and built into the J class 0–6–0.

Already it can be seen that Bulleid's experiences at the LNER were to influence his future design philosophy at the SR. It is difficult to judge exactly what part Bulleid played in Gresley's success but they made a very special team, with Gresley sitting in firm but gentle judgement on the ideas which streamed from Bulleid. Some interesting comments were made by Eric Bannister, a junior draughtsman who worked under Bert Spencer at Gresley's King's Cross office and carried out many tasks for Bulleid: 'He was an interesting person in many ways, a very nice man and interested in everything', although he did strike Bannister as being 'rather eccentric', and Bert Spencer would ask 'what other mad idea has he got?' The locomotives produced at this time were a clear indication of the talent Gresley had in picking the good ideas from the bad. In the future Bulleid would not have this restraining influence when he became the CME of the SR.

No. 34070 *Manston*, an unrebuilt 'Battle of Britain', with a Down passenger service passing south of Hildenborough station. Note the semaphore signal-post constructed out of redundant rail.

Norman Simmons, Hugh Davies Collection

With Bulleid's arrival at the SR on 1 October 1937, steam motive power on both this railway and the future British Railways changed significantly. The steam locomotive stock on the Southern was in the main elderly and less than efficient, having serious difficulties in dealing with the heavier trains of the time, including the new Pullman services, as well as the boat-trains and the West of England services. At the same time passenger receipts were increasing, not only on the suburban services but also on the longer-distance trains and, further, the economic limits of electrification were starting to be reached.

Thus Bulleid was faced with serious conflicts of views and constraints on any future designs. On the one hand the Board members were intent on furthering the electric services which produced such good financial returns. They were almost totally focused on this area of motive power. Yet it was also acknowledged that faster and heavier longer-distance services were required to meet demand; but any new design would have to fit around and contend with the fast acceleration and high frequency of electric trains across the system. Bulleid firmly believed that a new building programme was required if services were not to break down altogether. The report written by Bulleid on his arrival at Waterloo was used to impress on the Board the reality that new motive power must be provided.

Bulleid won over John Elliot, then Assistant General Manager (later Sir John Elliot, who became Chairman of the Railway Executive). His support, together with that of Gilbert Szlumper, the newly promoted General Manager, enabled Bulleid to convince a less than enthusiastic Board as to the benefit of new locomotive stock. Of course, it also helped that the SR chairman lent support to Bulleid's ideas and plans.

In the meantime Bulleid was able to apply some experiments with the existing Maunsell passenger classes. He fitted the complete 'Lord Nelson' class with the Lemaître multi-jet exhaust system, and some of the 'Schools' and 'King Arthur' class were also modified. Significant improvements were made to the steaming of these locomotives over the unmodified members of the class, with accompanying improvements in usage, although the classic shape was changed dramatically with the installation of the large diameter chimney, and not for the better. But for all the improvements, the results could only be considered as stopgap measures and new locomotive designs were essential.

Interestingly, during the period 1933 to 1934, Maunsell produced proposals for a wide firebox four-cylinder 4–6–2 design which was a development of the 'Lord Nelson' class. This was later truncated to a three-cylinder 2–6–2 scheme, but neither this nor the Pacific design found favour with the powers that be. Part of the problem with any new design was the reluctance of the civil engineer, George Ellson, to allow the use of leading pony trucks on locomotives. Ellson had suffered a nervous breakdown after the tragic accident when a 'River' class 2–6–4 tank locomotive was derailed at speed in 1927 with fatal results at Sevenoaks. Ellson had only recently taken up the post of civil engineer at the time of the accident, and Maunsell blamed the track while Ellson blamed the locomotive. In the end the track was given new ballast and the 'River' class locomotives were rebuilt as 2–6–0 tender engines.

No. 35019 *French Line C.G.T.* at Eastleigh on 6 September 1956. Nos 34030 and 30096 are in the background.

B.K.B. Green, Initial Photographic

This had long-lasting effects on the judgement of the civil engineering department, so much so that when Bulleid proposed a 2–8–2 design he was overruled and even when he modified the design of the leading pony truck the design was accepted with great reluctance. The 2–8–2 design had a boiler pressed to 220 psi and a 30 in piston stroke on the outside pistons, with a maximum axle loading of 19 tons – a design which was clearly inspired by Gresley's P2 class. In addition Bulleid produced an initial layout for a 2–6–2 design which would have been used instead of the final design for the lightweight Pacifics, but again this was frowned upon by Ellson. Around the time of the 2–8–2 design a 4–8–2 drawing was also produced, but this scheme was rejected too. The long, rigid wheelbase, the size of the coupled wheels and the fact that it was too long for the existing turntables all provoked adverse comment.

Bulleid recognized early on that a new design was needed for the heavy boat-trains on the Eastern Section of the SR, particularly the 'Night Ferry' and 'Golden Arrow' expresses, and that these same designs would have to be capable of working some of the major routes in the Western Section. A different, lighter design was required for the more restricted holiday routes on the West of England services. As a result the smaller 2–6–2 design ultimately became the 'West Country' and 'Battle of Britain' Pacifics.

Surprisingly, Bulleid obtained permission to produce two 2–8–2 locomotives which he had modified to include the fitting of the Helmholtz arrangement of pony truck. In the end Bulleid decided not to go ahead with this design as he considered it would be difficult to gain general acceptance, and as a result he pursued the Pacific design, believing this would be much more acceptable to both the civil engineer and the Board.

The Pacific designs were originally considered for the heavy boat-trains between Victoria and Dover but became the standard express locomotives where heavy, high-speed services were provided. On 22 March 1938 the Southern Railway Rolling Stock Committee gave authority for twenty new main line steam locomotives to be constructed, from an original request for thirty. This decision was formally approved by the Locomotive and Electrical Committee on 30 March. The cost estimate was for £110,000. The design of these locomotives was yet to be defined but Bulleid had outlined that the locomotive had to be capable of hauling trains of 500–600 tons at start-to-stop average speeds of 60 mph (on the Continental boat-trains) and 70 mph (on the Western Section). The outbreak of the Second World War was to interrupt the design work, with the result that the first locomotives did not appear until 1941. The original orders were Nos HO 1068 and HO 1189, both for ten locomotives. A further order, No. HO 1190, was cancelled, this being originally for twenty-five mixed traffic locomotives. There was clearly some confusion over the description of this design even when they had been built and placed into service. This confusion was apparent at the most respected of levels both in the press and within the SR. *The Locomotive Magazine* called No. 21C1 *Channel Packet* an express engine while in July 1941 the same magazine described *Union Castle* as a mixed traffic engine. At the same time an internal SR document referred to the Pacifics as express passenger engines.

While the designs were being brought together, outside events conspired to assist Bulleid in his quest to modernize the steam traction on the SR. First, events at Munich awoke the country to the inevitable: war with Germany. As this realization increased, the requirements for better and more modern steam traction were acknowledged and the Locomotive and Electrical Committee of the SR agreed to extend the original locomotive order to thirty. With the threat of war, delays to the production inevitably occurred and while Bulleid was willing to accept some standard features on his new designs, this was only subject to there being no significant delays to the final production. Unfortunately this was not the case, and Bulleid decided that as delays were going to occur he would modify the design to include original ideas of his own. This of course increased the delays.

The design work was carried out predominantly at the Brighton drawing office, but both Eastleigh and Ashford were involved and the original intention was for Eastleigh to carry out the production of the locomotives. The records and drawings indicate that there was a certain restriction of information between all of the departments within the SR, so much so that the full implications of manufacture at Eastleigh were not properly understood until quite late in the initial stages of the project. Then it was found that the manufacturing techniques

No. 35014 *Nederland Line* ex-works at Eastleigh in immaculate condition.
B.K.B. Green, Initial Photographic

and machinery were not up to the design requirements for the large high-pressure boilers and all-welded fireboxes that Bulleid had specified for the design. Consequently the initial order for the boilers was given to the North British Locomotive Company at a cost of £2,850 each. It seems that there was much secrecy about the design as neither the Rolling Stock Committee nor the Locomotive and Electrical Committee, nor indeed the civil engineer, were aware of the full extent of the design. Requests for information still being made in vain by the civil engineer as late as October 1939, some two months after the first boilers had been ordered from the North British Locomotive Company.

Fundamentally, the locomotive was a three-cylinder simple engine; however, simple it may have been but conventional it was not. The design was a total breakaway from previous locomotive design, having a host of innovative concepts. These included significant numbers of labour-saving features for the footplate crews which were all very welcome, until they started to go wrong!

The boiler on the 'Merchant Navy' Pacifics was free steaming and probably one of the best boilers to be fitted to any British steam locomotive – ever. The firebox was all welded, to save weight and money and to enable repairs to be carried out at the running sheds rather than at the works. Nicholson thermic syphons, supplied by Beyer Peacock Ltd, were fitted to assist the water circulation as well as giving some additional support to the Belpaire firebox crown. Subsequent work placed doubts on the need for the syphons, as efficiency tests showed little difference between a modified boiler without syphons and the standard boiler.

The consensus was that it was not viable to remove the syphons, but with British boiler sizes and hand firing the advantages were limited. The boiler had a total heating surface of 2,176 sq. ft and the firebox was 275 sq. ft including the syphons, giving a total evaporative surface of 2,451 sq. ft. The grate area was 48.5 sq. ft and the superheater surface measured 822 sq. ft. Altogether it was a magnificent boiler and producer of steam.

Apart from the chain-driven valve gear and the airsmoothed casing, innovations included BFB wheels which were based on the US Boxpok design and built in collaboration with Firth & Brown, the Sheffield steel makers. BFB stood for Bulleid, Firth, Brown and the design was patented in 1940.

Another innovation was the use of clasp brakes, which were able to be fitted because of the increased space (over conventional designs) between the wheels and frames. The clasp brakes gave a greater brake-block surface in contact with the wheels and also reduced the unequal thrust on the horns when only single blocks were used.

However, probably the two most original components of the Bulleid Pacifics were the airsmoothed casing and the chain-driven valve gear, of which the latter is described in more detail later in this book. But for all the criticism levelled at both of these design aspects there were sound reasons for their inclusion, and while it is easy with hindsight to find fault with the concepts, the overall considerations were sound, the intention being to lessen the workloads of crews and shed staff alike while at the same time increasing availability.

The experience that Bulleid had gained over the years indicated that the use of an alternative type of valve gear was a valid concept. Evidence suggests that Bulleid's original plan was to use gearing and a shaft drive, both of which were reasonably common on existing Continental and some British locomotive designs, the Lentz poppet-valve gear being an example. This concept, by definition, required a drive which would be immersed in some type of oil bath. The final design, though chain driven, could be considered to be due as much to the circumstances of wartime as to Bulleid's original ideas. However, previous experience from his work in the French factory of Westinghouse had shown that chain drives could be successful. All the machinery in the French factory was driven by chain rather than the belt drives used in Doncaster. Bulleid, upon his arrival at the French plant, asked how many men were made available for daily maintenance and repair of the chain system. He was told 'none'. In Doncaster it was normal for at least two men to be available for belt-drive problems. The difficulties suffered with the valve gear could be put down to the design and the available technology for the oil bath sump as much as to the valve gear itself, particularly as the effects of wear and stretch in the chain drives were compounded by the inaccuracy and inefficiency of the steam reverser, itself an innovation.

Later, when consideration was being given to the rebuilding of the Bulleid Pacifics, examples of the 'Merchant Navy' class were tested at the Rugby stationary test plant between 1952 and 1954. The reports from these tests severely criticized the enclosed chain-driven valve gear for some of the more irrational behaviour of the test locomotive. Bulleid, on hearing these comments, responded vehemently, and was totally unrepentant. He wrote:

> I have no knowledge of any locomotive Walschaerts or Stephenson valve gear giving such good valve events. The valve gear was successful. The unusually even beat of the engines, the acceleration and their high speed capabilities testify to very efficient steam distribution. I have always felt that the chain drive was not fully understood. It must be remembered that gear drive was originally planned and then discarded as too expensive, that extreme accuracy must be maintained as regards centres, and that it was not seen how the relative movement of the axle to the frame was to be dealt with. This was a case where time was too short! The flexibility of the chains overcame these difficulties. The chain drive was only part of the valve gear and as the chains were not expensive they were regarded as consumable stores. The effect of a five inch sag in the chain is negligible as regards over length and does not of itself affect the phasing of the valve events. If excessive wear did occur there still should not be any phase error as all the values would be equally affected. Any defect was to be found in front of the enclosure rather than in it. The copious lubrication ensured the maintenance of an oil film between all working parts and the oil was sufficiently great to prevent it becoming overheated. If there was an irregular beat it was usually a cylinder out of order. This cannot have been due to the chain drive, but was rather a defect in some other part of the individual cylinder valve gear and probably in the shaft operating the valve itself.

There are clearly a number of contentious issues in Bulleid's response and whether or not his view is valid can only be assessed against the evidence of the in-service behaviour of his Pacific designs.

The airsmoothed casing gave an interesting aesthetic shape to the locomotive and has always been stated as being part of the desire to ease the work on shed by enabling the locomotive to be cleaned by passing through the carriage-cleaning machinery. No records exist to show that any 'Merchant Navy', 'West Country' or 'Battle of Britain' locomotive was ever cleaned in this manner. It is accepted, however, that given Bulleid's desire to keep servicing costs down and locomotive availability high this is a feasible explanation. Consideration should also be given to the point at which the initial design was produced. At that time both the LNER and LMS had benefited from highly significant publicity from their streamlined trains that ran on a daily basis, in particular, the LNER with its world steam record gained by the A4 *Mallard*. The chairman of the SR, who was something of an eccentric, was also known to have wanted to gain some serious publicity for his company; it is possible that he saw a way of satisfying this with the radical shape of Bulleid's Pacifics and he may have even encouraged Bulleid in this area of the design. Interestingly, while Bulleid never used the term streamlined for his locomotives he did use both the description of express and mixed traffic, while the original order was for express engines.

Rebuilt 'Merchant Navy' No. 35024 *East Asiatic Company* passes Hook with the 'Bournemouth Belle' on 20 April 1960.

B.W.L. Brooksbank, Initial Photographic

The Second World War had a serious effect on the production of the Bulleid Pacifics. Eastleigh was inundated with war work and as a result was forced to pass the tender and preparation of the mainframes to Ashford. There were also difficulties with the delivery of the cylinder castings, which when they did arrive were mostly found to be defective. All these problems severely tried Bulleid's patience, but he postponed part of the order and continued with the labour and materials that were available. Consequently, on 17 February 1941 No. 21C1 steamed in the works yard and became the first Pacific to leave the works. The following day two return journeys to Winchester were made and after some adjustments other test runs were made to Brockenhurst, Basingstoke and Salisbury, the last of which included a train of sixty-three goods wagons and two brake vans.

The final cost of the first Pacific was £23,840, with an additional £11,368 debited to design and allied expenses. No. 21C2 *Union Castle* cost £20,146 and the remainder of the first ten locomotives of the class cost between £18,470 and £19,144 each. This was significantly higher then was originally budgeted for, £110,000 for twenty (£5,500 each), and higher even than the various revisions including the final revision of £16,000 each. The SR Board's comments would be interesting to record! Thus it was that probably the most contentious Pacific design in British railway history was born.

The following years saw a number of significant teething troubles with the locomotives but Bulleid was never totally involved with solving them as he believed that these things should be sorted out by his staff while he moved on to new ideas. Also, Bulleid was not good at receiving bad news about his designs and so his subordinates were reluctant to report the problems to him. As a result the only person who could really solve some of the difficulties was not kept totally in touch with the operational problems.

July 1942 saw the last of the first ten 'Merchant Navy' Pacifics, No. 21C10 *Blue Star*, entering traffic, by which time the SR had adapted itself reasonably well to wartime conditions albeit with heavier and slower trains and frequently overcrowded services. Consequently, consideration was given to meeting the expected demands on the West Country services which at that time were being worked by Drummond T9 4–4–0 locomotives and 'N class 2–6–0s, the latter also being required for goods traffic elsewhere on the network.

The need for new and more powerful locomotives on the West of England lines was sensible in view of the fact that it was then considered (rightly with hindsight) that the electrification would be unlikely to reach Devon and Cornwall, particularly via Salisbury and Exeter. Steam was to remain the prime motive power on these routes for some considerable time. What was less sensible was the lack of use of the power available in the 'West Country' and 'Battle of Britain' classes of locomotives. The services beyond Exeter were unprofitable, with summer trains having a maximum of six coaches on average and the overall year average not being more than three or four coaches at most.

The original drawings for the West of England motive power, produced in December 1942, showed a three-cylinder 2–6–0 design with fairly conventional features. At this stage of the war the quality of coal fell so significantly that a narrow firebox was inefficient, hence the design was modified to include a wide firebox; as a result, and with the addition of a front bogie to improve ride, the design progressed to a 4–6–2 arrangement.

Wartime conditions had a further impact on the design of the new locomotive. Even though by 1943–4 the threat of Allied defeat had receded, the collection of materials and supplies for a new product took time and organization, and was fraught with difficulties, in particular if the design was totally different from existing schemes. Under these circumstances Bulleid designed a locomotive with all the details of the 'Merchant Navy' class, but smaller and lighter. Ten new Pacifics were ordered from Brighton in September 1944, with work commencing during December of that year. The first of the class, No. 21C101 *Exeter*, entered service on 21 June 1945 having been completed in the preceding May. The delay was due to a boiler defect and faulty cylinders.

After the first forty-eight 'West Country' class locomotives had been built it was realized that most of the next order would be allocated away from the West Country region. It was therefore agreed that other names should be considered for the locomotives. In the end names recalling the air battles of 1940 where chosen and a further forty-four locomotives were given names associated with that time. These were known as the 'Battle of Britain' class and although they were separately classified they were in fact exactly the same locomotives as the 'West Country' class. A further eighteen locomotives were given West Country names following the completion of the 'Battle of Britains'.

All the classes received a number of modifications over their lifetimes, including the complete rebuilding of all the 'Merchant Navy' class and a significant number of both the 'West Country' and 'Battle of Britain' classes. The Bulleid Pacifics in the original form produced continuing controversy and argument, but they were never ignored and had an important impact on the future of British Railways designs. In fact, some said that the Bulleid Pacifics were the first step in a new generation of steam locomotives and that the BR Standard Pacifics were 90 per cent Edwardian in concept, materials and manufacturing.

CHAPTER THREE

THE SOUTHERN RAILWAY PEOPLE

One of the surprising aspects of Bulleid's tenure at the SR was his ability to persuade the senior management to spend hard-earned cash on new and radical designs of steam locomotives – and this within an environment which was focused on extending the electrification of the Southern's services. The chairman of the SR, R. Holland-Martin, was a man of diverse and varied interests with a somewhat eccentric approach to life, by no means a typical company chairman. He knew Bulleid well and was open to new ideas. Certainly Bulleid had plenty of these and was adept at putting them across. Holland-Martin was also impressed with Bulleid's enthusiasm for Gresley's P2 and A4 designs and he became a powerful supporter of Bulleid's cause.

The General Manager of the SR, E.J. Missenden, who was appointed prior to the Bulleid designs being put forward, gave Bulleid his full backing and, like his chairman, was able to make sure that the CME received more than his fair share of the resources. According to Michael Bonavia in his work *The History of the Southern Railway*, 'Missenden was a very experienced railwayman, who had risen from the bottom of the ladder . . . he delegated well keeping a sharp eye on the performance of his subordinates . . .'

Interestingly, while the designs had management support, Eastleigh Works initially objected to the building of the locomotives. This was a pretty difficult period for the workshops with air raids causing severe disruption, and staff were less than impressed with building a new locomotive design that was intended for non-existent express services. Bulleid's announcement that they were also designed for heavy freight duties was what succeeded in helping to change the situation.

Missenden was corresponding with the Minister of War Transport, Rt. Hon. Lord Leathers, and letters between April and September 1941 confirmed the contention that the 'Merchant Navy' class locomotives were mixed traffic engines. Missenden emphasized the usefulness of the class to the war effort with the high tractive power contributing to the movement of war materials and military personnel throughout the SR. Clearly the effort put in by the SR management was highly successful.

During the design stage of his Pacifics Bulleid had always tried to keep in mind the men who drove and maintained them. Thus the concept of the oil bath for the

'Merchant Navy' No. 35029 *Ellerman Lines* and BR Standard tank No. 82014 resting at
Eastleigh shed.

Bob Barnard, Hugh Davies Collection

valve gear was produced, along with the electric lighting, and it was also part of
the reasoning behind the airsmoothed casing. But how successful was Bulleid in
easing the workloads? Certainly the footplate crews liked the locomotives in their
original form, but when problems resulting directly from the design started to
appear the shed staff discovered some of the drawbacks and ultimately they
favoured the rebuilt locomotives. From the point of view of the footplate crews,
the unrebuilt Pacifics in their final form made life that much easier, even with the
unpredictability of the steam reverser and the risk of fires due to oil leakage. The
boiler and firebox enabled steam to be produced well in access of anything
required for the Southern routes; for example, Salisbury crews have said that if
the firebox was filled with coal on leaving Nine Elms they had no need to pick up
a shovel again before Salisbury. This is very anecdotal, but real evidence exists of
firemen filling the firebox at Winchester and not touching the shovel again on the
journey to London.

   During the last years of steam in 1966, Driver E. Pistell of Salisbury shed
organized a testimonial for the unrebuilt Pacifics and of the 150 drivers who were
eligible to comment 50 signed in agreement. In general, the consensus of the
footplate crews was that the Bulleid Pacifics were 'good 'uns' and that, in good
condition, they were able to master completely any duty that was put before
them. Criticisms from the footplate were concerned with visibility and difficulties

in solving problems with the internal motion, something which on standard Walschaerts valve gear was visible and accessible. While the fully enclosed valve gear brought benefit to footplate crews, it sometimes only exacerbated difficulties. Somehow, in spite of all the niggles and problems experienced, the enginemen of the time had an almost perverse loyalty for the locomotive and, generally, Bulleid's Pacifics produced strong emotions at all levels of railwaymen.

The preparation and disposal of the Pacifics gave some respite to the crews over the more conventional locomotives, particularly when oiling round at the beginning of a duty. The internal oil bath, which meant that only the outside motion needed oiling, was certainly an advantage, particularly for the more rotund of the drivers on the link. One of the most frustrating and tedious tasks was filling the sandboxes. This needed a ladder or staging on the unmodified members of the class but, in spite of this, it was still considered safer by some firemen than carrying out the same task on the rebuilt Pacifics. This involved carrying 'a 2 gallon bucket of hot dry sand across all the shed roads, then placing the bucket on the running plate, clambering up the buffer beam and edging around the plate to fill the sand boxes'. The perils of this task can be appreciated particularly when steel studded boots are worn with the running plate wet and greasy. Spillage was inevitable and the sand invariably ended up on the motion and slide bars. Covers were added to the slide bars but these then produced difficulties when oiling round and were eventually discontinued. Bulleid originally thought that the sandboxes would be filled via overhead pipes, but even in this case ladders would have been required to attach the pipes to the sandbox openings.

On the subject of sand, some drivers at Nine Elms had picked up a useful ploy to help steaming by using a couple of buckets of grit which had been sifted from the sand hoppers. The driver would deliberately make the locomotive 'dance' on the incline out of the running shed and, with the firedoor open, the fireman would throw a bucket of the grit onto the tube plate. This disappeared through the tubes and with it went all the muck, straight out of the chimney!

At the other end of the duty, disposal was not without its difficulties. Cleaning out the smokebox needed a longer handled shovel than normal because of the extra length of the smokebox over conventional locomotives. On the plus side the amount of char and ash in the smokebox was never that great as the multi-jet blastpipe ejected most of the ash up the chimney. This was one good reason why stationmasters were very keen on preventing the Bulleid Pacifics from using the blower while they were waiting in the station, particularly on washing days. The local people would not be very pleased to find their washing covered in soot from a waiting Pacific. This was all part of the station staff requirements when trying to be good neighbours.

The disposal of the fire was another task for which Bulleid had given consideration to the footplate crews. On the 'Merchant Navy' class a hopper-type ashpan was fitted, while on the Light Pacifics rocking grates were also fitted. The hopper ashpan doors, while a good idea, did give some problems in service and it was not uncommon for the doors to be levered opened using a coal pick. The ash

'Battle of Britain' No. 34059 *Sir Archibald Sinclair* light engine at the Down end of Salisbury station.

Norman Simmons, Hugh Davies Collection

should have been removed using a rake or picker, but because tools always seemed to go missing it was not unheard of for the fireman to give the sides of the hoppers a good bang to dislodge the ash! At Nine Elms a number of small rakes were produced by the shed blacksmith especially for the top link crews.

The Pacific cabs were considered to be 'just the job' by the crews with all the controls laid out to hand, although the first impression was one of a mass of untidy piping. The cab floor was exceptionally large giving a feeling of comfortable spaciousness, with the steam and water valves for the injectors controlled by hand wheels under the fireman's seat. The overflows for these could be sighted through two small cut-outs in the cab floor and these were lit at night by electric light – a total luxury! From the fireman's point of view, the first ten 'Merchant Navy' Pacifics were the cause of many a cracked head as the Detroit sight feed lubricators seemed to have been fitted in just the position where the fireman would bring his head up during the firing swing.

The firing position was generally good, with the firehole and the shovelling plate both located at about the correct point above the cab floor so that the fireman did not have to bend too much during the swing. The acceptance of the Ajax steam-operated firehole doors varied from area to area. The operation required a certain knack to be able to time the swing and door opening in one fluid movement, but it seemed to have been used consistently by crews from Salisbury and Exmouth Junction, although it received less appreciation from the Eastern Section crews.

Apart from the difficulties caused by smoke and steam, the view from the cab was also obstructed by the large Davies & Metcalfe vacuum ejector which was situated in such a way as to protrude across the driver's window. This coupled with the normally narrow window did cause a number of serious complaints and the ejector was finally moved. On the later locomotives and Light Pacifics a D-type ejector was fitted. The tender was also fitted with a cab which included lockers for both the driver and fireman. The coal bunker was equipped with a coal watering pipe, controlled from the footplate, which helped to keep the dust down, as did the sliding door above the shovelling plate. The tender cab was joined to the footplate roof and during hot weather the cab became just a little warm, with it not being unknown for even the driver to be working in shirtsleeves.

The crew normally filled the tender tank using the rear water filler and, while there were two fillers inside the cab, one on either side, they were normally not used other than to give an indication of the water level. Crews quickly learnt that one small mistake with water filling meant that the whole of the footplate would become a river, much to their disgust and annoyance! Once the Pacific was prepared it was time to drive it off shed and pick up the train for the duty turn.

Much criticism has been made about the valve gear and the steam reverser on the Bulleid Pacifics, but from a driving point of view the effort needed to operate the reverser on the unrebuilt members of the class compared with the screw-type on the rebuilt Pacifics was significantly less. Furthermore, the locomotive was very forgiving in terms of how the driver controlled his engine, with examples of running with full-fore gear and regulator only and at the other extreme using the 30 to 40 per cent cut off and full regulator. Clearly, account had to be taken of the ability of these Pacifics to slip when starting, but typically the driver would have his own technique to overcome this difficulty. A knowledgeable driver would be aware of the implications of a locomotive fitted with a combination of small diameter cylinders, short-stroke, large piston valves and big steampipes. These, together with the insensitivity of the regulator, would create problems when starting, particularly with a heavy train. One method was that used by Russ Coffin of Nine Elms who, upon starting, opened and closed the regulator in a definite rhythm with the exhaust beats, until the locomotive was on the move. At this point the cut-off could be reduced to around 45 per cent and the regulator opened wider. As the speed increased the cut-off could then be shortened until the running cut-off was reached, but it was essential to watch the steam pressure gauge, which, if it started to fluctuate, indicated that the cut-off was too short.

The steam reverser may have been easy to operate, but knowing exactly what percentage was set was almost pure guesswork even though the control was fitted with a marked quadrant. The accuracy was somewhat wanting but in all fairness this was not an uncommon situation on any screw- or lever-operated reverser. With the Bulleid Pacifics it was normal to work on the principle of a certain number of turns or notches on the lever.

The superb steaming capabilities of these locomotives helped them to be so forgiving as far as driving and firing were concerned and although the boiler was pressed to 280 psi it was not unusual to find them working from 110 psi upwards in the steam chests. Typical of the style of driving for the Bulleid Pacifics is that

undertaken by Driver Swain and Fireman A. Fordrey of Nine Elms shed during
the latter part of the 1940s, sometime prior to the exchange trials.

Nederland Line, No. 21C14, was working the 'Bournemouth Belle' with a train
consisting of ten Pullman coaches, at 397 tons tare, 420 tons gross. Swain
notched up to 20 per cent soon after starting out from London and between then
and arrival at Southampton the cut-off stayed between 20 per cent and 15 per
cent. A permanent way check reduced the speed to 20 mph after Wimbledon and
adverse signals caused a reduction to 45 mph just before Surbiton, but thereafter
the road was clear.

The boiler pressure started at 275 psi but the steam chest pressure was no more
than 170 psi out to Clapham Junction, at which point the regulator was closed
even further. Following the Surbiton check the cut-off was 20 per cent and even
with 130 psi steam chest pressure the speed increased until after Weybridge
Nederland Line was doing 75 mph. The cut-off was then reduced to 15 per cent
and with 240 psi in the boiler and 130 psi in the steam chest milepost 31 summit
was passed at 66 mph. Beyond Fleet the locomotive was opened out a little with
20 per cent cut-off and 150 psi in the chest, and consequently the speed increased
to 77 mph after Hook.

The locomotive was being worked under fairly easy conditions but even then
the timings were sharp. The 24.4 miles to Woking from Waterloo were passed in
just over 29 minutes and the 23.4 miles from Woking to Basingstoke were
covered in just under 20 minutes. The 35.8 miles from Surbiton to Basingstoke
were completed with an average speed of 68.4 mph. On the downhill section past
Winchester the train speed was 74 m.p.h. with no more than 60 psi in the steam
chest of *Nederland Line*. The 'Bournemouth Belle' ran into Southampton Central
having been just over 84 minutes for the 79.2 miles (81 minutes net). The
following 28.7 miles to Bournemouth Central were completed with ease in under
35 minutes, start to stop.

As previously noted there was some difference of opinion between shed staff and
footplate crews on the quality of the unrebuilt and rebuilt Bulleid Pacifics. The
maintenance staff were undoubtedly less than enthralled with the difficulties
involved with maintenance on the enclosed valve gear or access to boiler fittings via
the airsmoothed casing. The design tested the ingenuity of the fitters but the reality
was not always the same as the horror stories sometimes told. Valve and piston
examinations were dirty in a different sort of way with fitters and overalls being
smothered in oil whenever this work had to be carried out. Certainly at Nine Elms
massive amounts of spares were not required, as has been suggested at other sheds.

Maintenance was indeed a problem and this was exasperated by the lack of a
workshop manual or operator's handbook. To be fair, some of the initial
problems were the result of unfamiliarity with the class. Typical of this was the
fitter who, on examining a 'Merchant Navy' at Nine Elms, noticed the trailing
brake blocks were hanging some 4 in off the wheels. Adjustment according to the
normal standards of locomotive practice was carried out with the consequence
that the 'Merchant Navy' lost 20 minutes due to dragging brakes on the return
Waterloo–Salisbury trip.

During the early allocation at Nine Elms there was little major maintenance carried out and, apart from oil levels in the sump being checked or filled and sundry other small adjustments, there was a surprising lack of work booked on the Pacifics. The valve gear sumps needed regular topping up with 3 to 4 gallons of oil. At Nine Elms this was carried out by two ex-fitter's mates who had volunteered to work two alternate 12-hour shifts, checking and filling the sumps from 4 gallon drums. A further problem with the sump which added to the unpleasantness of the tasks involved was that there was usually water in with the oil in the sump, caused either by seepage from the boiler or by condensation when the locomotive had stood for too long.

Fitters used either flare lamps or, latterly, acetylene lamps to assist in the examination of the locomotives, but these themselves caused problems with the Bulleid Pacifics. It was not unheard of for the flare lamps to ignite the oil-soaked boiler lagging! Additionally, turbo generator failure could be caused from the lamps melting the rubber insulation of the lighting cables and causing a short circuit. While this may seem careless, it has to be remembered that the sheds were not well lit and the cable conduits were likewise not easy to see or necessarily placed in the best position for the maintainer. In any case the shed electrician was not very happy with these failures!

A further difficulty with the unrebuilt Pacifics was concerned with the screwed hexagonal–pentagonal retaining caps on the crankpins. These were designed by Reg Curl at Eastleigh and were located using an offset pentagonal-shaped block which was inserted into the outside of the crankpin. They became tight with use and sometimes the torque required to remove them was so great that the tool provided was not large enough to carry out the task. It was not unknown for a 35 ton breakdown jack to assist in moving the tool and on one occasion the complete locomotive was lifted off the rails without the extraction tool moving! The caps were finally removed on this occasion by the precise and careful use of an oxyacetylene torch.

Of course, the footplate crews and shed staff were not the only members of the organization behind the Bulleid Pacifics. A whole team of people were involved with the presentation and running of these original locomotives: cleaners, passenger staff, signalmen and station staff from around the routes served by the trains hauled by the Pacifics.

One aspect for which the design was a reasonable success was the cleaning of the locomotive, although care had to be taken with locomotives encased in limpet board which was prone to damage from heavy-handed cleaning. The overall design lent itself to the cleaners as, apart from the airsmoothed casing and the rounded top and front of the locomotives, the BFB wheels were easier to clean, and with both the inside motion enclosed and only the piston rod, slide bar and connecting rod on the outside, the cleaning task was simplified. However, for all the advantages over conventional locomotives, the task was still daunting, to put it mildly.

With the 'Merchant Navy' class being nearly 70 ft long and just under 13 ft high, and the Light Pacifics approximately 2 ft shorter, the area to clean, albeit

'West Country' No. 34016 *Bodmin* approaching Teignmouth along the sea wall section with a Down passenger service.

David Lawrence, Hugh Davies Collection

with the almost unobstructed sides, was large! The need for cleaning was made worse because of the softer exhaust of the large chimney and multiple blastpipe, with more soot and exhaust dirt being deposited on the casing. So, while the task of clambering over the inside motion to clean the rods and big ends was not a required task for the Bulleid Pacifics, the amount of work in dirty, cramped and poorly lit conditions was still considerable and the presentation of the locomotives during the early days exemplifies the pride in these locomotives.

Over the lifetime of the Bulleid Pacifics a number of high profile and luxury trains travelled the Southern metals, including the famous 'Golden Arrow', the 'Bournemouth Belle', the 'Devon Belle' with its well-known 'wings' on the smoke deflectors of the Bulleid Pacifics and, of course, the 'Atlantic Coast Express' (ACE). It was trains such as these, along with their train staff, which gave the SR and ultimately the Southern Region of British Railways a special place in the memories of its passengers. Memories like the journey to Exeter on the ACE with the dining car attendants travelling the train advising passengers when the next sitting was, the sheer delight of having a 'proper' meal on a moving train, or the pride of the youngster being served the next course by the uniformed attendant, while passing through a station where other less fortunate mortals are waiting for the local train. And why was it that when you were young the guards on these holiday trains were always big, happy, slightly overweight men, who had all the information at their fingertips, dispensed with a ready smile? They were the trusting figures who fronted the railway company and complimented the splendour of the train and locomotive. It always seemed to be the Bulleid Pacifics which had this wonderful service, never the lesser locomotives – or is this just a view through rose-coloured spectacles?

The other task which concerned the guard was the 'booked time lost' ticket which he issued to the driver if he considered that time lost on a journey was due to the locomotive of his train. The driver then had to record his reasons on the ticket before it was sent to the depot foreman. The footplate crew hated this system, particularly when the guard decided to send the ticket direct to the depot foreman. This seemed an unfair way of doing things, especially as the ticket also included section timings as well as overall timings. Drivers could still be in trouble when section timings were down, even if overall the train was on time or early.

Along with the spread of the electric services further across the Southern network went the extension of the electric signalling systems, which in turn gave higher frequency services and a change in the methods of working for the signal staff. Consequently, where the third rail services reigned supreme the special relationship between the signal-box and footplate crew tended to diminish, particularly around the London areas and the suburbs. These areas of the Southern were given to fast, frequent electric services, the paths of which steam trains had to fit around, so the signal staff were under constant pressure to meet schedules and had very little time for the niceties of accommodating steam.

The ACE at one time divided at Okehampton and the section with the dining car went forward to Plymouth. The division was carried out by the shunters based at that station and, as the split would change depending upon the original composition of the train, a message with the information was sent from the inspector at Exeter once the train had left. Typically the make-up would be something like 5 Plymouth, 3 Bude, 2 Padstow, but the division was only made between the Plymouth and Bude sections at Okehampton, the second split being made at Halwill Junction.

The dividing of the ACE was the first duty on the late turn; the shunter came on duty, read the special notices, grabbed the message regarding the split and rushed off to await the train. On one particular night the message stated 4:3:3 so, as soon as the train stopped, the shunter jumped between the requisite coaches, released the couplings, returned to the platform and gave the right away. With that, the gangway shield was put on, the corridor door was locked and the coupling adjusted for the new locomotive. At that moment the shunter looked up to the stationary coach where a waiter stood with a load of empty plates and a look of absolute horror on his face. The conversation went something like this:

'Too late chum, you should have been back there before I split the train.'

'No, I shouldn't. You have gone off with the kitchen car, I have all the diners back here!'

The message that night should have read 5:3:2, as was normal.

The SR had a number of important London termini, with both Victoria and the old LSWR terminus, Waterloo, having the pride of place. Waterloo was the station which had it all: boat-trains from the USA and the Far East, trains to

No. 35014 *Nederland Line* at Waterloo, recently rebuilt, with the 'Bournemouth Belle' on 14 December 1957.

B.K.B. Green, Initial Photographic

famous sporting events and a varied mixture of famous and infamous passengers, from film stars and presidents to criminals. Victoria included the famous, luxury express services to Paris, the 'Golden Arrow' and the 'Night Ferry', both of which were the province of a number of the great and the good of the day. The 'Night Ferry' used shortened versions of the Wagons-Lit Continental coaching stock (to meet the SR loading gauge) with sleeping cars of the International Sleeping Car Co. via the Chatham route to Dover, while the 'Golden Arrow' comprised British Pullman cars.

There were other special expresses hauled by Bulleid Pacifics, in particular the boat-trains operated for the major oceanic passenger lines, services like the 'Statesman' run for US lines or the 'Union Castle Express' and the 'South American', all programmed to meet the respective passenger liner's arrival at Southampton and transport the passengers onward to London. Film stars, politicians and the rich and the famous were all to experience their first taste of travel in the UK behind one of Bulleid's Pacific locomotives. A particularly special boat-train from London was that hauled by No. 21C4 *Cunard White Star* on 16 October 1946. The service carried passengers for the first sailing of the RMS *Queen Elizabeth* after release from troopship duties during the Second World War.

In November 1950 *Cunard White Star*, now No. 35004, was again used for a special train, that of the royal train carrying the Queen of The Netherlands from

Dover to London. The Bulleid Pacifics were used on all the special and royal trains right up to the end of steam as they were the natural choice for these high profile and important services. For example, 'West Country' No. 21C129 (then unnamed, but later named *Lundy*) took King George VI and the then Queen to the Oaks at Epsom on 7 June 1946 and during June 1950 'Merchant Navy' No. 35019 *French Line C.G.T.* was also used for a royal train to take the King and Queen from London to Sherborne.

Arguably the most unusual service for the Bulleid Pacifics was when 'West Country' No. 34092 hauled the train taking the most powerful men of the then USSR, the joint leaders, Nikita Khrushchev and Marshal Bulganin, on their journey back to Portsmouth after the state visit to the UK in April 1956. The locomotive headcode for this was individual to say the least, having a single disc on the centre line above the smokebox door with the figure 1, then the letters spcl and a further two white discs, one to the left of the smokebox door at the halfway point and the second on the right side of the buffer beam.

One of the saddest duties carried out by one of the Bulleid Pacifics was hauling the train for Sir Winston Churchill's final journey after the pomp and ceremony of his state funeral in London. Churchill was taken from Waterloo to Long Hanborough station, near Oxford and close to Blenheim Palace where he was born. His final resting place was nearby at Bladon. The funeral train was hauled appropriately enough by 'Battle of Britain' class No. 34051 *Winston Churchill*, and included five Pullman vehicles and a bogie van with corridor connections. The train left Waterloo at 13.25 on 30 January 1965 and arrived at Long Hanborough at 15.30. The footplate crew for this sombre occasion was Driver A.W. Hurley and Fireman J.C. Lester. The Pullman vehicles and the mourners were brought back to London behind 'Western' class diesel No. D1015 *Western Champion*, the 'Battle of Britain' having returned light to Nine Elms engine shed. Churchill's funeral train carried another example of an unusual headcode, with three white discs used to form a 'V' shape to emulate the famous Churchill victory sign.

Over the years a number of nicknames have been applied to various locomotive classes, in most cases being indicative of some affection for the locomotives themselves. It is unclear when the Bulleid Pacifics were first given the nickname of 'Spam Cans' or who gave it to them, but the original airsmoothed shape does bear a certain similarity to the wartime tins of spam which almost became staple diet during that period. While the name was originally used for the 'Merchant Navy' class, it was also extended to the original 'West Country' and 'Battle of Britain' classes.

The other nickname for the 'Merchant Navy' class, 'Flannel Jackets', is believed to have been derived from Cockney rhyming slang based on the first member of the class, *Channel Packet*, and originated at Nine Elms shed during the early days of working with the Bulleid Pacifics. Interestingly, a further nickname for the Bulleid Pacifics was that given by railway artist Geoffrey Wheeler, who described them as 'shufflebottoms' because of the subdued 'shuffling' exhaust note of these locomotives at six 'shuffs' per wheel revolution – 'six beats to the bar!'

However, regardless of the nicknames or the problems, both in the early days
with smoke and steam, and subsequently with oil fires and difficulties of
maintenance, the Bulleid Pacifics did give good service across the length and
breadth of the Southern Railway system. The locomotive was one that crews and
shed staff alike either loved or hated outright. Similarly, among enthusiasts the
design produced controversy and strongly polarized opinions and to a certain
extent it still does so today, even in preservation.

Clearly, the design of these locomotives was radical. The intention was to
produce a design which solved some of the more aggravating problems when
dealing with steam traction, both in terms of availability and the workload and
comfort of the footplate crews. That the resultant design was a success is highly
debatable; whether this was due to the wartime conditions and lack of correct
materials is also arguable, but these powerful giants still create an emotional
response and are remembered with affection by many who served them. There
was a need for such a locomotive and this was filled by the highly original designs
of Bulleid.

CHAPTER FOUR

DESIGN AND CONSTRUCTION

On 10 March 1941 the first of the last Pacifics built before nationalization was named *Channel Packet* at the Eastleigh Works of the SR. No. 21C1 also happened to be the first Pacific built by the SR and was among 140 'Merchant Navy' and Light Pacifics built over the ten-year period between 1941 and January 1951, when the last 'Battle of Britain' class, No. 34110 66 *Squadron*, was completed.

The other major railway companies had all built Pacific locomotives, including the short-lived *Great Bear* of the GWR that was rebuilt as a 'Castle' 4–6–0. Both the GNR under Gresley and the later LNER produced Pacific designs which, after the Grouping, were augmented, although the Raven design of the NER was soon withdrawn. The Gresley designs multiplied and increased in stature, culminating in the fastest steam locomotive in the world, the A4. With the appointment of Stanier as CME for the LMS in January 1932 this railway also built Pacific designs, with the first, No. 6200 *The Princess Royal*, appearing in service some 17 months after Stanier's appointment. Ultimately Stanier's Duchesses equalled the grace and power of the A4s, and were probably at the pinnacle of design and engineering ability.

The SR however, was concentrating its efforts on the electrification of the system with the resultant decrease in the quality of steam traction. A number of things conspired to bring about this company-wide attitude in the 1930s. The SR was, by and large, a passenger railway with significant traffic into the heart of the city of London, as well as holiday and European boat-train traffic. All this helped to make the SR a very financially successful company, which regularly paid dividends of 5 per cent. In the early 1900s the London County Council's electric tram services had attacked the railway services out of London with a resultant loss in receipts. The railways fought back by modernizing the system and building electrified suburban services into the heart of the city. These became a great success and led the way to the future of fast, regular services from the suburbs of London on the SR.

The Depression of the late 1920s and early '30s produced less effect on the south of England than on the industrial north and consequently both the SR and the passenger receipts were less troubled by these problems. As the country slowly returned to prosperity so property prices in the South also rose, which in turn meant a slow migration of the middle-class workers further from the centre of the capital. With this migration went a demand for reliable, fast and clean transport from the Home Counties to the city. The SR was happy to oblige, with electrified trains reaching the depths of Kent, Sussex, Surrey and Hampshire. This created a snowball effect: more homes were built at the limits of the suburban services followed by SR adding more electrified route miles, thus increasing the reach. Ultimately, the SR provided electrified rail services to Brighton and Worthing in 1933, Sevenoaks, Eastbourne and Hastings in 1935, Portsmouth in 1937 and Bognor Regis in 1938.

By this time the economic advantages for pushing further afield with electric services were becoming difficult to justify and, although the receipts from these services were increasing significantly, longer distance trains were suffering from lack of investment in motive power. Even at this time the steam locomotive on the SR was considered an evil which should eventually be eradicated. Funds were allocated on a limited basis for maintenance, re-boilering and modernization, and very sparingly for new construction. The consequence of this strategy was the serious risk of a total breakdown in the steam services on the long-distance trains.

Bulleid took over as CME on 1 October 1937 having understudied Maunsell from the previous September. R.E.L. Maunsell had been appointed CME for the SR in 1923 and was responsible for both the 'Schools' and 'Lord Nelson' classes, he also designed the modifications to the Urie 4–6–0 N15 class which later became the 'King Arthur' class. The electrification programme, the increase in boat-train and longer distance passenger services all produced a situation where the existing steam motive power was having difficulties in meeting demands. The electric trains limited the boat-train speeds because of extensive track occupation and the limited size of the locomotives hauling the increased loads also contributed to the problem. A clear need was apparent for a locomotive with increased power and adequate acceleration, and while Maunsell attempted to produce Pacific designs in 1933 and a 2–6–2 design in 1934, both were rejected by the civil engineer and the locomotive committee. This was the cauldron that Bulleid moved into when he took up his post of CME. That he was able to convince the SR to even consider a Pacific design under the circumstances was highly indicative of Bulleid's abilities and persuasive powers.

During his time with the LNER Bulleid had become closely associated with the designs of the 2–8–2 P2 and, of course, the A4. Also, with his gift of languages, he had become fully conversant with the ideas and designs of André Chapelon, having been involved with the tests carried out with the P2 No. 2001 *Cock o' the North* at the French testing plant in Vitry-sur-Seine. This locomotive was fitted with Lentz rotary cam poppet-valves and gave some conflicting results at the test plant compared with the runs on the road.

Soon after Bulleid became CME his General Manager, Sir Herbert Walker, retired from the company and his place was taken by Gilbert Szlumper. Szlumper was very keen on the electrification programme but also recognized that changes were needed in the short term to overcome the problems experienced with steam traction. Similarly, the chairman of the company, Robert Holland-Martin, was also prepared to give support to Bulleid in his quest to find a solution to the

A fitted van train passes Farnborough hauled by a smart-looking 'Merchant Navy', No. 35003 *Royal Mail*.

Bob Barnard, Hugh Davies Collection

motive power problems he was facing. Thus, with this softening of attitudes, Bulleid was able to consider new designs and improvements to existing locomotive stock.

Initially Bulleid considered ways of improving the boat-train power and this resulted in his ugly modification to the Maunsell designs. The modifications were based on a design used by the *Nord Belge* railway and later the French *Nord* locomotives and consisted of a large divergent–convergent chimney fed by five 2⅜ in nozzles on a 12 in pitch circle. This idea was continued in the Pacific designs, and in addition, Bulleid added free steam passages based on Chapelon designs and new cylinders fitted with 10 in piston valves. The pistons were fitted to all of the 'Lord Nelson' 4–6–0 class except No. 851 *Sir Francis Drake* and No. 863 *Lord Rodney*.

While these designs were taking effect Bulleid was tirelessly working behind the scenes to encourage the company to move ahead with new designs, but even with the support of senior management he was not totally successful. On 22 March 1938 the request for thirty new express locomotives was reduced by the Rolling Stock Committee to twenty of a design as yet unspecified. This decision was formally ratified by the Locomotive and Electrical Committee on 30 March 1938 with the cost estimated at £110,000. The door had been opened for Bulleid to commence his modernization plans for steam traction, albeit on a scaled-down level. However, as the idea had been accepted and the decision made, it was considered that further orders could be gained in the future.

The type of locomotive had still not been decided at this stage; Bulleid had been outpaced by the overall circumstances caused by the outbreak of war and had not fully settled on the form the design should take. This was partly due to the influence of the civil engineer and his fear of leading trucks, partly to the diverse power requirements on the Eastern and Western Sections of the SR and also the inbuilt resistance of the company itself to steam power. The most urgent requirement was for a new powerful locomotive on the sharp gradients of the Eastern Section and originally Bulleid envisaged an eight-coupled locomotive for the heavy 'Golden Arrow' and 'Night Ferry' express services, while on the Western Section he considered that the 'Lord Nelsons' and a new designed Pacific would more than cope with the work.

Detailed investigations confirmed these findings and so Bulleid proposed a 2–8–2 design with 6 ft coupled wheels and a working weight of 112 tons. This locomotive had a boiler pressure of 220 psi and a 30 in piston stroke, clearly influenced by Gresley's three-cylinder Mikados. The design was modified to a 4–8–2, after assessment by the civil engineer, in order to overcome the objections to the leading truck. Three sets of Walschaerts valve gear were included, along with steel fireboxes and BFB wheels plus a number of Doncaster ideas. Owing to the urgency of the requirements for the Eastern Section Bulleid was prepared to accept some Doncaster ideas if this meant expediting the delivery of locomotives into service; however, this did not include the use of conjugated motion. After the initial delays were exasperated by the general situation and the reluctance of the SR to accept his original designs, Bulleid decided to produce a Pacific design which would be satisfactory for both the Eastern and Western Sections and at the same time include a number of revolutionary design ideas of his own. This, of course, added to the delays, and they became even more complex with the redesign of the original 4–8–2 boiler for the new Pacific. It seems that at this stage neither the Rolling Stock Committee nor the Locomotive and Electrical Committee was fully acquainted with the situation and the civil engineer was still requesting details of the design as late as October 1939, two months after the first two boilers had been ordered from the North British Locomotive Company (NBL).

The new locomotive design was mainly undertaken by the Brighton drawing office with assistance from both Ashford and Eastleigh. Around this time Bulleid brought in a new draughtsman to lead the drawing office design teams, C.S. Cocks, a Doncaster man who fully supported Bulleid and his ideas but who brought a little coherence to the designs. At the time it was whispered that Cocks was brought in because Bulleid considered the SR drawing office too cautious. Under the circumstances and with the radical approach Bulleid was taking, it was perhaps not surprising!

The distribution of the work made it difficult for the uninformed to readily appreciate the details of the design and this had some serious consequences. The intention was that the locomotive should be built completely at Eastleigh Works, but this was never fully investigated until some way into the design process. It was then discovered that the equipment and techniques available at Eastleigh were not up to

The first of the 'Merchant Navy' boilers, showing firehole, double regulator and insulation blanket. Note the driving wheel splashers fitted to the frames.

National Railway Museum, York

the design of the boiler and the all-welded steel firebox. The first ten boilers were subsequently ordered from the NBL with the thermic syphons subcontracted to Beyer Peacock & Co. The quoted cost from the NBL on 19 August 1939 was £2,850 per boiler. The order was accepted on 4 October 1939, although records indicate that the real cost was closer to £3,046 each. When the second batch of Pacifics was considered, NBL was again contracted to produce these boilers and the quoted cost in May 1941 was £2,855, an increase of only £5! However, the next batch of boilers was actually manufactured at Eastleigh at an estimated cost of £3,700 per boiler, and a penalty of £374 was paid to NBL for having cancelled the contract. The site for building the boilers was changed because of the delay in proceeding with the next group of locomotives caused by wartime pressures and because Bulleid pressed for new boiler fabrication equipment at Eastleigh. He suggested the new equipment could save up to £1,000 over the outside contractor's price per boiler, although it is not possible to justify this claim because records of the cost of the new equipment are not available. The thermic syphons for the new boilers were again provided by Beyer Peacock at a cost of £304 per pair. It is interesting to note that the thermic syphons were missing from the order for the second batch of boilers from NBL; whether this is significant or not is difficult to judge. It is possible that it was a simple lapse and that they would have been added subsequently to the order, but it is also possible that they were not planned to be added at all.

Before the design of the Pacifics could be fully completed Europe was at war, leading to serious delays in building the locomotives at Eastleigh Works because of War Department commitments. The construction of the tenders and mainframes was transferred to Ashford Works in Kent. Further troubles were experienced with the late delivery of the cylinder castings, which, when they did arrive, were mostly found to be defective and had to be rejected. This was a particularly frustrating time for Bulleid, and without his courage and perseverance it is possible that the Pacifics would not have been completed, with the work being postponed to a more auspicious time. Bulleid merely postponed part of the order and continued with work that could proceed as parts and labour became available. In any case significant progress could not be made until the first of the boilers was delivered from NBL in November 1940.

The first of the new Pacifics was completed on 17 February 1941 and for the SR followed the new numbering scheme adopted by Bulleid. This was based on the Continental system which identified the wheel arrangement of the locomotive via its number. Typically an Atlantic was recorded as 2B1 and a Pacific as 2C1. Although this was very logical, Bulleid decided to modify the system to suit his own requirements, which unfortunately made the results of limited value. It is arguable that Bulleid's modified system made it a little easier to identify the running number by using the letter to divide the running number from the locomotive type designator. Whatever Bulleid's original idea was, it was certainly different! It is also worth noting that Bulleid was insistent that the Pacifics should be known as the 21C1 class, rather than the 'Merchant Navy' class.

The original names for the class were chosen to honour the British land, sea and air victories of the Second World War, but up to that time authentic victories were somewhat thin on the ground so the idea had to be dropped. A rectangular wooden trial name-plate had been prepared for the first locomotive with the name 'The Plate', to commemorate the Battle of the River Plate and the destruction of the German pocket battleship *Graf Spee*. Consideration was given to using capital cities of the UK and the Commonwealth but these names did not meet with the approval of the SR. Finally, after a suggestion made by the chairman of the Union Castle Shipping Line to use the names of the shipping lines which called regularly at Southampton during peacetime, the class became the 'Merchant Navy' class and despite Bulleid's insistence this was the class name applied to all the name-plates. The name-plates included the house flag of each shipping line with the left and right side plates being different to show the flags in the correct direction when the locomotive was running forwards. The first of Bulleid's Pacifics No. 21C1 was named *Channel Packet*, after the SR's own cross-Channel fleet. The ceremony was performed on 10 March 1941 at Eastleigh Works by the Minister of Transport, Lt. Col. J.T.C. Moore-Brabazon.

The estimated weight for the locomotive was 92.5 tons, of which 63 tons were carried by the coupled wheels. While the civil engineer was comfortable with this, he did request a reduction of 3 tons off the weight carried by the coupled

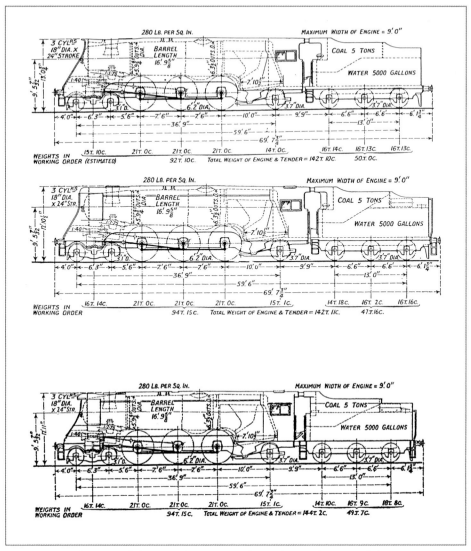

Arrangement drawing of the 'Merchant Navy' class. Above: the original design, No. 21C1. Middle: the design of the first ten, subsequently modified. Below: the later design, modified before rebuilding.

Railway Gazette

wheels. Both the first members of the class, *Channel Packet* and *Union Castle*, were found to be 7 tons over design weight, turning the scales at 99½ tons. This figure was totally unacceptable to the civil engineer and led to some severe measures being adopted to remove the extra weight. In fact he insisted that immediate measures were taken to reduce the weight of the next eight locomotives. Consequently, locomotive production was halted while remedial steps were taken to reduce the excess weight and for these measures to be approved.

PRINCIPAL DIMENSIONS OF THE 'MERCHANT NAVY' CLASS

Cylinder × 3 (diameter × stroke)	18 in × 24 in
Piston valve diameter	11 in
Bogie wheel diameter	3 ft 1 in
Coupled wheel diameter	6 ft 2 in
Trailing wheel diameter	3 ft 7 in
Wheelbase	6 ft 3 in + 5 ft 6 in + 7 ft 6 in + 7 ft 6 in + 10 ft 0 in = 36 ft 9 in
Boiler diameter	5 ft 9¾ in to 6 ft 3½ in
Boiler length	16 ft 9⅝ in (tube length 17 ft)
Firebox length	7 ft 10½ in
Heating surfaces	
Tubes (124 in × 2¼ in)	1,241.6 sq. ft
Flues (40 × 5¼ in)	934.3 sq. ft
Firebox and Thermic syphons	275.0 sq. ft
Total evaporative	2,450.9 sq. ft
Superheater	665.0 sq. ft
Combined total	3,115.9 sq. ft
Grate area	48.5 sq. ft
Working pressure	280 psi

The difference in approach that Bulleid took with his concept of the Pacifics extended down to the design of the frames. These were cut from 1⅛ in steel plate and fitted with welded hornblocks centred above the axleboxes. This gave one centre line for the frames, boxes, guides and springs, and cut out offset thrust. This principle had previously been one of the advantages of bar frames. Interestingly, for all the divergence of views stated about the Bulleid designs, this idea was perpetuated on the British Railways Standard classes.

The frame spacing was 3 ft 3⅞ in, which was significantly closer than normal. This narrow spacing was intended to allow the oil bath to be fitted between the frames as well as permitting the hornblocks to be centred, in turn ensuring that the axlebox thrust was applied centrally. The coupled wheel axleboxes were constructed of bronze, a material that Bulleid was very familiar with. These gave very little trouble, but when a coupling rod breakage occurred on No. 35016 *Elders Fyffes* it was found that the bronze axleboxes were cracked and brittle, and so they were replaced with cast-steel boxes.

Exceptionally good quality cast-steel stretchers were added to the frames and bolted to the horn cheeks at the front of the leading coupled wheels, between the leading and driving coupled wheels, and the driving and trailing coupled wheels. These horizontal stretchers added reinforcement to the horn stays. The weight reduction programme ordered by the civil engineer resulted in the stretchers being cut with lightening holes, which possibly exacerbated the problems with frame fractures that occurred later in the life of the Bulleid Pacifics. The later orders for the second and third series of Bulleid Pacifics included modified stretchers of fabricated construction. The stretchers on the next eight locomotives in the initial order were modified to reduce weight with a reduction of ³⁄₁₆ in across the thickness of the

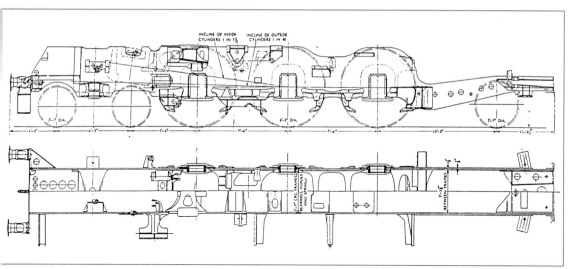

Original frame design for No. 21C1.

National Railway Museum, York

stretchers, which alone produced a saving of 23.5 cwt. The mainframes themselves already had lightening holes and these were enlarged and others added. These mainframe changes were all continued on the later 'Merchant Navy' locomotives.

The horn stays gave additional support for the steam brake cylinder and the main brake shaft. The layshaft and the three-throw crank axle were supported by the horn stay fitted between the leading and driving coupled wheels, and the front support for the boiler was attached to the top cross-stay over the leading coupled axle. This stay also carried the middle cylinder slide bar and the valve plunger guides for all three cylinders. The trailing ends of the frames which slimmed to the rear and curved upwards, shaped rather like a swan's neck in order to clear the trailing truck, were bolted to the cast-steel dragbox. The boiler was supported by a steel casting behind the trailing coupled wheels, which was also the anchorage for the trailing truck pin joint and the carrier of the trailing spring hanger bracket.

The trailing truck was a delta design with three-point suspension and a spring side control with the weight transmitted via sliding pads at the rear. The truck was constructed of a one-piece steel casting and was pivoted to a frame stretcher at the rear of the frames. The final ten locomotives had fabricated trucks as a weight-saving exercise and during repairs these were changed between all the members of the class. Lateral control of the truck was by the use of springs situated below the bearing pads; the springs had a maximum compression of 2 tons when the maximum transverse movement of 5 in was reached.

The leading bogie design was based very much on that of the 'Lord Nelson' class, although the 7 ft 6 in wheelbase was shortened to the LNER practice of 6 ft 3 in. The bogie pivot had a side play of 3¼ in controlled by spiral springs. The springs had an initial compression loading of 3 tons raising to 5¾ tons at maximum throw-over.

The Bulleid Pacific delta rear truck on 'Merchant Navy' No. 35010.

Author's Collection

All the wheels on the locomotive were of the BFB design with 6 ft 2 in diameter coupled wheels. The design of the cast-steel wheels was based on the USA Boxpok design, but Bulleid decided not to use propriety wheels. Instead he produced a number of changes and with the collaboration of Thomas Firth and John Brown, steel makers of Sheffield, he produced the BFB design. The advantages of this design were the avoidance of retaining rings, the inclusion of set bolts and greater and more continuous support to the tyre. With this design the tyre was retained by shrinkage, with a single turned lip on the outside and a small lip cold-rolled over the centre once the tyre was positioned. The wheel centres were lightened by a number of cavities and holes, giving a semblance of eight large half-spokes and a weight some 12 per cent less than similarly sized spoked wheels.

The diameter of the coupled wheels was less than those of Pacifics built by other railway companies, but the coupled and locomotive wheelbases were longer. This was in order to keep the locomotives within the lower lineal loading gauge imposed by the bridges of the SR, in particular those of the Eastern Section. With the longer wheelbase, significant space was available between the coupled wheels and this enabled the clasp braking system to be fitted. Each intermediate brake hanger carried two blocks, one for the wheel ahead and the other for that behind. By applying brake pressure to both sides of the coupled wheels the problems of wheel and axle displacement and frame flexing under severe braking were all avoided. Braking was only applied to the coupled wheels and was provided by

The BFB wheel design. Note the later British Railways four-bolt design of locking the coupling rods.

Author's Collection

The mechanism for the Bulleid clasp brakes.

Author's Collection

two steam cylinders of 8 in diameter. These produced a maximum pull of 57 tons, equivalent to 97 per cent of the adhesive weight and 60 per cent of the working order weight. The use of steam braking on the engine helped to save weight, but the tenders had no restrictions and were vacuum braked with a brake cylinder at each end of the frames producing a pull of 24.7 tons.

When designing the valve gear for the Pacifics Bulleid was up against a number of difficulties and, like all engineering judgements, a compromise was needed. Bulleid had been working with three-cylinder designs during most of his professional life and, like Gresley, he considered that three cylinders produced the best method of providing power. At the same time Bulleid, also like Gresley, did not favour divided drives or the resultant longer frames and shortened connecting rods which were unavoidable when inside cylinders drove the leading coupled axle. Furthermore Bulleid was less than impressed with the derived valve motion he had experienced on the LNER, but with the 'Merchant Navy' class it would be impossible to accommodate standard Walschaerts motion between the frames if the inside cylinder was to drive the second coupled axle, owing to the intervention of the leading coupled axle. Maunsell had found a solution to the problem, but in service it was unreliable and led to increased maintenance and a high failure rate. The conclusion reached by Bulleid's thought processes left him with little option other than to produce a brand new design.

A number of schemes for the valve gear were studied at Brighton including a derived motion driven directly from the driving axle, but in the end they were all found to be impracticable and Bulleid produced a separate three-throw crankshaft. This allowed the enclosure of all three sets of valve motion in an oil bath with a hoped-for reduction in maintenance and preparation. Bulleid accepted that the enclosure would produce very much reduced accessibility, but he considered that reduced wear and less maintenance would overcome any objections.

Bulleid's original intention had been to drive the crankshaft by means of gears and a propeller shaft in a similar manner to the rotary cam poppet-valve motion. Wartime restrictions and other priorities meant that the required standards of gearing could not be obtained, hence a chain drive was substituted. This design was patented by Bulleid in 1942 under patent Nos 547,156 and 547,180. The chains used were inverted tooth chains manufactured by Morse and were of 1⅛ in pitch and 2 in wide. Two chains were used, one horizontally from the driven crank axle to the intermediate sprocket-wheel and a second driving vertically to

'Merchant Navy' class interior of the motion casing, looking forward, showing the main chain drive, motion drive, eccentric rods and inside cylinder slide bar. A dummy axle is fitted in place of the crank.

National Railway Museum, York

the three-throw crankshaft. This arrangement allowed for movement of the driven crank axle on its springs without disturbing the workings of the valve motions. The three-throw crankshaft revolved at the same speed as the crank axle and each of the cranks were phased with its own big end and thus imparted the motion to the relative piston valve. The horizontal chain consisted of 118 pitches with a total length of 11.8 ft and the vertical chain had 73 pitches with a total chain length of 7.3 ft. The intermediate sprocket-wheel shaft could be adjusted to take up the wear in the chain drive, but in reality correct tensioning was only given to the vertical chain.

The chains themselves were an expensive item costing £128 each in 1944, a price which rose to £200 in 1956 and £280 when the last were purchased in 1965. Chain wear was considerable and at around 30,000–36,000 miles they were scrapped as part of the valve and piston examination. The wear on the chain

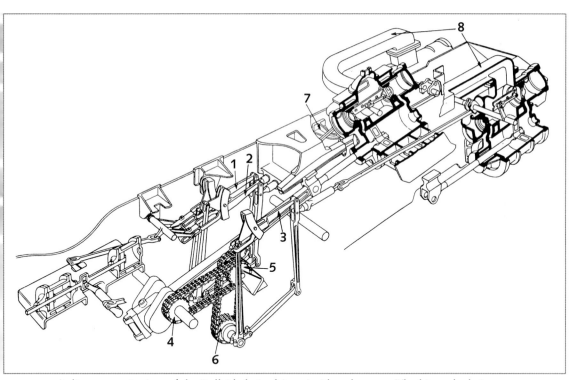

A diagrammatic view of the Bulleid chain-driven inside valve gear. The big end, chain gear and connecting rod were immersed in 40 gallons of lubricating oil.

1   Extreme left-hand valve gear driving middle engine
2   Inside valve gear driving left-hand outside engine
3   Middle valve gear driving right-hand outside engine
4   Main driving axle
5   Intermediate chain drive, mounted on brackets
6   Final chain drive for three-throw jockey shaft
7   Bracket for second valve drive
8   Exhausts leading to middle engine exhaust

pins and holes as well as the sprocket teeth could result in an elongation of the chain by as much as 6 in. While it is accepted that the slack could be taken out by use of the cut-off, the thought of this sag in the chain being snatched back from the slack position during a violent slip on starting is horrendous.

Owing to the restricted space into which the three-valve motion was positioned, the maximum throw of the expansion links was restricted to 37.5 per cent of the maximum valve travel, the distance being made good by the proportionally unequal length of the rocker arms which multiplied the motion from the crank axle in the ration of 8:3, thus giving the required valve travel of 6 in. Bulleid noted that while slackness could develop in the chain drive, a slack of 3 in could be absorbed when the chains were under load and further valve irregularity would be corrected by adjustment of the cut-off.

The inside cross-heads and slide bars, the inside connecting rod complete with big ends and crank axle, plus all the three valve motions were housed in an oil bath which contained 40 gallons of oil in the sump. In the sump two pumps driven from the three-throw crankshaft passed oil continuously at 18 psi through perforated pipes over the moving parts that were not immersed in the oil. The weight of the single set of Bulleid–Walschaerts valve gear was estimated as being some 205 lb lighter than the equivalent single Walschaerts gear but this took no account of the additional weight of 330 lb for the oil contained within the bath. Thus, while the unsprung weight was lower, the total weight was much the same as conventional Walschaerts gear.

The use of an oil bath for the inside valve gear was innovative and in principle could give significant advantage, but a steam locomotive is not like a motor vehicle so that the problems are different even if the solution is the same in theory. In particular, the reciprocating and rotating masses create movement between themselves and between the locomotive frames. Frame flexing could not be compensated for in the sump design and any movement could result in cracks and oil leaking from the sump. A further problem was that during movement of the valve gear when the locomotive was moving, pressure could build up in the sump producing additional stress. Condensation was another difficulty which was exacerbated by the enclosed motion, as was the ingress of steam from the inside piston draincocks and the steam brake cylinders, and although the oil specification was changed to a non-emulsifying mineral oil the problem was never fully overcome. Daily checks now included oil level checks and drawing water from the sump before operation. With the poor seals and joints it was not surprising that the Pacifics suffered from wheel slip and fires because of oil thrown up into the casing insulation. Possibly, if the Second World War had not occurred, the results may have been different, with a better design of geared drive and more technology and engineering expertise being put towards solving the problems of sealing the oil bath and sump.

On the subject of oil consumption by the Bulleid Pacifics, a Nine Elms driver has suggested that during the British Railways' era a cheaper grade of sump oil, Red Ilo, was used instead of the specified Duckhams oil. Apparently, when Duckhams was used the locomotives were able to run from one week to the next without needing to be topped up. The same source attributed some of the problems of corrosion in the sumps to this cheap oil, which was of a low viscosity. However, this account flies against accepted information and is difficult to confirm today.

Steam locomotives all need to have the rotating parts balanced and with Bulleid's Pacifics the back of the driving wheels hid plates which contained the lead balances for dynamically balancing the wheels. In addition, the pockets formed by the BFB wheels also contained lead weights, but there were no reciprocating balance weights. Opinion is at odds on the subject of reciprocating balance: too much will cause large hammer blows on the track, but too little could lead to severe sideways oscillations. Bulleid dispensed completely with the reciprocating balance, and with the three-cylinder drive was able to counter any tendency for lateral motion. Consequently, there was no normal hammer blow from the wheels but there was 'true' hammer blow from the vertical forces of the inside cylinder although this would decrease with speed and above 50 m.p.h. had little effect. Speed tests, observed by Bulleid, over Barnes Bridge indicated that there was no hammer blow, although it is questionable whether additional stresses were placed on the frames and axles.

The three cylinders were produced separately to ease the problems with casting and machining, but even then difficulties were experienced with late delivery and rejected castings. To be fair these were being produced under the severe pressure of wartime conditions. All the pistons drove the centre coupled axle, with the outside pair inclined at 1 in 40 and the inside piston inclined at 1 in 7.75, which allowed the rod to clear the leading coupled axle. The main rods were 11 ft long outside and 8 ft inside. All the cylinders had a bore of 18 in with a 24 in stroke which gave a tractive effort of 37,515 lb at 85 per cent boiler pressure. The steam for the pistons entered the cylinders at the top flange, which led to a cored feed pipe, itself giving entry to either end of the steam chests. The volume of this pipe and the two end steam chests was 2.6 cu. ft, which was some 5 per cent greater than the cylinder volume with full cut-off.

The port area through the valve liners was 40.7 sq. in and this opened up to an area of 254.5 sq. in through the cylinder barrel. The exhaust of the inside cylinders passed into the cavity below the blastpipe while that of the outside cylinders passed through the exhaust pipe flange and the external pipe to the centre cylinder casting, where the three exhausts joined under the blastpipe.

The piston valve design was another of Bulleid's innovations, unusually for the time having outside admission but with the valve gear arranged for inside admission. Furthermore, they did not have circular-section spindles connecting the heads nor were they spindle driven at the rear. The valves were connected by a double girder welded to the end plates, while a cross-pin in this girder took the drive from a rocker shaft and arms, which in turn were driven by a 50 in rod from a guided plunger off the combination lever of the valve motion. This eliminated the need for a valve stuffing box, but in service was to prove problematical as the arm of the rocking spindle was prone to failure.

The arrangement of the cylinders and valve chest was symmetrical with 11 in diameter valve heads, which was approximately 61 per cent of the cylinder diameter, probably the highest ratio of the time. The relatively small diameter of the cylinders (18 in) was possible because of the higher steam pressure. The diameter helped to keep the locomotive within the loading gauge and also reduce the reciprocating masses. If high steam pressure is used then the steam passages must be as direct as possible and of a sufficient size to allow the unfettered passage of steam from boiler to cylinder. The Bulleid Pacifics met this requirement in full and were therefore remarkably free running, being supplied by a boiler which produced abundant amounts of steam while not overworking the footplate crew.

The design features of the Bulleid Pacifics have been heavily criticized, but generally everybody is in agreement that these locomotives had the best and most free steaming boilers of any British locomotive, past or present. The boiler design contained many unconventional features, not least the all-welded steel firebox which included Nicholson thermic syphons. The boiler barrels were of a conventional riveted steel construction, but on the initial ten boilers ordered from the North British Locomotive Company the boiler barrel was tapered on the underside of the front ring and was parallel on the rear ring. Subsequent boilers were built with the front ring parallel and the rear ring tapered at the underside. This change in the design was to help save weight, both in materials and water content while at the same time keeping the heating surface area the same.

'Merchant Navy' boiler showing front tube plate, position of poppet valves and clack valves.
National Railway Museum, York

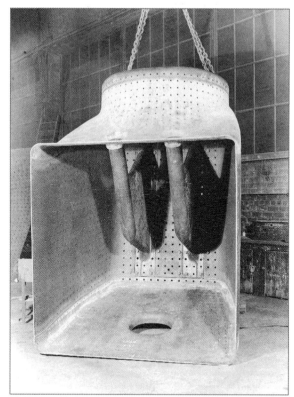

Steel inner firebox showing thermic syphons, viewed from the foundation ring.

National Railway Museum, York

The decision to use an all-welded steel firebox was based on a number of interlocking requirements, although as the design was established before the war started it is unlikely that a saving of the scarce commodity, copper, was part of the plan. With temperatures in the firebox of over 440°F it was not uncommon for copper fireboxes to loose elasticity and strength on the water side of the firebox. Additionally, a weight saving of almost 1.5 tons was gained by using steel instead of a riveted copper box, and problems caused by steel tubes fitting into copper tube plates, which were well known, were avoided. There was also a cost benefit and a maintenance advantage, as the fireboxes could be repaired using welding techniques at the running sheds.

The Belpaire firebox had a wide grate which extended over the rear frames and an area of 48.5 sq. ft. Owing to the very high pressure of the boiler Bulleid was concerned about the safety aspects in the event of low water in the boiler affecting the firebox, so he used two thermic syphons inside the box. While they did assist in promoting efficient water circulation, the prime consideration was to give greater support to the crown of the firebox. They also provided additional support for the brick arch which was thus built in three sections and placed higher in the firebox. The extra height gave a greater amount of free air space over the fire. Whether the syphons themselves added to the efficiency of the boiler is debatable; during tests in the early 1950s on the test plant at Rugby a conventional boiler without syphons was found to have the same evaporation rate as a standard boiler. Bulleid was not the first to use syphons on locomotive designs in Britain, having been preceded by both Gresley with his V4 2–6–2 No. 3402 and Bowen Cooke of the LNWR with his 'Claughton' No. 42 in 1921. As further protection, in case low water caused the crown sheet to collapse, the firebox was fitted with six fusible plugs. Again these were different from the normal practice, having a soldered or drop-in pellet rather than the more common lead-filled core.

The working boiler pressure was 280 psi, which was higher than usual at that time and so affected judgements on the boiler design. Bulleid used this boiler pressure to enable the locomotive to meet the required loading gauge while still being able to produce the necessary tractive effort. The higher the pressure, in theory, the smaller the diameter of the pistons, although obviously there is a limit.

Three Ross safety valves were fitted on the front ring of the boiler. They were fitted this far forward because of fears that turbulence from the water circulation at the syphons could cause steam and water to be lifted from the boiler if they were fitted conventionally. They were moved back to the rear ring of the boiler when it was found that braking caused the valves to expel water and steam. The steam dome was situated on the rear ring of the boiler and it covered a poppet-valve style of regulator with an internal push-pull operating rod which actuated the main valve via a crank. The regulator handle was initially fitted to both sides of the cab, but on later members of the class the regulator was only fitted for the driver, on the left-hand side of the cab. Initial movement of the regulator open a small pressure-equalizing pilot valve which gave the driver better control of the main regulator valve.

The water supply for the boiler entered via two clack valves which were placed on the right-hand side of the front ring of the boiler fed by the two Davis & Metcalfe No. 11 Monitor-type steam injectors. This design of clack valve was later adopted for use on the British Railways Standard class locomotives.

The smokebox for the Pacifics was fabricated from welded steel and, instead of being circular and supported by a saddle as was conventional, it took a highly irregular form which gave rise to the unusual oval-shaped door. Bulleid was not unfamiliar with smokebox doors of different shapes as the Gresley A4s were fitted with a door shaped to fit the streamlined casing and the Gresley P2 2–8–2, with its sloping smokebox top, also had an unusual smokebox door. The shape of the Bulleid door was directly caused by the inside valve chamber protruding well into the base of the smokebox and also because the casing front was cut to assist in smoke lifting. Although the smokebox was over 8 ft long, the interior space was limited by the extra piping used for the outside admission steam valves, the large diameter steam pipes and the blower pipe and superheater header. The superheater contributed some 665 sq. ft. to the total heating surfaces and consisted of forty elements at 1½ in outside diameter with a superheat temperature of approximately 400°C. The steam pipes were initially of cast construction but these cracked because their rigidity did not allow for frame

Fabricated and welded smokebox for No. 21C1, showing air slot to chimney.
National Railway Museum, York

movement relative to the boiler and smokebox, so they were later constructed from Aiton convoluted steel pipe, which was flexible.

The smokebox itself suffered from splitting throughout the lifetime of the original design. Part of the problem was that the relatively thin sheet steel used to fabricate the smokebox flexed under exhaust pulsing which led to fatigue cracks at the welds. When the Bulleid Pacifics were rebuilt the smokebox was changed to a more conventional tube-shape, although the oval door was retained.

All the Bulleid Pacifics were fitted with the Lemaître blastpipe via a divergent–convergent chimney, similar to the design fitted to the 'Lord Nelson' and 'Schools' classes. The exhaust steam was discharged through five nozzles of $2\frac{5}{8}$ in diameter, which were placed in a circle around the vertical centre of the chimney, 1 ft $11\frac{5}{8}$ in below the bottom of the chimney. The chimney was constructed from sheet steel, with a smokebox opening of 2 ft 8 in leading to a choke of 2 ft 1 in, and terminated in a plain top which was almost flush with

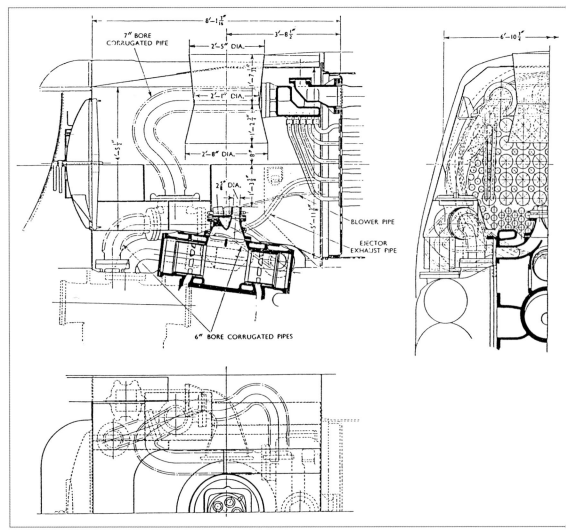

View of the smokebox and blast arrangements for 'Merchant Navy' locomotives after 1945. Compare this with the later design of the rebuilt locomotives.

National Railway Museum, York

the outer casing where the diameter was 2 ft 5 in. No. 21C1 was fitted with a circular cover which pivoted so that it could swing to cover the top of the chimney while it was out of steam in the sheds. No. 21C2 was also fitted with this cover, but after the smokebox modifications the cover proved to be impracticable. It has to be said that the idea of a crew actually placing the lid over the chimney when disposing of the locomotive sounds improbable and, even if they did, I don't think it is very likely that the crew preparing the locomotive the next time round would remember to remove the lid!

Probably the second most contentious aspect of the Bulleid Pacifics, after the chain drive valve gear, and certainly the most obvious was the airsmoothed casing. While it has often been repeated that this was to aid the preparation of the locomotive by allowing it to pass through the carriage cleaning plant, it is difficult today to justify the additional problems caused by this casing just to simplify cleaning. Looking over the design as a complete entity it is fairly clear that the locomotive was formulated from the very beginning to have a casing of some kind. Bearing in mind that the origins of the locomotive were from the last years of the 1930s when both the LMS and LNER were enjoying consistent success and publicity with the streamlined 'Duchesses' and A4s, and add to this the known enthusiasm of the SR chairman, R. Holland-Martin, for the streamliner's success and his desire to grab a little of the action and it could be construed that the casing was also a way of giving the SR some glory.

When the Second World War broke out, the control of the four main railway companies passed over to the Railway Executive Committee which was set up by the government. Interestingly, during the design stage of the 'Merchant Navy' class it was government inspectors who attempted to stop the construction because the class was not considered imperative for the war effort, and it was only when the locomotives were described as airsmoothed and mixed traffic that the situation eased. This was despite the *Railway Gazette* describing No. 21C1 *Channel Packet* as a 'streamlined 4–6–2 express engine'.

The casing was originally constructed of 16 swg steel sheeting although this was changed to asbestos limpet board on the last eight of the first batch of ten. Visually, the difference could be seen by the horizontal fixing strip along the centre of the casing. The casing was attached to channel section bearers which were fixed to the mainframes. At the cab end the casing matched the profile of the Belpaire firebox and at the smokebox end the casing was carried forward forming one-piece smoke deflectors, curved from the top of the front casing forward to the buffer beam. Various modifications were carried out to the casing at this point to try to alleviate the smoke and steam dispersal problems, none of which were totally successful.

On *Channel Packet* the side casings were swept round higher than the chimney and the front plate of the smokebox rose vertically to meet them. The front plate had a horizontal slot cut above the smokebox door, which was intended to force air through a smaller slot in the casing just in front of the chimney to lift the exhaust. Unfortunately, a shallow recess behind the smokebox front plate caused air to overflow and create areas of low pressure along the casing sides and, as a result, both the steam and the exhaust were drawn downwards and drifted around the cab windows. These problems resulted in changes to No. 21C2 *Union Castle* that included cutting the top of the smokebox front plate to expose the top plate which sloped back to the chimney centre line. The slot in the top of the casing and the chimney opening were also combined to give a square aperture with rounded corners. This change produced better results during trials and consequently the other eight of this batch were corrected during construction.

While the increased opening did provide some improvement, this was not the complete answer. Further experimental work continued during 1942 with a larger increase in the size of the rectangular airflow slot on Nos 21C6 *Peninsular & Oriental S. N. Co.*, 21C8 *Orient Line* and 21C9 *Shaw Savill*. No. 21C10 *Blue Star* was then used as a mobile test unit from December 1942 with the additional modification to the chimney height. The changes proved to be less than successful as the exhaust tended to gather like smog around the cab windows. This resulted in a one-tenth size model being produced which was then tested under varying conditions at the University of Southampton wind tunnel. The model had a removable front end which allowed various different designs to be tested.

There is some suggestion that two smaller models were also used during these tests. One, similar to the original shape of No. 21C1, had vertical slots within the casing on either side of the smokebox, while the other had the casing completely curved inwards on the sides and the top of the smokebox. Neither model had smoke deflector plates, but both were complete with fairings behind the chimney.

Ultimately the tests resulted in a compromise solution and No. 21C10 was modified to include a separate top cowl extending forward and across the top plate of the smokebox. Initially, short individual smoke deflectors were fitted, which stood proud of the casing at the rear but were joined to the casing at the front with an inward curvature. Tests on the road using cine cameras through the driver's window showed significant improvements in smoke clearance, but the increased width of the smoke deflectors diminished the forward vision for the driver. The plates were modified to a flatter shape on the other members of the first batch of locomotives during 1943 and 1944. The changes gave an increased flow of air upwards to the chimney and also an airflow along the sides of the casing which reduced the low pressure areas. A number of further changes were made to the airsmoothed casing over the lifetime of the class, none of which were totally successful in dealing with smoke and steam clearance.

Sanding on the Bulleid Pacifics was generally less than ideal, which was surprising bearing in mind that the propensity for Pacific designs to slip when starting because of the transfer of weight away from the coupled wheels was common knowledge. Initially steam sanding was only applied to the middle driving wheels on the first five locomotives. This was found to be woefully inadequate and additional sanding was fitted to the other driving wheels on the final five of the first batch. On later locomotives hand-operated sanding was applied to the leading wheels of the tender. One of the problems of the airsmoothed casing was the restricted access for the daily checks and procedures needed to keep the locomotive in service, in particular the filling of the sand containers. Despite a number of changes, this was never an easy job as the fillers were about halfway up the sides of the locomotive. Bulleid had designed the sandboxes in this way so that the boiler heat would help keep the sand dry.

With the inside motion and all the valve gear immersed in oil, mechanical lubrication of the other parts of the locomotive was carried out by two six-feed Wakefield lubricators which supplied oil to the cylinders, valve chests and rocker shafts. These lubricators were positioned below the smokebox front plate and were driven by ratchets from the valve rocker shafts. Their position made them prone to dust and smokebox char, even though they were supplied by a single reservoir which was designed to prevent this from occurring. In practice,

The original design for the sandbox on the Bulleid Pacifics. Being located under the casing, it was hoped that the sand would be kept dry by the heat of the boiler.

Author's Collection

the reservoir was always at risk from contamination and whichever solution was applied it made the filling difficult or the effectiveness of the lubricators less. On all of the first batch of ten locomotives there was a Detroit lubricator in the cab on the fireman's side but this was perfectly positioned for the fireman to be able to crack his head on it during the firing swing! On subsequent batches it was changed to a third Wakefield lubricator, fitted below the smokebox door with the other two. The axleboxes were lubricated via worsted trimmings fed from oil boxes situated on the footplate and mounted on the firebox backplate.

The ashpan was separated into three and the design allowed a free flow of air to pass over the grate area. In addition, they were fitted with self-cleaning hoppers that could be operated from ground level, which helped to overcome some of the dirty disposal problems normally associated with locomotives of this size. Air doors were fitted to the front and back of the ashpans, but there was no provision for dampers. This aspect of the design was revised when the Pacifics were later rebuilt. The middle ashpan was fitted with an additional door to ease the removal of the accumulated ash. This modified design later formed the basis of the ashpan on the British Railways Standard locomotives.

Ashpan for No. 21C1, showing the front damper door and hopper.

National Railway Museum, York

The cab on the Bulleid Pacifics was very roomy and comfortable for the footplate crew. The top of the cab roof was joined to the tender by a flexible sheet which helped to keep the elements out, but in the summer the temperature in the cab became overpowering for the fireman, particularly while firing heavily and travelling slowly. It was not unknown for the driver to be stripped to his vest in very hot weather, let alone the poor fireman! The cab was fitted with two sliding side windows and on later Pacifics the rear sides of the cab sheeting were turned in and fitted with metal framed glass windows. On No. 21C1 the driver had a bucket-type seat of the type found on some LNER locomotives while the fireman had a tip-up seat. The driver's seat was changed on subsequent members of the class to be similar to the fireman's.

Electric lighting was available both inside the cab as well as around the locomotive for servicing at night and during bad light. The power was provided by a steam-driven turbo generator, type TGH, which was rated at 350–500 watts and manufactured by J. Stone & Co. Ltd of London. The generator on the first batch of ten locomotives was mounted under the lubricators in front of the smokebox, but on subsequent batches the generator was mounted under the cab on the driver's side. The system illuminated the gauges in the cab using ultraviolet light, which allowed the instruments to be seen but the rest of the cab to remain dark, thus avoiding destroying night vision. Lamps also illuminated injectors and enabled inspection of the driving wheels, the bogies and the mechanical lubricators. In addition, sockets for hand lamps were provided over the centre driving wheel.

View of the footplate of No. 21C1 in April 1941. The restricted view from the windows can be clearly seen, as can the danger to the fireman's head!

National Railway Museum, York

The locomotive was fitted with electric route lights on both the front of the engine and the rear of the tender; these lights could be switched independently to provide the correct route indicators for the SR at night. The lamps themselves were fitted with brackets so that during the daytime the standard white discs of the SR could be fitted, one of which would carry the duty code in black letters. The siting of these discs caused some problems on the first twenty of the class as the second level lamps and brackets at the front of the locomotive were positioned such that the disc protruded outside the casing. This presented a danger to passing trains and also during high winds, when the discs were liable to fly off at speed with serious risk to life and limb. Additionally they obstructed some of the low positioned signals from the footplate crew. Despite this, the discs were not moved until after the completion of the first twenty of the class and it was not until April 1946 that No. 21C4 *Cunard White Star* was the first to have the brackets moved to the smokebox door.

Bulleid had applied a lot of effort to the design of the cab for his Pacifics and the result was good, ergonomically. The logical separation of the controls allowed both members of the footplate team to work together without interference with each other. The driver's side was fitted with the regulator (though on No. 21C1 it was duplicated on the fireman's side), steam reverser, brake valve and ejector, blower, steam chest pressure gauge, lubricating pressure gauges and cylinder cock controls. The fireman's controls included the boiler pressure gauge, firedoor opening treadle and control gear, steam heating controls, electric generator controls and the water and steam controls for the live steam injectors. The blower and whistle controls were duplicated for both the fireman and the driver, as were the Klinger-pattern water level gauges. The manifold mounted on the boiler backplate supplied steam to the vacuum brake and injectors, and was controlled by a valve on the left of the steam dome. A sliding opening was provided in the casing to access this control. The vacuum brake ejector, which on the first members of the class caused significant obstruction to the driver's view from the left-hand spectacle, was repositioned after the completion of the first batch of locomotives. Additionally, the Detroit lubricator which was in the fireman's way was also removed after the first batch was completed.

The firebox door was of a power-operated Ajax-pattern design, manufactured by Whitelegg & Rogers Ltd. The idea was to make the firing task easier for the fireman and at the same time reduce the problems associated with the ingress of cold air into the firehole. The door could be opened either automatically by using the floor level treadle or manually by a lever above the firedoor. The foot-operated treadle admitted steam to a cylinder which in turn opened the firedoor.

An unidentified 'Merchant Navy' locomotive under construction at Eastleigh Works, probably one of the 1948–9 series. Note the further sets of Pacific frames on either side of the locomotive.
National Railway Museum, York

In theory it sounded worthwhile, but in practice the mechanism was imprecise and took time to get use to. It proved awkward to coordinate the firing swing with pressing the treadle and timing the door opening. Some firemen found it to be a real advantage and used the system very successfully, but most were less than enthusiastic with the design and commonly opened the door manually. The door was designed to allow some air flow to the fire via a number of small holes in the door, but firemen who were used to operating with the door partly opened found it difficult to work with the door completely closed, only relying on the air holes. Additionally, the lubrication for the door operation sometimes overheated producing some very unpleasant fumes which would make the footplate a very uncomfortable place. This design of firedoor was changed when the locomotives were rebuilt.

The steam reverser was another area of contention which caused difficulties throughout the lives of the unmodified Pacifics owing to creep and the inaccuracies of cut-off indication. The steam reverser was chosen because Bulleid thought that the difficulties caused by the wide firebox and triple ashpans would produce a linkage that was complicated and hard to use, in the event a description which fitted the steam reverser! The horizontal LSWR pattern reverser was used rather than the better SER Stirling version purely because of space availability, also the LSWR device was already in service on the T9, M7 and D15 classes without major problems. The combination of the steam reverser with its problems of creep, sometime caused by poor maintenance and the difficulties of the chain-driven valve gear, made the driver's job very difficult. Drivers, having become used to the foibles of the class, tended to use the regulator to adjust power output rather than using changes in cut-off with fixed regulator openings. The steam reverser had modifications made to the hydraulic mechanism but none of these seemed to completely cure the problem. The reverser was another device which was changed during the rebuilds.

The 'Merchant Navy' class was fitted with a number of different tenders and at build each of the three series of locomotives was coupled to a different style of tender.

TENDER STYLES FOR THE 'MERCHANT NAVY' CLASS

Locomotive No.	Tender No.	Water capacity gall.	Built
21C1–10	3111–20	5,000	Ashford 1941
21C11–20	3121–30	5,100	Ashford 1944–5
35021–30	3341–50	6,000	Brighton 1948–9

The tenders were fabricated from steel plating of $\frac{3}{16}$ in thickness and in profile conformed to the general shape of the coaching stock, although as the batches progressed the tenders became less and less streamlined. The tenders were of welded construction and the first two batches were constructed at Ashford where

No. 35015 *Rotterdam Lloyd* on the fast line at Farnborough with an Up service. The coal had overflowed onto the rear of the tender!

Bob Barnard, Hugh Davies Collection

modern welding equipment had been installed. The first batch of tenders was estimated to cost £770 each, but by the time they entered service the cost had risen to £945.

All the tenders ran on six wheels, of the same BFB design as those on the engine. They measured 3 ft 7 in diameter, with round-top axleboxes and, also like the engine, had clasp brakes using two 21 in vacuum cylinders giving a breaking force equivalent to 115 per cent of the tare weight. The cylinders operated different brakes on each wheel, the cylinder at the front of the tender operating the brakes on the rear of the wheels and the cylinder at the back of the tender operating the brakes on the front of the wheels.

All the tenders were constructed with double frames, the outer frames being set 6 ft ½ in apart and the inner frames 4 ft ½ in apart. The frames were externally similar to the 'Schools' class tenders and overall the initial design was heavily based on Maunsell practice. The self-trimming coal bunker, which had already been tried by Bulleid on the 'Lord Nelson' class as well as on one of the 'Schools' class, and in common with all the 'Merchant Navy' class, had a capacity of 5 tons.

The tops of the sides of the tenders, known as raves, curved in to match the profile of the Bulleid coaches. The raves were changed in shape as the class progressed and the different styles of tender were completed. At the front of the tender the profile matched that of the cab with the top of the side raves curved down to a line approximately level with the top of the cab windows and continuing to the rear of the tender. The coal bunker was hidden behind the raves and on the first two tenders, Nos 3111 and 3112, the raves extended across the width of the rear of the bunker. Behind the coal bunker and in front of the water filler were the three vacuum cylinders used for the tender braking system, mounted on wooden beams and secured by metal straps. The cylinders were interconnected and the pipe ran through the tender tank to the braking system.

Between the frames sat the well to the tender tank, which was 13 ft long and 4 ft wide with a depth of approximately 1 ft 5 in and held close to 400 gallons of water. Within the well was a strainer intended to generate relatively particle-free water for the injectors but, blockages occurred because there was no external access to this strainer and the whole tank had to be drained to allow cleaning to take place from inside.

The springs on the first series of tenders included top link hangers, but these were removed in the 1950s when British Railways modified the 5,000 gallon tenders. Two pipes ran down the undersides of the tenders, the vacuum pipe on the left and the lagged steam-heating pipe on the right. On the first series of ten tenders the side sheets hid these pipes, but later versions of them had these sheets shortened and the pipes were visible. The pipes were connected to the flexible connectors at the rear buffer beam. The vacuum brake hose was fitted with a long swan neck at the rear buffer beam on the first tender, but later in service this was modified to match the arrangement and height of the steam connection located a short way up the width of the buffer beam.

No. 34011 *Tavistock* running light engine through Farnborough. On the tender can be seen the cover over the vacuum cylinders, one of the lifting eyes and rear coupling light.

Bob Barnard, Hugh Davies Collection

The rear of the tenders was high, derived from a mixture of Maunsell and Bulleid design ideas. Because of their height, the original tenders were fitted with three foot-steps on the right-hand side as well as four handrails to assist the enginemen when mounting the tender; close to the handrails were the lamp irons, which were rather convenient for the same purpose! Two vertical handrails were positioned on either side of the tender running almost from just above the buffer beam to the top of the middle lamp brackets. The top handrail ran horizontally and was positioned centrally below the top lamp. A fourth handrail was situated to the right and below the middle step. In addition to these steps Bulleid added a ladder of rectangular steel complete with two steps secured to the buffer beam face and alongside the right-hand buffer.

The route lamps on the tender were similar to those on the engine, and were constructed of matt-black painted brass and powered by the turbo generator. These lamps could be individually switched and became standard on all Pacific tenders. During the late 1940s an additional lamp was fitted to illuminate the coupling; it had a separate switch and a hood to direct the light downwards. The third series of tenders had these included from new and the earlier tenders were modified as they passed through the works. In October 1941 No. 21C4 *Cunard White Star* entered service with tender No. 3114, on which the handrails and steps were replaced by twin ladders constructed of 1½ in diameter tubular steel. These ladders became the standard on all the Bulleid tenders, but the actual shape and size varied; the British Railways design differed from that of the SR era. The ladders on the first series of tenders were set inside the buffers, running from above the buffer beam to the top of the rear tender rave, and had three rungs.

At the end of the Second World War the high rave at the rear of the tender, some 2 ft high, was cut down to a mere 4 in and as a result the ladders had to be changed to suit. The ladders were again constructed of tubular steel with three rungs, but the rungs were closer together because of the shorter length and the top of each ladder had two semicircular loops secured to the top of the tender to provide handrails. The bottoms of the ladders were attached to the running plate above the buffer beam. With the provision of twin ladders, the single two-step ladder down from the buffer beam was removed and two tubular steel ladders were fitted in its place on either side of the tender below the buffer, with one stile attached to the face of the buffer beam and the other stile to the buffer shank itself. The first tenders did not have foot blocks on the buffers but these were added when the rear ladders were modified. The cab ladders were similar to the original rear ladders, being constructed of ½ in steel bar with three steps which were suspended from the front plate of the tender.

The tender was fitted with three water filler holes, one at the rear in the conventional location and a further two inside the tender cab on either side. The latter were intended to assist the crew in filling the tanks by avoiding the problems of climbing up the rear of the tender each time. Unfortunately, the water was difficult to turn off quickly so it was not unusual for the footplate to become flooded, causing wet feet and clothing, not to mention 'words' between the driver and his mate! Also, water surges could occur while braking, resulting in the added

A grimy 'Merchant Navy' No. 35023 *Holland–Afrika Line* leaving Basingstoke with a tank train. The tender is a high-sided 6,000 gallon version and the TIA box can just be seen on the top right of the tender.

Bob Barnard, Hugh Davies Collection

'fun' of flooding the footplate while on the move. Consequently, the water fillers were not popular and were only really used to indicate water levels as Bulleid did not include water level gauges on the tenders. The flooding problems were never satisfactorily solved even though various different types of lid were tried until, eventually, in the 1950s the front tank fillers were dispensed with completely.

Tender cabs were common at this time among the Pacifics of both the LMS and LNER and Bulleid had a wealth of experience of these while working with Gresley, but on the SR these were considered very innovative and long overdue. The tops of the tenders were joined to the cab roof by canvas sheeting and inside a number of new provisions made life more comfortable for the crew. The front tender bulkhead was fitted with lockers, initially two on the driver's side but later a third was fitted on the fireman's side as well. Wartime-built tenders were also fitted with hooks for the footplate crew's steel helmets. The coal door to the bunker was located centrally with a shovelling plate set below it. Above the coal door and offset slightly to the fireman's side was the larger entrance to the bunker space. The hand brake had a separate column with a rotating handle to operate the brake and was positioned on the fireman's side of the coal door. The tenders also had blackout sheets fitted on each side of the tender behind the water fillers that were designed to be brought forward over the entrances to the cab.

The first tenders had a number of problems with leaks caused both by the thin plating used in construction and by water surging. At times the leaks were so bad that one wag at Salisbury suggested they should be used by the local council as water carts to lay the dust in the streets. In an attempt to solve the problem tender

No. 3114, originally coupled to No. 21C4, was fitted with additional wash plates in January 1944 and in April of that year it returned to traffic behind No. 21C7 *Aberdeen Commonwealth*. The modification provided no appreciable difference so when No. 21C2 returned to the works for its first general repair between March and June 1944 it had its tender (No. 3112) modified with the wash plates resited, the side bracing strengthened and much of the welding relieved of excessive stress. These changes proved to be very successful and became standard. The balance of the ten original tenders were modified by December 1945.

The original two tender designs were not completely satisfactory for the crews, so a number of modifications were carried out starting with tender No. 3113 which was coupled to No. 21C3 *Royal Mail* when first built. The changes included replacing the blackout sheets with steel slides and the tender bulkhead arrangement was modified to include a fire-iron tunnel inside the side raves on the driver's side. The bulkhead was moved forward by 12 in to compensate for the loss of coal capacity, bringing the lockers flush with the lower front of the tender. In addition, a fireman's locker was fitted, but this was shorter than the driver's to allow room for the brake handle to rotate. For some reason, tender No. 3111, originally coupled to No. 21C1 *Channel Packet*, was fitted with the steel blackout sheets after the war in the autumn of 1945 and tender No. 3112 never received this change, although both were fitted with the modified crew locker arrangements and fire-iron tunnel.

Tender No. 3113 as modified by British Railways. The rear coupling lamp can be seen clearly halfway down the middle of the tender.
Author's Collection

The footplate crew had the advantage of a 1 in pipe set inside the coal bunker which was perforated to give a spray. This was designed to assist in laying the dust from the coal space and could be operated by the footplate crew from the fireman's side.

The tenders were fitted with two gravity-fed sandboxes just in front of the tender below the fall-plate, which were manually operated, with the delivery pipes facing towards the rear of the tender. The sanding mechanism was only fitted after the first series of tenders was built and was intended to assist adhesion during tender-first running. The subsequent batches of tenders were built complete with the sandboxes. All were removed when British Railways rebuilt the locomotives.

The original tenders were found to be less robust than those common to SR locomotives, primarily owing to the light steel plate used and the all-welded construction. From 1944 to 1945 these tenders were subject to strengthening and a number of serious repairs were made to split welds. Eight of these tenders were modified by BR in the late 1950s, by having the raves cut down; the other two, Nos 3115 and 3117, had to have more serious work and the original tender tanks were replaced by a BR design. Tender No. 3115 was also fitted with a mechanical stoker in 1948 when running behind No. 35005 *Canadian Pacific*.

The second batch of tenders fitted behind locomotives Nos 21C11–20 were similar to the later eight of the first batch. The new batch of tenders were built with an increase in water capacity to 5,100 gallons, but with the same coal capacity. As a result, the tare weight at 22 tons 1 cwt and the gross weight at 50 tons 2 cwt both increased significantly over the first batch of tenders.

The tenders were fitted with new pattern short-spring hangers and the later design springs, so although the holes for the long hangers were still drilled in the frames, they were not used. Overall, the frames, wheels and wheelbase were the same as the previous design. The lower edges of the tender side sheets were shorter, thus showing more detail of the frames and the pipe for the steam heating on the right-hand side and the vacuum pipe on the left. The cab ladders were the same as previously, but the two rung ladders fitted to the rear of the tender were attached under the tender tank on one side and to the face of the buffer beam on the other. The ladders were supported at the bottom by the rear guard irons. Both of the tubular ladders fitted to the back of the tender now finished short of the raves and had no handhold loops at the top as on the original wartime design.

The tender raves ran from front to back without any change in height and curved gently in towards the top. The coal bunker was of an insert design and the bunker raves curved to form the tender cab roof. The bunker raves were significantly higher than the tender, to the height of the locomotive cab roof. The tender raves were matched to the curve of the cab over the side windows. Tenders No. 3121–7 were fitted with oval front water fillers with flat tops, but the last three had these plated over before entering service. The rest of this batch followed suit shortly afterwards. The vacuum tanks were fitted on the rear of the tender in a similar manner to the others with the main tank filler positioned behind them.

No. 34005 *Barnstaple* arriving at St Pancras with a train from Manchester on 17 June 1948. Note the Stanier tender, SR owner's plate and British Railways' number above the buffer beam.

B.W.L. Brooksbank, Initial Photographic

A hinged glass spectacle was fitted between the tender and the bunker rave to give some protection to vision while running tender first. The gap between the raves became a space for the fire-irons and was fitted with stands to protect the water fillers which were also placed in this gap. Photographic evidence suggests that rather than opening the spectacle to reach the irons, the fire-irons were stowed on top of the spectacle. Another problem produced from this design was a build-up of coal in the gap during coaling which was difficult to clear out, so a covered tunnel for the fire-irons was eventually fitted on later batches of tender. The tender was still not provided with a water gauge but a crude indication in the form of a tap was added to the left-hand side of the bulkhead.

The third type of tender fitted to the Bulleid Pacifics was that initially coupled to locomotives Nos 35021–30, which had an increased water capacity of 6,000 gallons but the same coal capacity. They had a slightly lower tare weight than the second batch of tenders, but were a lot heavier than the original design. The gross weight was some 3 tons heavier than previously at 53 tons 6 cwt. The 6,000 gallon tenders had the same number of wheels of a similar design, but the wheelbase was now 7 ft + 7 ft 4 in. These tenders were built without the front water fillers and, apart from the rear tubular ladders having loops on the inner stile, were similar to the previous batch.

One change, which was ultimately retrofitted to all the other tenders, was the addition of a coupling light at the rear of the tender, placed just below the top route indicator lamp and illuminating downwards onto the coupling components.

This design of tender was the first to have the French TIA (*Traitement Intérgrale Armand*) water treatment which is discussed in more detail in chapter five.

During the life of the Bulleid Pacifics a number of modified and temporary tenders were fitted, all of which are covered in more detail later. Briefly, temporary LMS tenders were fitted to three 'Merchant Navy' class engines during the locomotive exchange trials in 1948:

No. 21C17 *Belgian Marine*	04/48
No. 21C19 *French Line C.G.T.*	04/48
No. 21C20 *Bibby Line*	05/48

No. 21C18 *British India Line* took part in the exchange trials but ran on the Southern Region with a standard Bulleid tender.

The tenders used were 4,000 gallon six-wheel types, finished in unlined black with 'British Railways' in white letters on the sides. This was completely at odds with the malachite green and yellow stripes of the engine. The SR was not blessed with water troughs and consequently the SR locomotive tenders were not fitted with water scoops. Therefore, LMS tenders were coupled to the locomotives to allow the 'Merchant Navy' class to compete on equal terms by giving them the use of water pick-up when running over the other region's long-distance routes.

Five locomotives of the third and last batch of 'Merchant Navy' class were temporarily fitted with tenders from the lightweight Pacifics while awaiting completion of the correct tenders. Two 'Battle of Britain' 5,500 gallon 9 ft wide tenders and two 'West Country' 4,500 gallon 8 ft 6 in wide tenders were used. These tenders were finished in malachite green, unlined, with a number of different lettering styles. These engines were:

Locomotive No.	Tender No.	Capacity (galls)	Date Fitted	MN Tender No.	Date Fitted
35021	3333	5,500	09/48	3342	11/48
35022	3335	5,500	10/48	3345	01/49
35024	3333	5,500	11/48	3346	02/49
35026	3260	4,500	12/48	3350	07/49
35027	3288	4,500	12/48	3349	04/49

'Merchant Navy' tender No. 3345 was specially modified to take pre-weighed sacks of coal and was attached to No. 35020 *Bibby Line* in May 1956. At this time No. 35020 was newly rebuilt and test runs were being carried out. To cater for the coal sacks, the vacuum reservoir cylinders were arranged on either side of the rear of the tender.

In October 1947 a reconditioned Berkley mechanical stoker was purchased for testing on the 'Merchant Navy' class and was fitted to No. 21C5 *Canadian Pacific* in March 1948. The size of the fireboxes on these locomotives, at 48.5 sq. ft, was probably reaching the limit of continuous firing by one man. Furthermore, it was considered that a mechanical stoker could have allowed lower grades of

Name-plate details of unrebuilt 'West Country' No. 34042 *Dorchester* on 5 August 1955.
B.K.B. Green, Initial Photographic

coal to be used with the attendant cost savings. Having said that, previous experience of using crushed coal on both the Great Central Railway in 1922 and the Southern during the 1930s had not been a total success.

The mechanical stoker fed the coal to a distribution plate in the firebox via a flexible and reversible Archimedean screw which was powered by a small steam engine fitted to the front of the tender coal space. The coal was delivered to the required parts of the firebox by four separately controlled steam jets and, in the event of a failure, the fireman had the option of manual firing as the Ajax firedoors were still fitted. The maximum firing rate with the stoker was 5 tons per hour, but it is doubtful if this rate was ever fully used all the time. One of the difficulties was the need for consistently small size coal; this proved hard to achieve with mechanical coaling plants and, even with the coal crusher that was part of the stoker, problems still occurred. To assist in combating sparks the Lemaître blastpipe nozzles were increased in size to 2⅞ in diameter, although reports of unburnt coal and smuts appearing on dining car tablecloths were still heard.

The tender modified to accept the stoker was No. 3115. Some coal space was lost and the water space had to be modified to compensate for the loss due to the stoker, so the tender tank top was raised by approximately 14 in and two four-rung ladders were fitted with their tops visible above the tender raves. The vacuum reservoirs were also partially proud of the raves. The smaller size of coal required by the stoker caused a greater amount of dust; a canvas cover was spread across the coal bunker to combat this, but in practice it was never totally successful.

No. 35005 *Canadian Pacific* ran various tests and trials with the mechanical stoker fitted, in particular at the Rugby test plant in February 1950 and with the London Midland Region (LMR) mobile test unit over the Rugby–Euston and Salisbury–Waterloo lines during the same year. Comparative tests were carried out with the stoker removed in April–May 1950, then it was refitted in June 1950 and the trials were completed in April 1951, after a total of 77,338 miles. All in all, the stoker was popular with the footplate crews but the essential requirement of small lumps of coal was too great a complication. Perhaps if very fine pulverised coal, similar to the grades used in the USA, could have been used then it may have produced some economical advantages, although, in addition, the size of the firebox was probably not really large enough to justify the use of a stoker. The report on the trials with the mechanical stoker concludes by saying: 'that for normal English conditions of firing with typical grades of coal, the mechanical stoker is less efficient in working than hand firing'.

In 1952 British Railways decided that all of the various regions should be able to test water and fuel consumption and as a result it was agreed that coal-weighing tenders should be used on all regions. At that time the LMR was equipped with four tenders, the Eastern Region also had four and the Western Region had two, but the Southern Region only possessed one coal-weighing tender. (The LMR and Eastern Region tenders survived until they were scrapped, but with the yard-arms removed.) The Southern Region therefore modified tender No. 3343, which was a standard 6,000 gallon third series tender. The modifications were commenced in May 1952 and consisted of removing most of the top of the tender and fitting an inset coal bunker with vertical upper sides and a curved top to the rear. At the side of the bunker was a small rave, approximately 8 in high, which provided a gap for tender-first running and space for the fire-irons. The weighing equipment was supplied by the Transport & Engineering Co. of Lancaster and was housed in a padlocked metal box at the rear of the coal bunker. The equipment consisted of a steel yard-arm giving the weight of the bunker, with two bars suspended by camshafts, one showing the weight in 10 cwt divisions from 0 to 8 tons and the second weighing 0 to 10 cwt in 7 lb divisions. The coal bunker was secured when the locomotive was on the move by large, handled screws.

Coal was weighed as part of the preparation of the locomotive when it was first lit up and before leaving the shed. Further measurements were taken at the start and end of the duty while it was still attached to the rolling stock, and finally when the locomotive was back in the shed. Measurements included weighing ash and smokebox char at the end of the duty turn.

Tender No. 3343 was also equipped with the standard lamps and ladders fitted to the third series designs, but the vacuum cylinders were changed to the large cylinders of the 'Lord Nelson' type and were attached transversely to the left rear of the tender. When it was first built the tender was not fitted with a side or top curvature, but this was changed very early in service when a cab was built for crew protection when running tender first. This tender had the weighing equipment removed in December 1961 and was then rebodied. During service the

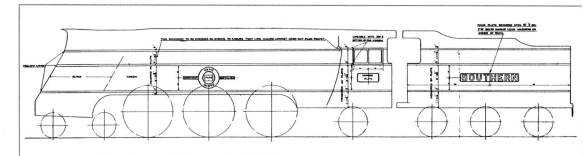

Original paint diagram for No. 21C1 showing the Southern lettering and the cast number and name-plates. This drawing shows Bulleid's requirements with the uppermost yellow band positioned below the top washout plug and in line with the top of the cab windows. Note that the black paint extends from the front side casing backwards to above the rear wheel of the bogie. In fact, contrary to Bulleid's wishes, No. 21C1 never appeared in this livery style and was out-shopped with the yellow band higher up the casing and no black at the front of the side casing.

National Railway Museum, York

self-weighing tender suffered badly from splitting tank welds, especially from the tank fronts. This tender was coupled to 'Merchant Navy' Pacifics Nos 35014, 35015, 35018 and 35024 during the time it was fitted with the self-weighing equipment.

Unlike the Pacific locomotives owned by other companies (particularly the 'Duchesses' on the LMS), the 'Merchant Navy' class only had four different principal liveries while in the original condition. Sometime before Bulleid's appointment as CME on the Southern Railway discussion had been taking place with regard to brightening the Maunsell green livery and Bulleid's arrival expedited the decision. A number of combinations of colours were tried, until in the middle of 1939 malachite green, edged in black and with yellow lining was chosen.

The first five 'Merchant Navy' Pacifics were turned out in malachite green but with a matt finish. This was in the hope that the small irregularities inherent from using large areas of thin sheeting for the airsmoothed casing would not be highlighted. The casing was finished with three horizontal yellow bands which ran the length of the casing and were continued along the tender. The top band cut above the highest washout plug, above the cab windows and continued along the tender rave. The middle band was at a level which included the bottom of the cab windows and the bottom line was some 3 in above the coupled wheels cut-out, both continuing along the tender sides. The casing was matt black from the top down to the guttering on the engine, and the top of the cab and tender were raves also black to match. The front of the locomotive, below the casing and the top of the tender were also black, as were the bottom of the cylinders and the casing forward of the buffer beams. The buffer beams and collars themselves were red, as was the background to the cabside number plates and name-plates. The wheels were green with black axle centres and tyres, while the rear of the tender was unlined green.

The original instructions given by Bulleid for the livery specified that the top horizontal yellow band passed along the casing just below the bottom washout plug and across the cab side sheets at the top of the cab windows. In addition, the front of the casing between the top and bottom yellow bands, to a point approximately over the rear wheel of the bogie and parallel to the angle of the casing front, was to be painted black. No. 21C1 *Channel Packet* was painted in this way while in the erecting shop at Eastleigh, but, for some now unknown reason, when the official photographs were taken it had been changed.

Drawings exist to indicate that had the Second World War not occurred then Bulleid may have used chromium-plated number and tender plates as well as external piping and handrails. The drawings show a name-plate placed on the casing side, above the cylinders, similar to the LNER A4s, as well as over the centre coupled wheel, the eventual position used.

With the weight reduction programme following the build of Nos 21C1 and 21C2, some changes resulted to the liveries. The cast number plates on the cab sides and front of the locomotive were removed and painted lettering was used instead. The front number was reduced to 6 in high while the cab side numbers were 9 in high. Both sets of numbers were in gilt lettering with the letter C being larger than the numerals to match the original design on the cast plates fitted to Nos 21C1 and 21C2. A further weight-saving exercise was the use of limpet board instead of steel plate for the airsmoothed casing. This needed additional horizontal strengthening using a rib which ran along the casing at a level just below the bottom of the cab windows.

Where locomotives had limpet board fitted and the extra rib, the middle yellow band was painted at that position to disguise the rib, thus placing the band some 2 in lower than on the first two locomotives. The risk of heavy handed damage to the limpet board was high and, because of wartime expedience, it was not unknown for holes to be made in the limpet board to aid maintenance.

A further change was a modification to the ownership plate on the smokebox door. It was originally an inverted horseshoe shape, but the footplate crews regarded this as unlucky and the plate was changed to a full circle on locomotives built after Nos 21C1 and 21C2. The extra space on the plate was used to include the date and place of construction.

The use of matt malachite green proved somewhat unsuccessful, as the paintwork soon become grimy and over a period of time assumed a dirty khaki hue with the yellow bands obscured or removed by the elements. This type of paintwork was not repeated. By July 1941, owing to wartime conditions, the SR decided that all locomotives except the express passenger locomotives should be painted unlined black. It was at this time that the sunshine lettering was produced to compensate in some small way for the austerity of wartime black. This lettering used 'old gold' yellow, green blocking and sunshine yellow highlights, complete with black internal lines. Nos 21C4–6 were hand painted with gilt lettering, black blocking and yellow highlights.

Early in 1942 the war situation meant that the SR was forced to paint even the express locomotives black, so the 'Merchant Navy' class started to be out-shopped in wartime unlined black. The first to enter service was No. 21C5 *Canadian Pacific* which, although originally painted green in the works, was changed to black prior to its naming in March 1942. The balance of the first batch and those of the second batch of Pacifics entered service in wartime unlined black. The locomotives originally painted in malachite green livery were changed to black as shown below:

No. 21C1 *Channel Packet*	December 1943
No. 21C2 *Union Castle*	June 1944
No. 21C3 *Royal Mail*	June 1942
No. 21C4 *Cunard White Star*	July 1943

In 1945, as the Second World War was drawing to a close, ideas of wartime austerity were changing and when No. 21C12 *United States Lines* entered Eastleigh Works for repairs to a broken chain in February of that year, a complete repainting of the locomotive was carried out ready for the naming ceremony in April. No. 21C12 was finished in malachite green, with three horizontal yellow lines running the length of the locomotive. The smoke deflectors fitted at that time were the short type and the two upper yellow lines from the casing continued across them. The casing above the top yellow line was painted black, as was the cowl and the top of the coal bunker. The rear of the tender was finished in unlined green and all the wheels were also painted green with black axle centres. The livery change was finished with a varnished top coat. Interestingly, while at Eastleigh this locomotive was initially painted photographic grey upon completion of repairs in February, prior to the change to green. Considering that as No. 21C12 was completed in December 1944 and released to traffic in January 1945 in unlined black, and only three months later at the time of the naming ceremony on 10 April 1945 the locomotive had already had three different liveries, No. 21C12 had become something of a chameleon. By August 1947 all of the locomotives of the first and second batches had been repainted in a similar livery to *United States Lines*, although there is photographic evidence that some of the post-war Pacifics were out-shopped with the cowls painted malachite green rather than black. Certainly, No. 21C9 was observed in this livery after repainting.

On 1 January 1948 the SR was no more with the formation of the nationalized British Railways. As a temporary measure, locomotives emerging from the works were finished with an 'S' prefix to the original Bulleid number and the wording 'British Railways' on the tender sides, in between the two yellow horizontal lines. The lettering was in the style of the original Southern lettering and as transfers were not available the sunshine lettering was hand painted. No. 21C5 *Canadian Pacific*, was the only 'Merchant Navy' to enter service between 20 March and 8 April 1948 with this notation, although No. 21C19 *French Line C.G.T.* received the 'S' prefix in the works but was renumbered prior to leaving.

Towards the end of March 1948 the full renumbering scheme had been announced for the whole system using a common method across all regions' locomotive stock.

An immaculate 'Merchant Navy' No. 35005 *Canadian Pacific* at Basingstoke with a West of England service.

Bob Barnard, Hugh Davies Collection

The 'Merchant Navies' lost the Bulleid notation and were renumbered 35001–35020. The first to carry the new number was No. 35005 *Canadian Pacific*. The renumbering scheme included a change to the method of displaying the front number, with the locomotives carrying a cast number plate on the smokebox door similar to the LMS type. This meant that the original circular Southern ownership plate had to be removed. After April all locomotives were renumbered before leaving the works, however, if there was no requirement for a repaint then they entered traffic with the new numbers but still with 'Southern' painted on the tenders. The exception to this was No. 21C2 *Union Castle*, which entered the works in August 1949 but returned to traffic still complete with the Bulleid numbering scheme. The reason may have been connected with the original cast number plates fitted to the first two members of the class or maybe a touch of pride in the old company. No. 21C2 was renumbered during the next visit to the works in January 1950.

An experimental lettering style was tried by Eastleigh Works in early 1948, using bold Gill Sans lettering in plain yellow with a black outline and numbers in the same style but plain yellow. By June 1948 the standard lettering style of medium Gill Sans commenced. In December 1948 the decision was taken to stop using the words 'British Railways' on the tender sides and use an emblem instead. For a period locomotives which entered the works for a repaint reappeared with blank tenders while awaiting emblem transfers.

The third batch of 'Merchant Navy' locomotives built (Nos 35021–30) entered traffic in malachite green in the style of No. 21C12 *United States Lines*. The exceptions to this were Nos 35024 *East Asiatic Company* and 35026 *Lamport &*

Holt Line, which were both painted in British Railways standard blue livery and were never painted malachite green. Owing to delays in delivery of the tenders some of green members of this batch were not lined. Locomotives fitted with the 6,000 gallon tenders were lined in the original SR style, with the yellow lines similar to the second series but with the taller coal bunker painted completely black.

In 1949 the cylinders were painted black to bring them into line with the general instructions of British Railways. This, in turn, also necessitated painting the front skirt between the buffer beams and the cylinders black, to avoid a somewhat odd appearance.

As part of the standardized 'corporate' image, BR had produced various different paint schemes for different classes of locomotives. During early 1949 the standard colours were announced and blue with black and white lining became the livery for the most powerful express locomotives.

The first 'Merchant Navy' to receive this was No. 35024 *East Asiatic Company*, when the locomotive entered Eastleigh to be coupled with its 6,000 gallon tender. Initially, the Eastleigh scheme was for blue to replace the malachite green and for 2 in horizontal crimson lines to replace the yellow lines. Why Eastleigh decided that the BR-decreed black and white lines should be changed to crimson is unknown. The blue paint, a middle to dark shade, was applied to the casing, including the cylinders, the cab and tender sides and the tender rear. The wheels were blue with black axle centres and tyres. The buffer beam and the background to the name-plates were red, while the top of the casing, front and all areas below the casing were black. The front number was a BR standard smokebox cast plate and the cab numbers were in yellow Gill Sans figures, edged in black. The tender sides were completed with the BR lion and wheel emblem centred between the crimson lines.

Having left Eastleigh Works on 12 February 1949, the locomotive travelled to Brighton for inspection on 18 February and entered traffic on the 22nd of that month. However, it returned to the works on 2 March 1949 and the crimson lines were changed to black and white lining, as per BR instructions. The original crimson lines were not approved! As standard for locomotives that had not been formally named, No. 35024 entered traffic with covered name-plates, although during service the name-plates were on full view at Exeter. The naming ceremony was carried out on 5 May 1949 at Waterloo. A further change to livery took place before the naming ceremony when the wheels and the complete splash skirt from the front of the locomotive to the rear of the tender were painted black. This became the final version of the blue livery and although No. 35026 *Lamport & Holt Line* appeared in blue in July 1949, up to that point malachite green was still used on locomotives coming out of the shops. Was this Southern independence or simply an attempt to use up stocks of paint?

The blue livery had been agreed contrary to expert advice and, as predicted, the paint did not wear well, so that by the middle of 1951 this colour was abandoned and Brunswick green was used instead. Nos 35011, 35014 and 35023 did not receive the blue livery, but went straight from malachite green to Brunswick green. The new colour scheme replaced the blue with Brunswick green and the black and white lining with orange and black, with no green showing between the lines. The other details remained similar to the blue livery. This style of livery stayed the same until the class was rebuilt, although some experiments with lining and emblem size were carried out, particularly on modified tenders where rectangular lining of the tender and cab side sheets was used. Typically, No. 35012 *United States Lines* was seen in service with this lining during July 1952. No. 35012 also had the small BR emblem on the tender, and the black splash skirt was limited to the area in front of the cab and the cylinders themselves. The cab sides and tender were similar to the lining on the rebuilt 'Merchant Navies' and, while the trial on *United States Lines* was brief, it is possible that it was designed to demonstrate the look of the rebuilt-style liveries.

All the name-plates on the 'Merchant Navy' Pacifics were works of art in themselves. They were cast in gunmetal using wooden patterns, with the circular section and the two wings being common to all the members of the class. The lettering varied in size on the circular section depending on the name of the shipping line, but the class name was in letters 2⅝ in high, raised by ³⁄₁₆ in. The plates were cast at the brass foundry in Eastleigh Works. In the centre of the name-plate was a vitreous enamel plaque showing the house flag of the company named, produced by Mead, McLean of London. During the time of the SR three name-plates were produced, two for the locomotive and one to be included within a coffee table as a gift for the person carrying out the naming ceremony.

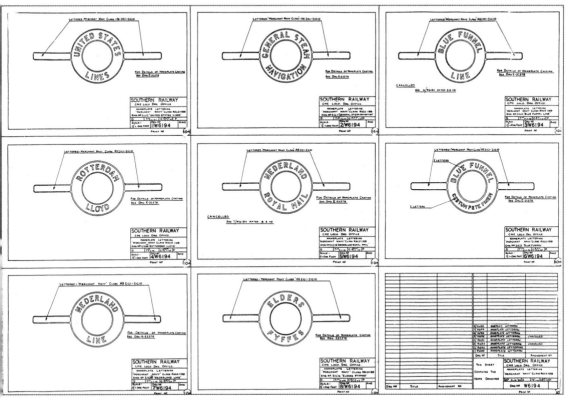

Southern Railway scheme for 'Merchant Navy' name-plates. Note the original names for *Nederland Line* and *Blue Funnel*, which were subsequently cancelled.

National Railway Museum, York

Initially, during SR and early BR times the raised letters were bright on a red background, but during 1952 BR decided that this should be changed to a black background. However, in the late 1950s this was altered once again to red. Unfortunately, Eastleigh either did not receive the information or ignored it, because the name-plates were still being produced with a black background as late as 1961.

The lettering in the circular plate containing the shipping company name was predominantly 3 in high, but some exceptions existed because of the length or style of the name. The differences are shown below:

Number	*Name*	*Letter size (in)*	*Special notation (in)*
35001	*Channel Packet*	4⅝	
35002	*Union Castle*	4⅝	
35003	*Royal Mail*	4⅝	
35004	*Cunard White Star*	4⅝	
35005	*Canadian Pacific*	4⅝	
35008	*Orient Line*	4⅝	
35009	*Shaw Savill*	4⅝	
35010	*Blue Star*	4⅝	
35014	*Nederland Line*	4⅝	
35020	*Bibby Line*	4⅝	
35007	*Aberdeen Commonwealth*	3⅝	
35013	*Blue Funnel*	3	Latin notation 2 in
35019	*French Line C.G.T.*		Top lettering as script 4 in and 2 in, initials 4⅝ in

No. 35013 was named *Blue Funnel Line* on 17 April 1945. However, in July of that year new plates were cast with only 'Blue Funnel' written on them, but including the Latin inscription *'Certum Pete Finem'*, which loosely translates to 'Make a good job of it'. No. 35006 *Peninsular & Oriental S. N. Co.* was one of only three members of the class which had the house flag of the shipping company flying in the same direction on both sides of the casing.

One illuminating aside concerns the name-plates on the 'Merchant Navy' class. During the wartime naming ceremonies it was common for Bulleid to attend, and a well-known correspondent of the *Railway Gazette* at the time once asked, 'Surely the CME of the Southern Railway has something better to do in this time of national crisis than to attend all these naming ceremonies?'

The 'Merchant Navy' Pacifics gave a good account of themselves while they were in good condition, but, although footplate crews generally liked them, the availability was poor and during the life of the unrebuilt Pacifics a number of modifications were undertaken to improve matters. These were predominantly concerned with smoke and steam dispersal, improving the steam reverser, attempting to cope successfully with the difficulties of the valve gear and dealing with slipping. In spite of these problems, the locomotives produced examples of outstanding performance and could never be forgotten.

CHAPTER FIVE

'MERCHANT NAVY' DESIGN CHANGES

The first Bulleid Pacific, No. 21C1 *Channel Packet*, began revenue-earning service at Salisbury shed in June 1941, but it was destined to suffer a host of minor problems which kept the locomotive on shed for days and sometimes weeks at a time, so much so that between 4 June 1941 and 6 January 1942 *Channel Packet* only ran 11,069 miles. In January 1942 the locomotive returned to Eastleigh to have new valve gear chains and for improvements to the oil bath. In the following September No. 21C1 was back at Eastleigh for the fitting of a new right-hand cylinder.

Similarly, the second of Bulleid's Pacifics, No. 21C2 *Union Castle*, did only marginally better, having completed only 15,411 miles when it was sent to Eastleigh on 27 January 1942 for work to the main steam pipes. Both locomotives had worked limited numbers of express services, with the majority of the low mileage achieved being accrued on goods services between Salisbury and Exeter or Salisbury and Southampton. Furthermore, the fuel consumption on the two locomotives was high, to put it mildly, No. 21C2 was reported on one freight duty as having consumed between 80 lb and 85 lb of coal per mile. Some of the difficulties experienced with the new Pacifics could be blamed on the unusual design of these locomotives as well as the newness and the learning curve for the footplate and shed staff. Salisbury shed estimated that for every Pacific 4½ hours were being spent out of service against 1 hour being spent on a 'King Arthur'.

The delayed construction of Nos 21C3–10 helped to reduce some of the more troublesome problems with the design and consequently these later designs gave comparably fewer difficulties than the first two locomotives. However, it was still felt necessary to allocate extra fitters to Salisbury and to Exmouth Junction sheds to deal with the maintenance problems. The fitters for Exmouth mainly came from the Kentish sheds.

Once all ten of the first batch of Pacifics were in service and being handled by a cross-section of crews, the areas of strength and weakness of the class became clearer. The steaming and power output was incredible, it would seem almost unlimited, despite the poor quality of wartime coal supplies. More power was available on the Southern than ever before and the ride at all speeds was very smooth and comfortable. Yet set against this was slipping, causing difficulties in starting even with moderate loads on the drawbar, slipping at speed, the restricted

Rebuilt 'Merchant Navy' No. 35025 *Brocklebank Line* leaves Basingstoke in 1957 with a Down train.

Norman Simmons, Hugh Davies Collection

lookout, high fuel consumption, oil leaks from the chain drive and oil bath, difficulties with the steam reverser and problems with steam and smoke obscuring the forward view. This, coupled with the obstacles in carrying out maintenance due to difficult access via the airsmoothed casing, generally made the locomotive availability less than ideal.

Simultaneous to the introduction of the class, Bulleid was running a number of test trains to gather data on haulage capacity and fuel consumption, and at the same time get a grasp on the difficulties of in-service operation. These were the start of many modification programmes throughout the life of the unrebuilt Pacifics which were unable to cure completely all of the problems with Bulleid's design. Ultimately, the only answer was to rebuild the class and remove or improve the troublesome features.

During the period 1941 to 1942 test trains provided a significant amount of data on the capacity of the 'Merchant Navy' class to haul heavy loads, the availability and also the fuel consumption. Runs of interest were No. 21C3 *Royal Mail* in November 1941 hauling a sixteen-coach special from Waterloo to Salisbury, and later that month hauling an 800 ton freight train between Salisbury and Exeter. No. 21C3 demonstrated the power of the 'Merchant Navy' Pacifics when working a seventeen-coach train to and from Bournemouth West. In addition, Nos 21C2 *Union Castle* and 21C4 *Cunard White Star* took charge of various eighteen- and twenty-coach specials between Waterloo and Exeter, proving without doubt that the Bulleid Pacifics were capable of working single locomotive loads unheard of on the Southern before.

COAL CONSUMPTION, MILEAGE AND AVAILABILITY AS OF
31 DECEMBER 1942

Locomotive No.	Mileage run	Coal burnt per mile lb	Months in traffic	Days in works	Days stopped on shed
21C1	35,082	56.2	18	96	213
21C2	39,892	57.8	18	102	197
21C3	38,548	56.7	15	106	168
21C4	25,911	59.1	13	108	172
21C5	29,688	60.3	12	81	103
21C6	35,992	61.5	12	36	88
21C7	23,892	58.6	6	33	47
21C8	24,625	57.4	6	27	46
21C9	26,802	58.7	5	5	34
21C10	24,224	56.3	4	6	29

From the table it can be seen that there was no apparent improvement in coal consumption as new members of the class entered service but availability did improve, slowly. The high fuel consumption was not just a failing of the design but was also caused by the crews being unfamiliar with the boiler. It was not uncommon for the fireman to do nothing with the shovel for the last 50–60 miles of a duty and while this is a reflection on the ability of the boiler to produce steam it also indicates that the fireman overdid the size of the fire. The Bulleid Pacifics were very forgiving of how they were fired, but when the optimum rate for the boiler had been exceeded then a lot of coal was consumed unnecessarily.

During the early days of service a number of mechanical failures occurred, mostly centred in the area of the valve gear. At this time Eastleigh really did not have sufficient knowledge of the stresses and strains set up in locomotive valve gear, particularly with such an innovative design as Bulleid's chain gear. Over the initial period of No. 21C1 *Channel Packet*'s service life the rocker shaft keyways on the middle piston valves failed twice, and No. 21C3 *Royal Mail* became incapacitated during a demonstration run for the same reason. The initial damage when locomotives were new was limited to sheared keyways, but as mileage increased the rocker arms also fractured and failed.

Bulleid instigated investigations and the cause was found to be momentary inequalities of steam pressure on the piston valve heads which produced excessive strain on the valve operating gear. The solution was to add balancing pipes between the ends of the steam chest and to fit additional bearings to support the rocker shaft. At the same time the piston valve liners were modified to stop valve breakages. The first locomotive to be so modified was No. 21C4 *Cunard White Star* in January 1944. The balance of the class were modified as they passed though the shops for new cylinders, as detailed overleaf:

Locomotive No.	Date	Mileage
21C1	12/45	143,639
21C2	07/45	139,675
21C3	02/44	91,235
21C4	01/44	124,306
21C5	01/46	158,606
21C6	02/46	173,100
21C7	08/45	138,575
21C8	11/44	113,569
21C9	09/45	153,174
21C10	03/47	205,633

During December 1942 No. 21C6 *Peninsular & Oriental S. N. Co.* suffered a catastrophic failure involving the valve gear. The locomotive was working the evening Exeter to Salisbury goods service when some half a mile east of Honiton one of the valve chains parted and thrashed violently around in the oil bath until the locomotive stopped. The damage caused was horrific, with oil thrown all over the boiler cladding, sleepers and lineside vegetation, all of which quickly ignited leaving the footplate crew absolutely helpless until the local fire brigade arrived. No. 21C1 *Channel Packet* suffered a similar but less damaging failure when the locomotive was backing down from the running shed to Salisbury station. The fire was rapidly placed under control by the shed staff, but long delays were caused while the locomotive was made fit to be moved back to the shed.

Rebuilt 'Merchant Navy' No. 35026 *Lamport & Holt Line* south of Brockenhurst with a Waterloo to Weymouth train on 20 June 1957.

M.H. Walshaw, Hugh Davies Collection

The oil baths for the chain-driven valve gear were a constant source of problems even after the final pattern had been fitted to No. 21C6 in April 1944. The oil baths held 40 gallons of lubricating oil and extended between the frames to enclose the chain drives, oscillating levers, the connecting rod big end and crank webs, the slide bars, cross-heads and piston rods. When the locomotive was running hard with a heavy load and at some speed, the disturbances caused by the violent movement of all these parts inside the oil bath would have been something to behold! Tremendous pressures were generated which led to distortion of the bath, and this was exacerbated by the flexing of the locomotive frames and the movement of the axles and steam chests all relative to each other. The net effect was that oil escaped from the seals, vents and cracks in the casing itself.

It is easy today to condemn the design of the bath, although it is significant that Eastleigh admitted that they had limited knowledge about the stresses caused by locomotive motion parts. As the end of the twentieth century approaches, with high-speed computer-aided design programs accurately predicting the results of events prior to a design actually being considered for production, it is easy to forget that even in the 1940s engineering design was still largely intuitive and based on human experience translated into plans drawn by hand. Consequently, any new design was always fraught with the prospect of problems. However, it rather begs the question that if the knowledge base was limited, why did Bulleid decide to proceed with this design?

The baths were fitted with vents to equalize the pressures caused, but unless they were clear they became a liability and in any case oil escaped via these vents even when they were clear. A lot of oil escaped from the axle seals and plungers, and at the same time the cracks in the bath allowed water and dirt to enter which caused corrosion of the motion pins, etc., particularly when locomotives were left unused for a period of time. The oil leakage reached the driving wheels, increasing slipping (which was always a problem with Pacific wheel arrangements), and soaked the boiler cladding, providing a fuel for fire underneath the airsmoothed casing.

A number of modifications were tried from 1942 to 1943, but it was only with the new design fitted to No 21C6 *Peninsular & Oriental S. N. Co.* that some success was experienced. Modifications were made to the vents, the seals and gaskets were improved to cope with the various movements and an attempt was made to divert the water dripping from the boiler away from the oil bath. The latter change met with varying degrees of success and water still had to drained off daily by means of a cock at the bottom of the sump. However, some water remained behind and, until a higher grade of non-emulsifying oil was used, the danger of corrosion still existed. In any case, if the locomotives were laid up for any length of time the oil baths had to be drained and refilled prior to the next use – an expensive, dirty and time-consuming exercise.

It was reported by Eastleigh Works that No. 21C16 *Elders Fyffes*, which went new into traffic in March 1945 and was officially named at Waterloo on 5 July of that year, returned to the works twenty days later after an explosion in the oil bath. The report stated that the 'oil bath had exploded after running hot'. It is difficult to reconcile this with the fact that the only bearing likely to run hot enough to cause an oil mist explosion was the centre big end, which was the very bearing that Bulleid had taken such pains to protect. It is still unclear as to exactly what did happen to cause the explosion.

The original batch of locomotives was built without sanding for reversing, which caused some serious difficulties, particularly when backing stock out of stations or into carriage sidings and when marshalling freight traffic. As a result, a simple provision was made by the addition of manually operated gravity-fed sanding, via containers which were fitted on the tenders so that they deposited sand between the tender and the locomotive wheels. In service these were never satisfactory, as the sand used to clog in the boxes and in strong winds a lot of the sand would blow away before the trailing driving wheels could reach it.

The other highly contentious area of the Pacific designs was without doubt the airsmoothed casing, which went through a number of changes during the life of the original members of the class. With hindsight, it is now probably fairly well understood that the slab-sided casing would cause problems with smoke and steam obscuring the view of the footplate. However, even though Bulleid was aware of the difficulties and admitted that the driver's view may be impaired, there was limited comparative data to help designers understand the problems. It was only after the locomotives were built and wind tunnel tests were carried out that the effects of low pressure areas on the sides of the casing began to be understood.

The initial attempt at solving the smoke-clearance problems, by using an enlarged aperture above the smokebox door forming a square opening with

Rebuilt 'Merchant Navy' No. 35013 *Blue Funnel* at Eastleigh shed. An unidentified Bulleid Pacific is receiving attention behind *Blue Funnel*.

Bob Barnard, Hugh Davies Collection

rounded corners on No. 21C2, was only partially successful. The modification was installed on the rest of the first batch, but in the meantime investigations continued in order to find a lasting solution. Lineside observations were made at sites determined by the footplate crews to be the worst and the conclusion was that low pressure air pockets along the firebox top and sides, coupled with the soft blast, was the prime cause of the problem. As a result of these difficulties No. 21C10 *Blue Star* was transferred to Eastleigh to be used as a mobile test bed from December 1942.

Initially, the front of the locomotive was modified to include a sharper-angled gap for the air flow at the top of the smokebox door and at the same time the chimney was lowered by $2^{13}/_{16}$ in. This provided no improvement at all and in fact made the situation worse, as the smoke failed to rise and instead collected around the cab like swirling fog, particularly in cuttings and when leaving tunnels. Changes to the chimney lip were then made, but these also proved unsuccessful so finally a scale model was produced for use in the wind tunnel at the University of Southampton. Contemporary records give the slight impression that the Eastleigh Works was reluctant to use the wind tunnel facilities, almost as a matter of pride.

Before the tests at the University of Southampton took place Bulleid had considered a number of alternative solutions. One of these involved the use of small steam jets positioned at the rear of the chimney on the top of the casing, presumably to break up low pressure pockets and give lift to the smoke. The control of these jets was left to the footplate crews to operate when the view became obscure. Other alternatives included new shapes for the casing similar to Gresley's A4s and *Cock o' the North* as originally built. The drawings concerning these modifications, especially the latter, gave a particularly pleasing design when combined with the other Bulleid features. While Bulleid was reviewing these designs, drawings were also prepared showing wedge-shaped cabs complete with three-sided windows; perhaps these changes were in mind some significant time before their inception.

The wind tunnel tests used a one-tenth size model with a removable front end which allowed different proposals to be attempted. The smoke and steam were simulated by the use of paraffin vapour. A number of different schemes were tested until a working solution was found; this was transferred to drawings and No. 21C10 *Blue Star* was taken to Eastleigh in April 1943 for modifications. The locomotive re-entered traffic fitted with a separate cowl extending ahead and across the top of the smokebox. It was shaped rather like an inverted trough, with short individual smoke deflectors which stood proud of the casing at the rear but curved in a similar manner to the original casing at the front. This was an error which was perpetuated by Eastleigh without reference to the wind tunnel results in an attempt to make the front of the locomotive less severe. This curve was not copied on the other locomotives in the first batch. The results of the changes improved the smoke clearance, but the view from the cab was now diminished by the extra width of the deflectors. These were redesigned to give a flatter configuration and the new shape was added to all of the first batch as detailed overleaf:

Locomotive No.	Date modified	Locomotive No.	Date modified
21C1	12/43	21C6	04/44
21C2	06/44	21C7	08/44
21C3	09/44	21C8	06/43
21C4	01/44	21C9	06/43
21C5	03/44		

The new design gave a better upward flow of air around the chimney and, by virtue of the additional air flow on the casing side, reduced the likelihood of low pressure areas.

The second batch of locomotives built between 1944 and 1945 was produced with a similar front end with separate vertical smoke deflectors which extended back to the rear edge of the outside cylinders and to approximately 6 in below the central yellow line. The chimney was completed with a fairing which at the rear extended to the top of the casing. By 1947 the smoke deflectors on the second batch were modified, with the length and depth increased by 2 ft and 5 in respectively. The result was an increase in effective smoke clearance and at the same time a more aesthetically pleasing front end. The first batch of locomotives was modified around the same time, while the third batch was built complete with the modified smoke deflectors. No. 35020 *Bibby Line* was fitted with different smoke deflectors from the rest of the class, seemingly because of the exchange trials, but in fact *Bibby Line* was spare and did not take part in the trials. The smoke deflectors were extended back almost to the rear of the front coupled wheel and covered the sliding opening to the front sandbox. Consequently, a new sliding opening was made in the smoke deflector and the sandbox was given a longer filler. *Bibby Line* kept these smoke deflectors until the locomotive was rebuilt.

The second batch of locomotives was completed with the fairing behind the chimney included. However, although some experiments were carried out on the first batch and at least three (Nos 21C1, 21C2 and 21C4) were fitted with the modified chimney, significantly none of the third batch was so fitted. The fairing was loosely based on the design for Gresley's P2 *Cock o' the North* and had a level surface from the top of the chimney to the top of the casing. In the early 1950s the fairing became standard for all Pacifics, although anomalies did exist: Nos 35019 and 35022 were fitted with single blastpipe chimneys and No. 35028 *Clan Line* was noted in March 1959 with a protruding chimney but no fairing. When the 'Merchant Navy' class was rebuilt the chimneys fitted were of a similar size to the early lipped versions, but with a petticoat below, based on the 'Lord Nelson' class design.

The airsmoothed casing covering the first of the class, No. 21C1 *Channel Packet*, was raised above the driving wheels to a level above the centres of the wheels and at each end curved downwards behind the cylinders and in front of the wide firebox. The casing continued over the outside cylinders with a rounded lower section and joined the bottom of the buffer beam. There was a slight increase in depth at the cylinders compared with the ashpans. The modifications to increase the effective smoke clearance left the rest of the casing basically the same, although by 1947 the rounded section at the front of the cylinders was removed.

'Merchant Navy' No. 35006 *Peninsular & Oriental S. N. Co.* waiting at Farnborough with a Down local to Salisbury. Judging by the amount of smoke the fireman is presumably preparing for the next part of the journey.

Bob Barnard, Hugh Davies Collection

For the first two locomotives built in 1941 the casing was constructed of 16 swg steel sheeting which was riveted and bolted together making access to the boiler fittings very difficult indeed. In theory, it was possible for the complete casing to be removed, rather like an inverted trough. While this did occur at Eastleigh Works, it was more likely that individual sheets were removed and stacked, if for no other reason than space constraints. With the weight reduction programme, Nos 21C3–10 were constructed using limpet board for the casing – a corrugated asbestos board which, while lighter, was also far more brittle and liable to local damage. Locomotives fitted with limpet board had a horizontal T-shaped bar which ran along the centre line of the casing and gave additional support.

The balance of the first batch of locomotives were built with a similar casing to No. 21C1, but with the casing continued joining the buffer beam halfway down with the curve under the cylinders formed from a separate portion. The second batch, Nos 21C11–20, generally followed the style and shape of the first ten, although the base of the casing was higher, that on the cab tender and firebox being at the level of the top of the buffer beams on the tender and engine. At the same time the curved cut-out over the coupled wheels was squared, with the casing behind the cylinders vertical and at the firebox end diagonal. The first of the new batch, No. 21C11, was built with a subtle difference to the style of the original members of the class, having the lower cylinder cladding carried forward enveloping the bottom of the buffer beam. The others in this batch were similar to the first batch. No. 21C11 kept this difference until 1947 when the casing was changed to become the same as Nos 21C12–20.

The third series locomotives were built with the same style of casing as Nos 21C12–20, but were fitted with larger smoke deflectors which extended back to a point approximately halfway along the slide bar. By the early 1950s maintenance was becoming a major issue across the whole of British Railways and the 'Merchant Navy' class had to sacrifice some aesthetics by having the casing removed in front of the cylinders and buffer beams to improve accessibility and maintenance. This change became the standard for all of the class.

The first members of the class suffered from reduced forward visibility which, apart from the problems with smoke, was also due to the limited size of the cab front windows – being narrow slits rather than recognized windows. To make the situation worse, small sun shields were fitted which projected forward from the cab sides, limiting the forward and side views and also trapping smoke and steam from the exhaust into the bargain. The cab was provided with two square, sliding side windows which, during the war, had the glass replaced by steel sheet. On Nos 21C1–2 the window frames were constructed of steel, but on Nos 21C3–20 they became wood, while the third batch was constructed with brass window frames. The first two locomotives built did not have rain gutters, but from No. 21C3 onwards a gutter was fitted high on the cab roof at the same level as the ladder angle on the boiler casing. During BR days the guttering was lowered to a point just above the windows.

The second batch cabs were constructed without the lower curve and became more vertical. They also included a major crew improvement with the rear of the cab side sheets turned in approximately 12 in, which gave some protection against draughts. In addition, to aid tender-first running, a glazed metal-framed window was set into the upper part, matching that of the tender.

Visibility was always a problem. In spite of the casing changes which improved the smoke and exhaust clearance, the small front window, glare and reflections from the casing and footplate created significant problems for footplate crews. Consequently, a major rethink on the shape of the cab was carried out to improve forward visibility. The result was that the top corner of the cab was cut back at a wedge-shaped angle and a large front window was placed in the increased space. The mid-line of the cab was also shaped into a shoulder. The first locomotive to be modified was No. 21C8 *Orient Line*, which appeared in a similar style to that of the 'Battle of Britain' Pacific No. 21C164 *Fighter Command*, but still with only two side windows and the remainder of the cab unchanged. The modification proved to be successful but for one small detail: the footplate crews had great difficulty in cleaning the front window because only two side windows were fitted. The design was changed again to include three smaller rectangular windows which could be moved to provide room when cleaning the front glass. The other nineteen members of the class were modified between 1948 and 1953 to include the wedge-shaped cab and three windows and *Orient Line* was changed to three windows in July 1949. The balance of the class were built from new with the modified cab and three side windows. The locomotives that were selected to run in the exchange trials in 1948 (Nos 35017, 35018, 35019 and 35020) were the first to receive the modified cab shape.

During the Second World War, with the blackout restrictions and the steel sheets fitted to the side windows, it was difficult, even in daytime, to see the hydrostatic lubricator. To solve this, starting with No. 21C2 a small window was placed above the main cab window on the fireman's side, this window was plated over from 1947.

One of the more irritating aspects of the 'Merchant Navy' Pacifics was the ever-present tendency for the steam reverser to creep. This was not a major problem if the locomotive was driven under full regulator, with the cut-off used to make adjustments to the power output. Unfortunately, because of severe vibration when the cut-off was appreciably shortened, drivers were very reluctant to practise this style of driving and it was not until after the rebuilds were in service that the use of the cut-off become more common. The lack of fine adjustment to the reverser also caused an unnecessary waste of fuel, as the locomotive was working less efficiently than circumstances would normally demand.

August 1944 saw No. 21C6 modified with an experimental hydraulic locking mechanism which was trialled over a number of test runs between Woking and Exeter to evaluate its effectiveness. Better control was available but even then creep still occurred, although this was considered to be unlikely to seriously inconvenience crews on regular express duties. The later-built members of the class were completed from new with the modified locking device, but records show that apart from No. 21C6, only Nos 21C5 (June 1950) and 21C10 (February 1945) from the first batch were modified before the class was rebuilt. Prior to the second batch of locomotives being built, Bulleid had produced drawings showing both a screw and a fine adjusting steam reversing system. Neither proved satisfactory, which is surprising considering the rebuilt locomotives were fitted with screw reversers based on those fitted to LMS express locomotives that had been in service for a number of years.

The reversing creep was further complicated by the basic design of the valve gear because the rocking levers multiplied the intended movement by 2.66:1 and, of course, any wear or inaccuracy was also magnified by the same ratio. Because of this the valve openings could vary while running, without the driver changing the cut-off, so that one valve could be just opening while the other had twice the aperture intended. Consequently, the valve gear and reverser had to be maintained in top condition. This tended to use up a lot of the fitters' time, something the design was actually intended to lessen.

The propensity of slipping when starting was never completely cured until the 'Merchant Navy' class was rebuilt, but the violence of the slipping led to a number of buckled or broken coupling rods. By 1953 this had reached such a level that a design for a stronger pattern was produced. It was plain and rectangular in shape, but with the rebuild of the whole class pending only a few unrebuilt locomotives were actually fitted with the redesigned coupling rods.

With the difficulties of filling the sandboxes it was inevitable that some sand was spilt. With the front boxes the result was the contamination of the slide bars and subsequent abrasion damage. September 1948 saw No. 35012 having the front sandboxes blanked off, and during 1949 and 1950 a number of locomotives

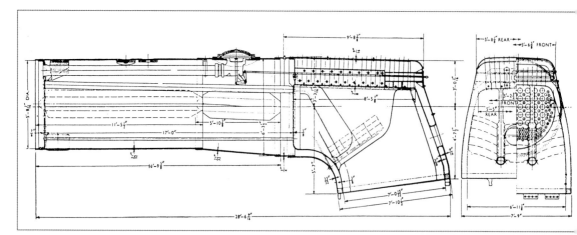

Arrangement drawing of the boiler fitted to the last twenty 'Merchant Navy' class.
National Railway Museum, York

(Nos 35001–2, 35005, 35009, 35014–15 and 35017–19) were fitted with slide bar covers to protect them from sand ingress. The covers caused maintenance problems of access to the slide bars and in any case were not the complete answer. From 1951 the front sand pipes were removed completely and the filler holes blocked off, but these procedures were not always carried out at the same time.

The airsmoothed casing made access to the boiler fittings very difficult and, while the sheets could be removed daily, access proved time-consuming, to say the least. Consequently, on No. 21C3 *Royal Mail* the casing was provided with two upward-opening hatches, one on the driver's side on the top casing for access to the steam manifold valve and the other on the fireman's side for access to the whistle valve. The whistle for the 'Merchant Navy' class had the note of middle C and was situated horizontally under the top casing on the fireman's side of the locomotive. At ground level it was not visible, but viewed from above it was contained within an aperture in the top casing between the safety valves and the steam dome. On No. 21C3 onwards the aperture was rectangular, occupying the width of the top portion of the casing with the whistle positioned along the centre line of the aperture.

The casing hatches were continued with the second batch of locomotives, but by 1947 the securing mechanism was changed to a lever with all locomotives being changed as they went though the works. The final batch was built with this change included. In 1952 British Railways changed the design of the hatches to a sideways-sliding cover which was provided with two grab handles. All the class received this modification prior to being rebuilt.

The Bulleid boilers were superb providers of steam and gave very little trouble during the lifetime of the class. Apart from the change in the position of the boiler taper on the last twenty boilers and the spares, very little change to the design was needed. The three Ross pop safety valves were sited in a triangular configuration in front of the steam dome on the front ring of all the boilers built.

During the early 1950s three changes to the safety valves took place, the first and possibly the least known was the creation of a well for the valves immediately in front of the whistle access. The well was designed to improve the accessibility to the valves and the bottom could be removed to reach the base of the safety valves. Ten of the class were changed, with five having a strengthening bar fitted across the well:

Locomotives fitted with the well	Locomotives fitted with the well and the bar
35010	35001
35015	35006
35016	35011
35024	35014
35026	35019

The position of the safety valves on the front boiler ring produced one unforeseen result: the valves lifted below the pressure set when heavy braking caused the water to surge in the boiler. Consequently, the valves were resited at the rear of the boiler between the firebox and the steam dome. The three valves were still retained, but were positioned in a shallow trough across the line of the boiler with

'West Country' No. 34094 *Mortehoe* leaving Southampton Central. The locomotive is fitted with AWS and has no shield on the casing.

Roger Holmes, Hugh Davies Collection

each valve at right angles to the boiler. The initial locomotive to carry the changes was No. 35024 in November 1952, No. 35008 was fitted a year later and twenty-four locomotives in total were eventually modified. All these were completed by January 1957. The other six were rebuilt prior to the change, but the valves were resited as part of the rebuild.

Modified from original design				Modified during rebuild
35001	35007	35017	35024	35009
35002	35008	35019	35025	35011
35003	35010	35020	35027	35012
35004	35014	35021	35028	35013
35005	35015	35022	35029	35018
35006	35016	35023	35030	35025

The final change to the boilers was the reduction in boiler pressure from 280 psi to the more common 250 psi. The decrease was originally considered in 1946 as a means of producing some economies in boiler repairs. The boilers were such good steamers that the reduction in pressure did not seem to cause any lack of capability and in any case it was very rare that the full pressure was used in the steam chest. The first 'Merchant Navy' locomotive to have this change was No. 35012 *United States Lines*, which left Eastleigh Works on 4 July 1952 set to 250 psi. No. 35024 *East Asiatic Company* followed in November of that year and at the same time was the first of the class to have the Ross poppet valves resited. The boilersmith at Eastleigh estimated that the reduction in maintenance and wear resulting from the decrease in boiler pressure would add some 80,000 miles between boiler lifts. An additional five spare boilers were produced for the 'Merchant Navy' class, initially three under order No. 2575 and subsequently a further two with order No. 3407.

During the tests of the thermic syphons at Rugby, carried out between 8 December 1953 and the end of January 1954, no appreciable advantage was found between a steel firebox without syphons and the standard boilers. The report produced by the Rugby testing station was inconclusive:

Maximum boiler output	Unchanged
Inlet steam temperature	40–60 degrees higher
Boiler efficiency	Marginally higher
Combustion	Unchanged
Smoke emission	No reduction
Clinkering of fire	A major problem with poor fuel
Ease of firing	Much more difficult
Fuel consumption	Unchanged

Conclusions: It would not be economically justified on boiler performance alone to remove the syphons, nor would it be worth while fitting them in any British coal-fired locomotive of similar or smaller size than the 'Merchant Navies'.

The Rugby tests involved No. 35022 *Holland-America Line*. Previously the boiler without the syphons had been carried by No. 35014 *Nederland Line* from

25 August 1951, although problems with erratic steaming occurred and difficulties were found with clinker build-up. After running only 781 miles a new and modified brick arch was fitted which produced instant improvements to steaming, but this was still below that experienced with the standard boilers. Clinkering still posed a problem and on long journeys a further problem was created, that of 'bird-nesting' on the tube plates. Additional modifications were made to the brick arch, resulting in an improvement in steaming and the effective reduction of the other difficulties to a manageable level.

Having been fitted with a firebox without syphons, this boiler was never refitted. Three locomotives were fitted with this boiler:

Built at Eastleigh, order No. HO 1189, No. 8, New steel firebox – no syphons	28/01/45
Fitted to No. 35014 Removed at 116,005 miles	25/08/51 01/10/53
Fitted to No. 35022 Removed at 233,736 miles	21/11/53 30/03/57
Fitted to No. 35017 Removed at 566,940 miles	30/03/57 05/07/63
Boiler broken up	09/08/64

Over the build period of the class two different types of rear truck were fitted. Both were of the delta design but one, the original, was cast and the other was steel fabricated. This change in design was a weight-saving measure and paralleled the introduction of fabricated frame stretchers. Throughout the lifetime of the locomotives the trucks were interchanged during overhauls at the works, seemingly without any recognized rational other than availability. Nos 21C1–20 were fitted at new with the cast trucks and Nos 35021–30 were built with the fabricated design. The cast trucks were fitted with either leather or Rexine covers over the wheel bearings to prevent ash and dust ingress, but the fabricated trucks were never so fitted. In any case, these covers were dispensed with on the cast trucks from 1946 onwards.

The BFB wheels fitted to the Bulleid Pacifics proved very successful, giving a 10 to 20 per cent reduction in weight and uniform support to the tyre, which was shrunk into a lip. This method of fixing the tyres became standard British Railways practice. Only one change was attempted during the unrebuilt period when No. 21C18 *British India Line* was fitted with fabricated driving wheels as an experiment. The results were not successful and the driving wheels were replaced with the original cast design.

After the end of the Second World War No. 21C2 was fitted with a Flaman speed recorder, providing both visual and paper records of the locomotive's speed. The speed recorders were sited beneath the fireman's seat at the side of the cab, with drive being taken from the rear coupled wheel on the fireman's side and held by an inverted triangular bracket attached to the casing. The drive was transferred via a horizontal shaft to the base of the cab. In 1948 No. 21C5 was also fitted with the Flaman recorder and later all the Bulleid Pacifics taking part in the exchange trials, Nos 35017–20, were so fitted. Two of these locomotives, Nos 35018 *British India Line* and 35017 *Belgian Marine*, kept the recorders well into the 1950s, but upon rebuilding all evidence of the Flaman devices was removed.

During the war little work had been carried out on the problems of boiler corrosion, scale reduction and sludge deposits, all of which reduced the times between boiler washout and also decreased the life of the boilers. The SR lines east of Exeter were supplied with water from chalk-based sources which contained significant amounts of calcium and magnesium bicarbonate. The water supply at the larger motive power depots was treated by a softening process that allowed the harmful salts to precipitate in a form of sludge, which was then removed. West of Exeter, where the hardness was lower, some water processing was carried out by way of bypass valves and chemical briquettes.

Some haphazard attempts to solve these problems had been made during the early 1940s but they were somewhat limited. However, it was noticed around 1943–4 that on the water side of the inner firebox plates of the 'Merchant Navy' locomotives significant amounts of scale were occurring and temporary repairs had to be made by welding additional diaphragm patches around the syphon holes. These repairs were necessary only a relatively short time after a locomotive first entered traffic and were a cause for concern, particularly with Bulleid's use of welded steel fireboxes. Consequently, expert advice was taken from T.H. Turner, a water treatment chemist, as to how these difficulties could be tackled. After investigation it was agreed in 1946 that the French *Traitement Intégrale Armand* (TIA) system should be used to reduce the scale, corrosion and pitting. Generally, the locomotives were not modified until the boilers were renewed, although the TIA treatment was introduced by Bulleid in 1947. All the boilers on the first batch of locomotives were renewed and from 1950 to 1953 the second batch was similarly treated, the last batch of locomotives being fitted from new. Without the intervention of the Second World War, it is considered that Bulleid may have introduced this system from the inception of the class, although no firm evidence exists to confirm this.

The TIA system consisted of a steam-heated holding tank set in the rear of the tender behind the coal bunker. The tank was approximately 3 ft long, 1 ft 6 in wide and 1 ft high, and the water treatment chemicals consisted of sodium carbonate, tannin, an anti-foam compound and occasionally sodium phosphate (Calgon). The chemical fluid was displaced automatically into the tender tank at a rate which was in proportion to the requirements set out by the daily analysis of the both the boiler and tender contents. The result was that the feed water was kept chemically capable of precipitating all the scale-forming salts in the form of a soft non-adhering mud, which was removed by a manual blow-down valve at the base of the firebox. By using the blow-down valve for approximately half a minute every hour, priming could be avoided and most of the precipitate could be deposited on the ballast. The TIA system made it possible to extend the boiler washout periods from 7 to 56 days, which neatly coincided with the routine inspection periods of the firebox plates and boiler stays. The tannin in the treatment chemicals helped to reduce the boiler corrosion by reducing the oxygen content of the water and the anti-foam compound (organic polyamides and polyoxides) helped to lessen the surface tension of the bubbles in the boiler water with the consequent reduction in boiler priming.

The ongoing review of costs made during British Railways times resulted in the TIA system being replaced from 1956 with a standard BR method using briquettes, which was simpler, cheaper and more compact. The briquettes were placed in a 10 in diameter steel tube which was 3 ft 6 in long with a circular lid on the top. The steel tube was fitted into the tender tank with the top protruding adjacent to the main water filler and along the lower section were six pairs of removable plugs set 4 in apart. Within the tube was a stand to support the briquettes which had four holes to allow water circulation. The level of water treatment was controlled by plug adjustment and by the composition of the briquettes themselves. These had a similar content to the chemical reagents used in the external water treatments of the 1940s, but also included anti-foam. The detailed composition was based on the hardness of the source water and an analysis of the boiler water supply, which was made every two days on water drawn from the glass draincock gauge, after blow-down and boiler filling. The water treatment controller would make decisions on any changes needed to the water treatment and issue details to the footplate crews on procedures for manual blow-down, both at the shed and on the road.

While the locomotives of the 'Merchant Navy' class were innovative, to say the least, and had a significant effect on the workings of the Southern Railway, it was not until they were rebuilt that, in engineering terms, they became a satisfactory design.

CHAPTER SIX

THE BULLEID LIGHT PACIFICS

The end of 1943 saw the country looking towards a happier future. With the war considered all but won, thoughts were no longer on an Allied defeat but on how long it would be before victory. The railways by this time had adapted well to the wartime conditions and, while the services offered were not up to the pre-war quality, standards were much improved and although the trains were heavier and slower they were able to provide reasonable timekeeping. Thus it was that the railways considered planning for the future peacetime. For the SR this proved to be particularly difficult because of the heavy investment, both financial and in resources, in the pre-war electrification schemes. The company was left with an ageing motive power fleet consisting of a number of diverse medium power locomotives and a limited number of modern express and mixed traffic locomotives.

At Christmas 1943 the outstanding motive power orders consisted of a further twenty 'Merchant Navy' class locomotives, fifteen Q1s, twenty-five diesel electric shunters and twenty other unspecified passenger locomotives. The latter had been originally ordered from Brighton in April 1941, but very little progress had been made so as a result no materials had been ordered. The passenger locomotives had been intended for the West Country where the majority of the major routes were worked by Drummond T9 4–4–0s and N class 2–6–0s, but because of the heavy military demands on the railways the N class were needed for freight duties on other parts of the SR system.

The early designs for locomotives to work the West Country services drawn up in December 1942 were for a compact and neat three-cylinder 2–6–0 of a similar design to the Gresley K4s built for the West Highland line but fitted with three independent sets of Walschaerts valve gear, a Belpaire firebox and BFB wheels. These locomotives were to have no unconventional features or any standardization with the Q1s or 'Merchant Navy' class. While the original intention had been for a 2–6–0, as the war progressed the quality and size of available coal fell, so the use of a narrow firebox was considered less than advisable. Consequently, Bulleid had the drawings changed to include a wide firebox, which meant a further stretch of the design to incorporate a rear truck to accommodate the larger firebox. With further reviews of the requirements Bulleid substituted a front bogie for the front truck to gain better riding over the West of England curves. The design had been increased from a moderately sized 2–6–0 to a main line Pacific with a fire grate size which was nearly as large as on the Gresley A4s.

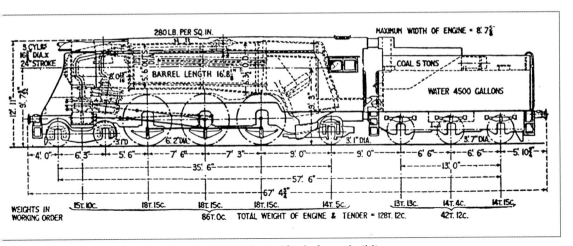

Arrangement drawing of the Bulleid Light Pacific, before rebuilding

Railway Gazette

The need for new and more powerful locomotives for the West of England was based on sound logic but the requirement for a Pacific design was suspect, to say the least. Even if the path from the 2–6–0 concept to the Pacific was rational in approach, the West Country loadings were extremely light, the all-year average being three coaches and the summer services seldom exceeding six.

As with all decisions, other factors affected the design, especially the need to provide more powerful locomotives for the Eastern Section's business services. In 1938/9 a requirement for more powerful locomotives on the Victoria Continental boat express services had been accepted, but with the electrification programme no provision for other express services was made. Now, with the realization that the modernization programme for the south-east of England was likely to be placed on indefinite hold, some additional powerful steam motive power was necessary to meet the post-war requirements of increased loads and improved services.

The war had tuned Britain's economy to the needs of supplying the military and the people, so a requirement outside the immediate needs of war presented huge difficulties in collecting materials and establishing an assembly line. This would have been more than doubled if two classes of significantly different design were built concurrently. Bulleid decided that, in the circumstances, one class must suffice and that the Eastern Section must have priority, and for similar reasons the 'Merchant Navy' details were included. The power of the Light Pacifics was generous to say the least and it is doubtful if they ever worked to full capacity over extended periods. For all the persuasive logic and the difficulties of the time, there does seem to be a touch of reluctance on Bulleid's part to proceed in this direction; one almost feels he may have been a victim of circumstances.

Gresley's solution when faced with a similar problem was to introduce the capable 'Green Arrow' 2–6–2s and he would have followed these up with a cut-down version, the 'Bantam Cocks', for less exacting duties. However, after Gresley's untimely death Edward Thompson built his B1 4–6–0s instead.

Following the temporary withdrawal from service of the Bulleid Pacifics because of problems with the axles in May 1953 it was these 2–6–2s and 4–6–0s which took over the Light Pacific services and carried out their duties with panache. They did so with considerably less maintenance and a significant reduction in fuel consumption. It was obvious to both observers and footplate crews that the 'Green Arrows' could haul the heaviest loads with ease, and any additional power was not only superfluous but probably also wasteful.

The Light Pacifics were constructed with all the principle 'Merchant Navy' features: BFB wheels, Bulleid Walschaerts valve gear fully enclosed in an oil bath, wide Belpaire firebox complete with an inner all-welded, steel box with thermic syphons, 280 psi boiler pressure, Lemaître blastpipe, electric lighting and an airsmoothed casing. The boilers were similar to the later 'Merchant Navy' locomotives with the boiler barrel front ring parallel and the rear ring tapered along the base to reduce water content and weight. In all 110 locomotives were built in the 'West Country' and 'Battle of Britain' classes but there was some contention about the need to build this number of power Class 7 locomotives.

PRINCIPAL DIMENSIONS OF THE BULLEID LIGHT PACIFICS

Cylinders × 3 (diameter × stroke)	16⅜ in × 24 in
Piston valve diameter	10 in
Bogie wheel diameter	3 ft 1 in
Coupled wheel diameter	6 ft 2 in
Trailing wheel diameter	3 ft 1 in
Wheelbase	6 ft 3 in + 5 ft 6 in + 7 ft 6 in + 7 ft 3 in + 9 ft 0 in = 35 ft 6 in
Boiler diameter	5 ft 9 in to 6 ft 3 in
Boiler length	16 ft 9 in
Firebox length	6 ft 11 in
Heating surfaces	
Tubes (112 × 2 in)	1,121 sq. ft
Flues (32 × 5 in)	748 sq. ft
Firebox and thermic syphons	253 sq. ft
Total evaporative	2,122 sq. ft
Superheater	545 sq. ft
Combined total	2,667 sq. ft
Grate area	38.25 sq. ft
Working pressure	280 psi
Tractive effort (85%)	31,000 lb
Weight in working order	
Bogie wheels	15 ton 10 cwt
Leading coupled wheels	18 ton 15 cwt
Centre coupled wheels	18 ton 15 cwt
Trailing coupled wheels	18 ton 15 cwt
Pony truck	14 ton 5 cwt
Engine total	86 ton 0 cwt
Tender (4,500 gall.)	42 ton 12 cwt
Locomotive total	128 ton 12 cwt

Basingstoke in 1957 with 'West Country' No. 34007 *Wadebridge* waiting to depart and BR Standard No. 73115 waiting alongside.

Norman Simmons, Hugh Davies Collection

The Bulleid Light Pacifics were fitted with a rocker grate which was something of an innovation for the SR. The design was fundamentally similar to those fitted to the LNER A2/1 Pacifics of 1944–5. To avoid damage caused by the burning of the grate firebars, front dampers were not fitted; instead, the hopper ash containers were open at the top. Generally the boiler, firebox and cylinders were smaller than those on the 'Merchant Navy' class which allowed the Light Pacifics access to routes that had previously been limited to Maunsell 2–6–0s. The reduction in size was not immediately obvious from the lineside and the shape and size of the name-plate was the only definite indicator to the casual observer.

While the majority of the Light Pacifics were built at Brighton, six of the 'West Country' Pacifics were built at Eastleigh Works in 1949 and 1950: Nos 34095 *Brentor*, 34097 *Holsworthy*, 34099 *Lynmouth*, 34101 *Hartland*, 34102 *Lapford* and 34104 *Bere Alston*. All the rebuilt members of the class were modified at Eastleigh.

The initial twenty locomotives built were constructed under the original order of April 1941, No. 2421, and were named after towns and cities of the West Country because at the conception of the locomotives it was considered that the West of England was the priority area for an improved service. In practice the class found itself spread across the complete SR system. Unlike the 'Merchant Navy' class the 'West Country' class, as they naturally became known, were from the outset considered for both passenger and freight services. However, for freight duties the design was intended to be limited to 'fitted' goods but in reality they worked the complete spectrum of goods and passenger services. Once again Bulleid used his own notation for the new class commencing with No. 21C101 *Exeter*.

The second batch of ten locomotives was built during 1946 under order No. 2561, dated 28 September 1944. All of this second batch recalled geographical areas of the West Country rather than the towns and cities of the initial order. The exception to this was No. 21C125, which was originally named *Rough Tor* and then was renamed *Whimple* almost immediately after leaving Brighton.

The tractive effort of the class was in theory less powerful than the 'Lord Nelson' class but, because of the larger and superior steaming capabilities of the Bulleid boilers, the 'West Country' class outdid the 'Lord Nelsons' in haulage capacity and turn of speed. As would be expected from a locomotive design incorporating so many of the Bulleid features found on the 'Merchant Navy' class, similar problems were experienced. In general, the Light Pacifics were good steamers with commendably smooth running, particularly when coasting or travelling downhill, and they had the same efficient clasp brakes and trouble-free BFB wheels, while at the same time giving excellent route availability. Clearly, problems with the steam reverser, oil leakages from the oil bath causing slipping, and the risk of fires, sanding and other failings exacerbated the situation and perpetuated the negative views that the Bulleid designs produced.

As with the 'Merchant Navy' class a similar design of valve gear using chain drive was fitted to the Light Pacifics and seemingly the design did not benefit from the lessons learnt as a result of the experience with the larger Pacifics. When the locomotive was running at speed the oil bath suffered from immense pressures and the complete structure was beset with vibration and racking stresses, all of which caused fractures and distortion of the casing. This, coupled with the poor design of the plunger and axle seals, produced significant oil loss, most of which found its way to the rail or boiler cladding. The situation was further complicated by oil being lost through the oil bath breather valves and the casing cracks allowing the ingress of water dripping from the boiler barrel. This latter problem also led to corrosion of the valve gear which became so severe that parts of the valve gear needed replacement at the first general repair.

Initially, to overcome this problem, a higher grade of oil was introduced, but this did not improve the situation so the running sheds were ordered to dip the baths on a daily basis and if water was discovered this was to be drained off. The water, being heavier than the oil, would settle at the bottom of the oil bath when the locomotive was stationary. Improved breather valves were fitted and automobile-type gaskets and seals provided, both of which helped to reduce the seepage to something close to a manageable level. The consumption ultimately averaged 23.8 pints per 100 miles, compared with 8 to 10 pints for the 'Lord Nelson' and 'King Arthur' classes.

The oil that seeped its way onto the rails and driving wheels caused slippage, but of equal importance was the fact that it was also absorbed by the boiler and firebox cladding, so much so that after approximately 20,000 miles service it created a significant fire risk. While most conflagrations were minor, a number caused significant damage and required the assistance of the local fire service.

The prime cause of ignition for these fires was thought to be sparks from the ashpan; consequently, No. 34042 was equipped in 1948 with an experimental steel protection sheet which ran along the base of the firebox and barrel. In February 1949 a further modification was added to Nos 34001, 34002, 34061 and 34062: the fitting of water sprays to the ashpans in an attempt to dampen the red hot ash and clinker. The sprays were not totally successful and were later removed, the protective steel sheet, however, became a standard feature on all members of the class. Interestingly, the first two 'Merchant Navy' class locomotives were built from new with driving wheel splashers under the casing and, while records are incomplete, the incident of fires on these two locomotives seems to be decidedly less than on other Bulleid Pacifics.

A further twist to the Light Pacific fire problem was that while the initial assumption was that sparks from the firebox were the cause, a further source of ignition was detected when a number of 'West Country' class locomotives were transferred to the Somerset & Dorset line. With the prolonged periods of braking needed on this steeply graded route over the Mendip Hills, white-hot metal particles from the brake shoes clung to the oil-sodden boiler cladding causing smouldering and sometimes being fanned into serious fires by the slipstream. The brake shoe design and the material were both changed, providing a simple solution to the problem.

The steam reverser gave footplate crews the same problems as on the 'Merchant Navy' class and tended to make inexperienced drivers reluctant to use less than 30 per cent cut-off or to make them close the regulator before notching up in case the movement was misjudged and the locomotive suddenly went into reverse, with all the attendant damage to the valve gear. The problems were not solved by experience as the steam reverser was incapable of fine adjustment, moved by itself and was extremely heavy on maintenance. Changes were made with the design, in line with those of the 'Merchant Navy' class but, while the inconvenience to most drivers was reduced, the reverser never lost its fierce action or lack of fine adjustment.

The oil seepage on the driving wheels caused enough of a disadvantage, but coupled with the insensitive regulator this problem could become a nightmare. The problems were exacerbated by Bulleid's desire to provide a smooth ride for his Pacifics. Consequently, the springing was evenly distributed, so much so that upon starting, when maximum adhesion was required, much of the adhesive weight was transferred to the bogie – not the best method for adhesive power! The permanent way gangs reported that the Bulleid Pacifics also produced excessive 'rail burn' at difficult, and sometimes not so difficult, starting points. The rails at these points had to be replaced at a higher frequency than normal.

The steam-operated firedoors were disliked as much by the firemen on the Light Pacifics as they were on the 'Merchant Navy' class, although those firemen who learnt how to understand them were strong defenders of the device. In particular, the South Western crews favoured the use of the firedoor, with Exmouth Junction men being enthusiastic users and Salisbury crews accepting the

Slide bar details on an
unrebuilt 'Battle of Britain'
class showing the method of
lubrication.
Author's Collection

device and using it. London men were less than impressed and did not use the
firedoor. Possibly the inbuilt conservatism of some footplate crews meant that the
firemen really did not want to attempt to understand the operation and tended to
ignore it.

Steam sanding was applied to the front of all the driving wheels from new.
However, as with the earlier Pacifics, filling the sandboxes was awkward and
became a drudge to carry out with the result that it was not always completed
properly, leading to either sand being spilt or sandboxes running out of sand. The
sand from the leading filler, if spilt, tended to end up over the outside slide bars,
causing untold damage to these components. To overcome this, dust covers of a
similar design to that on the 'Merchant Navies' were fitted to Nos 34039 and
34042 during June 1948 and as these appeared to be successful they were applied
to most of the class. Before all the class could be modified, the problem of access
to the slide bars for lubrication and maintenance was considered more of a
potential threat than the sand itself, and by the middle of 1950 the covers were
being removed again as the locomotives passed through the works. At the same
time the front sand containers were usually blanked off, although some
locomotives were still running with both the slide bar covers in place and the
front sandbox blanked off. No. 34005 *Barnstaple* was a typical example.

The smokebox suffered similar problems to the original Pacific designs, namely
cracking from exhaust pulsing, scouring, corrosion and vibration, causing leaks in

The enormous width of the blastpipe for the Bulleid Pacifics can be seen clearly on this 'Battle of Britain' class locomotive under repair.

Author's Collection

places where smokeboxes should not leak. The modifications followed the examples set by the 'Merchant Navies', but much of the front end vibration was the result of over-light construction and led to mainframe fracturing, loosening of the cylinders and steampipe breakages. The problems were investigated during 1947 when Nos 21C105 and 21C139 were fitted with indicator shelters in front of the smokebox and then employed on a number of express and freight workings.

The information produced from these trials led to a number of changes to the front end of the Light Pacifics, initially including modifying the front end stretchers so that the frame structure was more rigid. This change was applied to Nos 34034, 34039 and 34042 during May and June 1948, but the results were not totally successful. During June and July 1950 the bogies of Nos 34008 and 34064 were modified to include strengthened vertical and horizontal stretchers, and longer springs. These changes were successful and as a result they were incorporated into the rest of the class. However, steampipe fractures still occurred and, while tests using similar bellows-type pipes as fitted to the 'Merchant Navy' class proved unsuccessful when fitted to Nos 34008, 34009 and 34034, trials were carried out on No. 34041 in September 1950 using solid-drawn steel pipes. These were not 100 per cent satisfactory but performed better than previous designs and proved less susceptible to cracking. Consequently, they became the standard for the Light Pacifics and were fitted as replacements, where needed.

In March 1947 No. 21C156 was used on an opportunistic occasion for a return trial run between Brighton and Norwood Junction. The original electric locomotive intended for the trial had failed with a defective tyre, so a 'Battle of Britain' class locomotive was used instead.

SPECIAL TRAIN WORKINGS 30 MARCH 1947

Locomotive: No. 21C156 *Croydon*
Working: 09.45 Brighton to Norwood Junction
Load: 492 ton gross

	Scheduled time	Actual time	Boiler pressure psi	Steam chest °F	Cut-off %	Water
Brighton	09.45	09.45	240	–	50	full
Preston Park			244	600	38	full
Patcham Tunnel			247	634	38	½
Clayton Tunnel			240	658	26	½
Hassocks			237	658	26	½
			237	658	30	½
Keymer Junction	09.56	10.05	237	658	30	½
Wivelsfield			237	670	30	½
			240	670	35	½
Haywards Heath			250	670	30	½
			257	680	30	⅜
Balcombe			245	680	27	¼
Balcombe Tunnel			232	680	27	¼
Three Bridges	10.00	10.12½	coast			
			240	612	38	⅝
Gatwick			coast			
Horley			240	570	27	full
Salfords			260	610	27	full
Earlswood	10.15½	10.26½	242	645	40	full
Redhill	10.17	10.28	243	650	37	full
Mersham Tunnel			coast			
			247	607	27	full
Coulsdon North	10.23	10.37¼	260	607	20	full
Purley			253	570	27	full
Purley Oaks			coast			
Windmill Bridge Junction	10.30	10.44¼				
Norwood Junction	10.32½	10.46½				

Notes: Permanent way slack at Clayton Tunnel and Coulsdon North.
Signal check at Balcombe Summit and Gatwick.
Safety valves blowing off at approx 260 psi.

Locomotive: No. 21C156 *Croydon*
Working: 12.58 Selhurst to Brighton
Load: 492 ton gross

	Scheduled time	*Actual time*	*Boiler pressure psi*	*Steam chest °F*	*Cut-off %*	*Water*
Selhurst	12.58	12.58	250	–	full	full
Windmill Bridge Junction	13.00	13.01¾	247	560	40	full
East Croydon			247	560	40	full
South Croydon			230	580	37–27	full
Purley Oaks			232	588	32	full
Purley			225	590	32	full
Coulsdon North	13.07½	13.09¼	230	600	35	full
Merstham Tunnel			242	600	35	full
Merstham			240	600	27	full
Redhill			245	coast		
Earlswood	13.15	13.23½	250	620	27	full
Salfords			245	620	35	full
Horley			232	610	35	⅝
Three Bridges	13.22½	13.30¾	220	610	40	⅜
Balcombe Tunnel			185	610	30	⅜
Balcombe			180	605	32	⅜
		13.38	170	605	32	⅜
Haywards Heath			177	600	32	⅜
Wivelsfield			178	600	32	⅜
Keymer Junction	13.34½	13.41¼	175	610	32	½
Hassocks			180	617	32	⅜
Clayton Tunnel			coast			
		13.49	205	590	35	⅞
Patcham Tunnel			205	570	35	¾
Brighton	13.45½	13.55½				

Note: Permanent way slack at Coulsdon North and Clayton Tunnel.
The rake was used frequently and rocker grates operated at Hassocks.

The test report for these runs comments that 'in view of the heavy working which was required . . . the water consumption of 27.8lbs per DBHP hour is considered satisfactory', but 'considering the high calorific value (14,620 BTUs per lb) of the coal supplied . . . the coal consumption of 4.15lbs per DBHP hour cannot be regarded as satisfactory.'

The firebox on the Light Pacifics provided good service although the rocker grate was something of a limited success, needing constant attention from the shed staff. The lack of dampers, contrary to expectations, did not cause a problem as the experienced fireman knew that it was always possible to take a Light Pacific 'off the boil' by piling too much coal across the front of the grate. It was not uncommon to stand or even run short distances with a hole in the middle of the fire to control the steaming rate and only have the grate fully covered when working hard or at the start of a journey. Intriguingly, while the footplate crews

'West Country' No. 34045 *Ottery St. Mary*, without the nameplate shields, at Salisbury shed.
David Lawrence, Hugh Davies Collection

found no difficulty with the lack of dampers, the powers that be had some concerns and, consequently, tests were carried out with dampers fitted to the inside ashpans. In May 1948 Nos 34004–6 were so fitted and later during the same year and during early 1949 similar changes were made to Nos 34002, 34011, 34015, 34040, 34056, 34061, 34064 and 34076. The footplate crews made very limited use of the dampers and in most cases were not aware that they were fitted. The modification was not a great success and most of the dampers were removed, although No. 34040 was still so fitted when working the Somerset & Dorset line and was considered to be the poorest steamer of the Light Pacifics based there.

The firebox was given some tough treatment and it could have been expected that a significant failure would occur, but this was not the case due in part to the welded tube ferrules, the TIA water treatment and the construction of the brick arch. The arch had three sections with three large bricks in each section, and was supported by the thermic syphons. Consequently, a collapsed arch was a very unusual occurrence; with one brick down, or even three, it did not impair steaming sufficiently to warrant a replacement locomotive being put on the service.

All the Bulleid Pacifics were renowned for sparks being thrown from the chimney and in 1948 No. 34034 was fitted at Brighton with an experimental spark arrester. The device performed very well in stopping the release of sparks, but in doing so degraded the steaming capabilities of the boiler so much that on a rostered service via Bournemouth the locomotive had to stop for a 'brew up' on a number of occasions. The official records show the spark arrester being carried until October 1948 but shed staff observations suggest that it was not present in August of that year. During January 1949 further attempts were made to find a solution to the spark throwing and tests were carried out using an LMS design of spark arrester fitted to No. 34033, but this also caused the locomotive to be reluctant to steam and it was removed in June 1949.

A less-publicized modification was the valve gear adjustment applied to No. 34040 in October 1948 and to Nos 34011 and 34015 in December of the same year. The maximum cut-off in full forward gear on the Bulleid Light Pacifics was 70 per cent, a generous margin given that slipping occurred on starting. However, it was adjusted to a maximum of 77 per cent on the above locomotives, although records do not indicate whether any improvements were achieved. The modification had been removed from all locomotives by September 1950, which presumably indicates that it was not successful.

Problems were also experienced with the hopper doors which had a habit of opening themselves while on the road, sometimes with dramatic results. The difficulties normally exhibited themselves when locomotives came to a halt at stations or signals and sometimes during the bump when coaches were being coupled. While at Woking station in December 1948 one of the outside hopper doors dropped on No. 34063 *229 Squadron* and welded itself to the third rail! Later that month No. 34076 *41 Squadron* had the same problem at Brighton. A modification was made to No. 34061 *73 Squadron* in February 1949 which proved successful and as a result the rest of Light Pacifics were modified to the same standard.

As the last of the batch built under order No. 2561 were completed a further fifteen were commenced at Brighton under order No. 2885 and these entered traffic between June and October 1946. This batch, Nos 21C131–45, had some minor changes which included the modified regulator. They were also fitted with standard LMS-style buffers, which had parallel shanks rather than the tapered pattern common to the SR. However, Nos 21C29 and 21C30 had tenders fitted with the LMS buffers, but the engines were out-shopped with SR-pattern buffers. Additionally, this batch was equipped with the Firthag-style steel chimney. A less obvious change was the resiting of the coupling rod knuckle pins ahead of the crankpins on the driving wheels.

As this latest batch of Light Pacifics was being completed another order (No. 3213) was raised to include a further twenty-five locomotives and again these were to be built at Brighton. The original concept had been to continue the West Country names on this new order and in fact a list had been drawn up by the SR directors. However, after due consideration and the realization that the majority of the new locomotives would be allocated to depots outside the West Country, it was considered that another theme would be more appropriate and names associated with the Battle of Britain were chosen to commemorate that desperate time in Britain's history. This was an astute decision, as the publicity gained for the new locomotives did no harm to either the SR or Bulleid's design. Of the twenty-five locomotives built under this order only the first three were named after West Country areas: Nos 21C146 *Braunton*, 21C147 *Callington* and 21C148 *Crediton*.

The balance of the order were named after places or people associated with the Battle of Britain and, while these locomotives were exactly the same as the 'West Countries', they were given a new class nomenclature: the 'Battle of Britain' class. This new class was identified not only by a different name but also by a change in design of name-plate. The 'West Country' locomotives had each carried the name, coat of arms or similar insignia of the place named and the class name on a cast plaque, but the 'Battle of Britain' locomotives carried the squadron number, personality name, organisation title or place name, below which was the class name, on a plaque in the shape of an aircraft wing, and the relevant associated crest on an oval plaque. The exception to this were the name-plates carried by No. 34090

The naming ceremony of 'Battle of Britain' class No. 21C155 *Fighter Pilot* at Brighton on 19 September 1947. Left to right: Group Captain Douglas Bader, Wing Commander W.G. Clouston, Air Chief Marshal Sir Keith Park.

National Railway Museum, York

Sir Eustace Missenden which used a combination of 'West Country' scrolls for the name and a 'Battle of Britain' plaque (on the horizontal axis) for the coat of arms.

Of all the West Country names considered for this order all but four of the names were used on later orders of Light Pacifics. The unused names were: Broad Clyst, Pinhoe, Wenford and Woodbury. Worthy of note was that No. 34093 was named *Saunton* even though other names were still available and this name was not part of the 1946 list.

At the onset of nationalization a further twenty Light Pacifics were built, Nos 34071–90, all 'Battle of Britain' class. While this order could be considered as outstanding from SR times, a further order for an additional twenty Light Pacifics was placed in March 1949 and this caused some consternation in railway circles as it was difficult to find justification for a total fleet of 140 Pacifics of all types on the SR. At that time there were ongoing energy crises every winter and the heavy fuel consumption of the Light Pacifics only exacerbated the situation. Furthermore, it was fairly common for the 'West Country' locomotives to be seen along the lines of Somerset and Devon with only two or three coaches and for the running sheds to have a number of these locomotives at rest in the yards. Records are strangely mute about the justification for this final order of Light Pacifics, but it must have been substantial because the decision was made fairly quickly.

The penultimate twenty locomotives constructed, Nos 34071–90 (under order No. 3383), were completed between April 1948 and February 1949 and could be considered the first genuine 'Battle of Britain' class locomotives. They were fitted with 9 ft V-shaped cab fronts and the 5,500 gallon tenders, and included a number of changes found necessary because of operational experiences. These included ashpan water sprays, fire protection sheets above the driving wheels, strengthened smokeboxes, longer smoke deflectors and flexible steampipes. In addition, the top of the chimney was visible when viewed from the side as a result of the changes to the smokebox. An electric coupling light was fitted to the rear of the tenders to assist with coupling at night; this was similar to that on the 'Merchant Navy' class and was added to the 4,500 gallon tenders as a standard feature.

This batch of Light Pacifics entered service with an increased working weight compared with Nos 21C101–70:

Bogie	16 ton 4 cwt
Leading coupled wheels	19 ton 5 cwt
Centre coupled wheels	19 ton 16 cwt
Trailing coupled wheels	19 ton 4 cwt
Trailing truck	13 ton 9 cwt
Engine	87 ton 18 cwt
Tender (fully laden)	47 ton 15 cwt
Engine and tender	135 ton 13 cwt

Note: The total weight of a locomotive fitted with a 4,500 gallon tender weighed at Eastleigh in September 1957 was 130 ton 16 cwt.

The final batch of Light Pacifics was built as 'West Country' class except for the last two which took 'Battle of Britain' class names. While on paper Brighton was to build all twenty of this batch, owing to difficulties with procurement of steel for the firebox and the chains for the valve gear, construction was somewhat protracted. In addition, Brighton was heavily involved with the design, construction and build of the 'Leader' class. Assistance was requested from Eastleigh Works and, as a result, six 'West Country' class were assembled there instead. The frames for all the locomotives of this order were cut at Ashford and the cylinders, bogie, motion and steel fireboxes were constructed at Eastleigh. The locomotives entered traffic between September 1949 and January 1951, No. 34110 being the last to leave Brighton Works.

No. 34110 *66 Squadron* entered traffic without the standard Royal Air Force badges below the name-plate because the contractor who normally supplied these was unable to find a replacement for the craftsman preparing them, who had retired. The frames for *66 Squadron* had been laid up at Brighton in March 1950, but on orders from British Railways headquarters all work was stopped for several months. This was to allow time to investigate a number of alternative designs for the Bulleid Pacifics using the original boiler and tender. Records exist showing that at least two design ideas were examined, both using the original boiler with a conventional smokebox, standard boiler cladding and a single blastpipe. The designs differed in the cylinder and motion layouts, with one

No. 34051 *Winston Churchill* heading west past West Moors station with a short cattle train on 14 October 1961. How the mighty have fallen.

David Lawrence, Hugh Davies Collection

requiring the use of two 20 in × 28 in outside cylinders with normal Walschaerts valve gear and the other considering the use of the original Bulleid cylinders and three sets of independent valve gear. Both designs were rejected because new frames would be needed, unlike the later Jarvis rebuilds. Consequently, No. 34110 left Brighton on 26 January 1951 as a standard member of the 'Battle of Britain' class.

The approximate costs for the Light Pacific classes were:

Order No.	Locomotive Nos	Date	Cost
2421/2561	21C101–30	1945/46	£17,000
2885	21C131–45	1946	£19,100
3213	21C146–70	1946/47	£20,200
3383	34071–90	1948/49	£22,100
3486	34091–110	1949/51	£24,700

Note: The comparative cost of a BR Pacific was £17,520.

As with the 'Merchant Navy' class, visibility from the footplate was poor. The information gathered from the smoke deflector trials on the 'Merchant Navy' locomotives was applied to the Light Pacifics, with the result that smoke deflector plates were fitted from new. Even so, smoke and steam still caused a problem, as did the small forward windows on the cab. The early members of the class were fitted with the narrow 8 ft 6 in cab and, even with the change of vacuum injector on the driver's side, the lookout was poor and could cause potentially hazardous situations. Consequently, during the latter part of 1946 Nos 21C137, 21C139 and 21C141–2 had different lengths of coloured tape attached to the smoke deflector plates and casing, and cameras were fitted to the footplate to record the behaviour of the steam and smoke exhaust. A review of all the camera evidence showed that the smoke deflectors were not giving sufficient lift to disperse the smoke from the casing and that the deflectors should be lengthened.

No. 21C108 *Padstow* was modified in January 1947 to include this change and was worked up and down the Redhill–Tonbridge line to observe the wind currents and exhaust gases. A significant improvement was noted and as a result Nos 21C122 and 21C140 were modified with the extended smoke deflectors in February 1947. This change became the standard for the Light Pacifics and the first to be fitted from new was No. 21C158 *Sir Frederick Pile* in March 1947. One anomaly was No. 21C162 *17 Squadron*, which ran during May and June 1947 with the leading ends of the deflector plates curved inwards. This produced no noticeable improvement and the straight ends were therefore replaced. Some of the small changes which were made on the Light Pacifics followed the same pattern as on the 'Merchant Navy' class, with similar unsatisfactory results, perhaps indicating a certain lack of communication within the design teams.

While the problems caused by the soft exhaust may have been brought to a manageable level, the amount of forward vision was still very restricted from the small front windows on the cab. In July 1947 No. 21C164 received a new cab front plate and angled windows, which increased the forward view by around 38 per cent and also reduced the reflections at night. No. 21C65 received the modification prior to leaving the works and, like the prototype, it had only two side windows. However, just as on the 'Merchant Navy' class this made the front windows difficult to clean and so Nos 21C166–70 received V-shaped cabs with three side windows. This became the standard for all the Light Pacifics and was retrofitted to Nos 21C101–65, the last being No. 21C115 in March 1957. The original SR-built Light Pacifics were constructed with 8 ft 6 in wide cabs so that they could meet the limited clearances on the Charing Cross to Hastings services. In practice, they did not run on this route and as a result the Pacifics built after nationalization were fitted with standard 9 ft wide cabs, and benefited from a corresponding increase in visibility.

The 'Battle of Britain' and 'West Country' class locomotives were coupled to tenders of two differing designs and capacity: 4,500 gallons and 5,500 gallons. The details are shown below:

Locomotive No.	Tender No.	Width	Capacity gall.	Class
21C101–48	3251–98	8 ft 6 in	4,500	WC
21C149–70	3299–320	8 ft 6 in	4,500	BB
34071–90	3321–40	9 ft 0 in	5,500	BB
34091–108	3351–68	9 ft 0 in	5,500	WC
34109–10	3369–70	9 ft 0 in	5,500	BB

Note: The tender numbers were not always allocated in strict numerical order and the ten missing numbers, 3341–50, were used by the 6,000 gallon tenders coupled to the 'Merchant Navy' class Nos 35021–30.

No. 34089 *602 Squadron* entered traffic on 31 December 1948 coupled to tender No. 3290, a 4,500 gallon pattern, and ran until March of the following year with this tender. This change was due to the delays in constructing the 6,000 gallon tenders for the 'Merchant Navy' class and their entry into service temporarily coupled to the Light Pacific tenders. Tender No. 3260, a 4,500 gallon type which had been coupled to No. 35026 *Lamport & Holt Line*, was damaged in Eastleigh yard after removal from the 'Merchant Navy' locomotive with the result that it was not returned to service until August 1949, an additional delay of 8 months. This tender was eventually coupled to No. 34039 *Boscastle*.

The Light Pacific tenders suffered from the same problems as those fitted to the 'Merchant Navy' class. The 4,500 gallon tenders gave considerable troubles with split welds, bulging plates and wash plates, and also corrosion. Most were partially rebuilt, strengthened and fitted with stronger wash plates. Three, two of the first batch and one of the second, were completely rebuilt, while one of the later 5,500 gallon tenders was also rebuilt:

'Battle of Britain' No. 34054 *Lord Beaverbrook* with a Bristol to Portsmouth train passing Sholing on 19 March 1955.

M.H. Walshaw, Hugh Davies Collection

Tender No.	Capacity (gall.)	Batch
3261	4,500	1st
3273	4,500	1st
3313	4,500	2nd
3354	5,500	4th

The rebuilt tenders could be identified from the rest because they were 9 ft wide and had higher side plating than the other cut-down tenders, built with rectangular manhole covers and British Railways lockers as well as more robust rear ladders. The BR rebuilds were further identified by the small oval plates denoting the tender numbers which were sited on the opposite side to those of the genuine Bulleid tenders. These tenders were nominally quoted as holding 5,250 gallons, but when tested were found to hold 5,340 gallons and weigh a total of 47 tons 18 cwt, as against the weight of a 4,500 gallon tender of 42 tons 12 cwt. The coal capacity of all the Light Pacific tenders was 5 tons.

When the original intention to work the Hastings routes had been decided against, the opportunity was taken with the introduction of the 'Battle of Britain' locomotives to increase the cab width to 9 ft and, starting with No. 34071 *601 Squadron*, the tenders were also widened. This increased the water capacity to 5,500 gallons. Tenders were regularly exchanged when locomotives came into the works and also occasionally at the running sheds, but it was not until the rebuilds came out of the works that the original narrow locomotives, Nos 34001–70 were coupled to the larger capacity tenders. The building of the 5,500 gallon tenders was intended to have been shared by Brighton and Ashford, but they were all built at Ashford and left there in either grey or Brunswick green livery. The tenders were transferred to Brighton where they waited in storage at Lancing until needed, and then they were coupled to the locomotives at Brighton.

The high sides of the Light Pacific tenders caused as many difficulties to the footplate crews when taking on coal and water as did the 'Merchant Navy' tenders. In 1952 three of the Light Pacific tenders entered service with the side raves cut down to give easier access: Nos 3310 (June), 3263 (September) and 3280 (November). The cutting down was an aesthetic disaster, even more so than on the 'Merchant Navy' class. This was probably because of the smaller overall size of the Light Pacifics, but the change relieved the crews of much of the aggravation caused during refuelling. Consequently, it was somewhat surprising that no further Light Pacifics were modified in this way until 1957 when, as locomotives were rebuilt, they received the cut-down tenders. At the same time the unrebuilt locomotives began to receive the modified tenders until 105 tenders had finally been cut down, leaving only Nos 34069, 34072, 34074–5 and 34078 coupled to the high-sided tenders. These unmodified tenders were condemned during 1963–4.

Nos 21C166–70 entered traffic fitted with the TIA feed water treatment system, No. 21C166 being equipped in September 1947. As with the 'Merchant Navy' Pacifics this greatly reduced boiler maintenance and allowed longer times between boiler washouts. The TIA equipment became the standard for the class until there was a move to the cheaper and simpler British Railways water treatment, which was substituted between 1955 and 1957. As would be expected, these changes followed the pattern of the modifications resulting from the expensively gained experience of the 'Merchant Navy' class and were used to the advantage of the Light Pacifics. In an effort to conserve fireboxes, the locomotives equipped with the TIA system were allocated to areas of hard water and the unmodified Light Pacifics were moved to Exmouth Junction. The first twenty genuine 'Battle of Britain' class locomotives, Nos 34071–90, were intended to be completed from new with the TIA water treatment, but Nos 34074–6 did not have the equipment fitted; this was rectified in November 1948.

The experience of steel firebox boilers which had been gained with the 'Merchant Navy' class was used with good effect on the Light Pacifics, so much so that only two completely new replacement fireboxes were ever fitted to boilers before the end of steam traction in July 1967. The boiler details are shown below:

Boiler No.	Date when new	First locomotive No.	New firebox date	Mileage when renewed	Locomotive fitted to
1290	05/46	21C130	07/60	615,471	34077
1330	04/47	21C160	09/54	300,744	34089

In total, 120 boilers were produced for the Light Pacifics; 12 were made by Eastleigh Works, the same number came from the North British Locomotive Company and the balance of 96 were produced by Brighton Works. The Eastleigh boilers were built in two batches. The first ten cost £3,480 each and were delivered during 1945/6, and the final two were delivered in 1950 as replacement boilers at a cost of £3,620 each. The boilers from the North British Locomotive Company (order No. D6917, 30/01/46) were delivered between July 1946 and April 1947 at a cost of £3,210 each. The Brighton-built boilers cost on average £3,360 each, but ranged in price from £3,140 to £3,575. The boilers built outside Brighton were initially fitted to the following locomotives:

North British Boilers	Eastleigh Boilers	
	1st Batch	2nd Batch
21C139	21C101	34055
21C141	21C105	34064
21C144	21C107	
21C148	21C109	
21C150	21C112	
21C158	21C114	
21C160	21C116	
21C162	21C120	
21C164	21C122	
21C166	21C135	
21C167		
21C169		

Notes: 1. Boiler No. 1261 was initially fitted to No. 21C101 when under construction at Brighton, but this developed faults during the steaming tests prior to entering service and was replaced by the first Eastleigh boiler, No. 1266. No. 1261 was repaired and fitted to No. 21C110 where it remained until December 1947 when the mileage was 93,464.
2. Locomotives Nos 34071 and 34082–3 were completed with second-hand boilers originally fitted to Nos 21C124, 21C121 and 21C127 respectively.
3. Two Light Pacific boilers were commenced by Eastleigh in May 1951 but were not completed until August 1953 when both the boilers were installed as stationary boilers at Ashford, one at the Locomotive Works and the other at the Carriage and Wagon Works. In October 1967 both the boilers were derelict and by January 1969 had been removed for scrap.
4. Ten spare boilers were produced for the 'West Country' and 'Battle of Britain' classes under order No. 3211.

In March 1951 No. 34093 was fitted with a boiler modified to 250 psi. Trials showed that there was no appreciable reduction in power or performance and so this change was applied to all the Light Pacifics, starting with Nos 34011, 34043, 34053, 34065 and 34069 during 1952 and to the balance during 1953–6.

No. 34104 *Bere Alston* under general repair at Eastleigh. Note the fitter inside the smokebox.
National Railway Museum, York

The boilers were constructed with three safety valves sited on the barrel top, ahead of the dome. The valves were positioned in a triangular configuration with two side by side preceding the third. In April 1952 No. 34082 had the latter safety valve removed and the other two recessed into the barrel top. However, in June 1952 No. 34089 not only lost the third safety valve but had the remaining valves resited on the rear of the boiler barrel to overcome the risks of discharging water from the valves during heavy braking. This became the final position of the safety valves for all the Light Pacifics, and the change was often carried out in conjunction with the lowering of the boiler pressure to 250 psi.

Immediately after the Second World War good quality coal for locomotives was difficult to obtain in sufficient and reliable quantities and, in addition, winter conditions caused acute shortages of solid fuels of any type. Consequently, in August 1946 the government decided to instigate a plan which had been considered during the war to convert locomotives to oil firing. The intention was to convert 1,217 locomotives across the system to burn a heavy oil known as Bunker C, which was too heavy for compression ignition engines. In all, 110 locomotives on the SR were proposed for modification, including 20 Light

Pacifics, 16 N15s and H15s, 34 Ns and Us, 10 D15s and 30 T9s and L11s. However, it appears that the Treasury was not fully informed of the details of the plan with the result that no sooner had the scheme started in 1947 than the funds to purchase the extra oil required could not be found and locomotives had to be laid off or returned to coal firing. There were also fairly vociferous objections from the National Coal Board and the National Union of Mine Workers, both fearing a significant loss of jobs and revenue following the removal of a large and traditional market for coal. Only two 'West Country' Pacifics were in fact modified: No. 21C119 *Bideford* at Eastleigh Works during June and July 1947 and No. 21C136 *Westward Ho* at Brighton Works between December 1947 and February 1948.

The modifications consisted of the addition of a 1,600 gallon welded oil tank positioned in the coal space, with the vacuum cylinders resited on either side of the water tank filler cover and tubular ladders fitted at the tender rear to give better access for refuelling. The rocker grates and ash hoppers were removed and a 'Mexican Trough' system installed with a single burner. This was found to cause great difficulty in the maintenance of steam as the thermic syphons severely restricted the efficiency of the burner and, far from maintaining steam pressure, led instead to the production of masses of dense black smoke! A second burner was added and after adjustment some improvement was found, but the steaming still remained erratic. Further trials took place, but by September 1948 No. 21C119 was converted back to coal firing after only 8,220 miles service.

The problems experienced with No. 21C119 caused a rethink on the suitability of oil-burning equipment for No. 21C136 and the Laidlaw-Drew Swirlyflo system of oil burning was fitted at a cost of £640. This design was considered more advanced and would give a greater opportunity for reliable steaming. The locomotive returned to traffic on 28 February 1948 with the short-lived British Railways regional prefix, as No. S21C136. Initial tests gave an equally poor power performance as had been experienced with No. 21C119 but, as experience was gained, adjustments made and teething troubles were overcome, excellent service resulted, with a plentiful supply of steam available. Various goods and local passenger trains were worked around Eastleigh until the problems were solved. Then Waterloo express services were operated and finally the 'Atlantic Coast Express' was successfully rostered, as well as other major West of England express duties.

A number of test trains were undertaken with No. S21C136, including a twenty-coach train between Eastleigh and Weymouth and a special consisting of eighteen new coaches with assistance from S15 No. 30510. This train travelled from Eastleigh to Basingstoke, but the S15 only gave assistance during starting and then became part of the train load. On passing Winchester No. S21C136 was blowing the safety valves and at the Basingstoke stop the boiler pressure was showing 265 psi. The tests showed how successful oil burning could be and they were deliberately extended to enable detailed information to be acquired which would assist in any future oil-firing plans. In November 1949 the locomotive was returned to coal firing after having travelled 15,044 miles.

'West Country' No. 21C101 *Exeter* at Exmouth Junction on 27 July 1948, still in Southern
Railway livery and numbering, with an unidentified 'Merchant Navy' at the rear.
B.K.B. Green, Initial Photographic

The results of these trials had shown that oil firing was a practical solution and
could provide improved availability and reduced footplate workload with heavy
trains. In addition real savings could be made by avoiding coal handling, ash
removal and disposal of the locomotive, and of course the removal of all the dirt
and grime associated with coal firing.

The first of Bulleid's Light Pacifics, No. 21C101, was out-shopped in the SR
malachite green. Although after nationalization the locomotives initially had
'British Railways' lettered on the sides of the tenders, ultimately the tenders were
left blank until the supplies of the new BR lion and wheel emblem were able to
meet the demand. Four of the Light Pacifics received the BR lion and wheel symbol
while still in SR malachite green livery: Nos 34036, 34071, 34079 and 34090. The
large cast SR circular plates on the smokebox were replaced from June 1948 by
cast number plates similar to the LMS style, and at this time a start was made on
removing the painted locomotive numbers from the front of the casing.

One interesting aside to the nationalization issue was a comment made by Sir
John Elliot who at one time was Chief Regional Officer of the Southern Railway,
under Sir Eustace Missenden, and who eventually became Chairman of the Railway
Executive. He was quoted around the time of nationalization as saying, 'Let the
Southern go their own damned way – we have enough troubles with the others.'

The early members of the Light Pacifics were worked to Eastbourne for
photographs to be taken in the shed yard, but in fact a number of the locomotives
assumed false identities for these photographs. Typical of this was a photograph

Name-plate of rebuilt 'Battle of Britain' No. 34090 *Sir Eustace Missenden* at Nine Elms on 20 July 1964.

Colin Stacey, Initial Photographic

of No. 21C105 in works grey, lined in white bands, which was in reality No. 21C107 suitably re-numbered and renamed. Similarly, No. 21C102 was represented by No. 21C103. In October 1948 No. 21C112 became Nos 21C108 and 21C109 on successive days. A noteworthy consequence of this change of identities was a photograph of No. 21C116 *Bodmin*, complete with the number 21C115 – apparently the paint shop became confused!

On 3 August 1949 No. 34039 was the first of the Light Pacifics to leave the works in the new BR Brunswick green livery, fully lined in black and orange. The background to the scroll and name-plates was black and the overall effect was a little sombre, probably due to the large expanse of dark green casing. Details of the dates when the liveries were changed can be found in Appendix 4. 'Battle of Britain' No. 34070 *Manston* retained the malachite green until March 1953 which shows how hard-wearing this paint was.

During 1948 the Railway Executive was determined to find a common livery style for all types of locomotives on all the disparate constituents of the nationalized railways. A number of experimental liveries were tried and on the Southern Region the locomotives designated for this were 'West Country' No. 34011 and 'Battle of Britain' Nos 34056, 34064–5 and 34086–8. All the locomotives were painted in apple green with two wide-spaced cream bands which were edged with red and grey. The tender rears and all the buffer beams were unlined, while the tender lettering and cabside numerals were unshaded yellow, edged in black. No. 34086 was the only apple green locomotive to carry the BR lion and wheel emblem on the tender and only No. 34011 retained the SR circular smokebox plate and the painted front numerals. The locomotives with experimental liveries were allocated to a wide

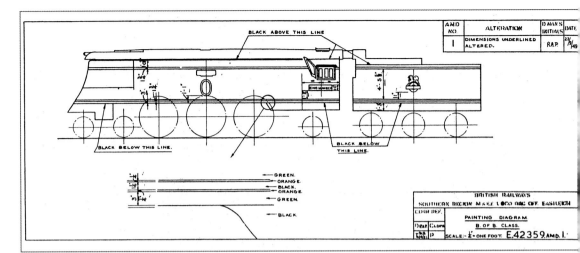

British Railways paint scheme for the 'Battle of Britain' class, in Brunswick green.

National Railway Museum, York

number of routes in order to allow as many members of the public as possible to see the various ideas and voice an opinion.

Surprisingly, a significant number of people expressed an interest; 11,408 travellers wrote to the Railway Executive giving their views and, probably not surprisingly, the preference was for the original malachite green of the old SR, 82 per cent preferring the old to the new. The apple green livery did not wear well while in traffic and rapidly became grimy and streaky in spite of regular cleaning, and by the middle of 1949 all interest had been lost in the experimental livery. Starting from 1950 all the locomotives were quietly repainted in Brunswick green livery as they passed through the works.

When No. 34090 *Sir Eustace Missenden, Southern Railway* was named at Waterloo station on 15 February 1949 the locomotive carried a special livery for the occasion. Overall, the locomotive was malachite green and the wheels were also painted malachite green, with yellow tyres instead of black and the hubs outlined with a narrow yellow line. The tender carried the lion and wheel emblem, on which the wheel was painted with a yellow tyre to match the engine although the wheel itself remained black. The name-plate was curved and the scroll was similar to the style of the 'West Country' class, but the plaque carrying the SR coat of arms followed the 'Battle of Britain' style, although with a longer horizontal axis. Below the plate was another curved scroll lettered 'Southern Railway', 'Battle of Britain Class'. Really, this locomotive could only be very loosely considered to be in the 'Battle of Britain' class, being more a celebration of the Southern Railway than anything else.

A curious aside related to the details of names and name-plates is that during September 1960 when Nos 34068 *Kenley* and 34058 *Sir Frederick Pile* were under overhaul at Eastleigh Works the oval plates on both locomotives were inadvertently swapped. They were never changed back again and the locomotives ran with the

Still in Southern livery but with the initial British Railways numbering scheme, No. S21C167 *Tangmere* is resting at Bricklayers' Arms shed on 20 March 1948.

R.J. Buckley, Initial Photographic

incorrect ovals until being withdrawn. Also, 'West Country' No. 34023 *Blackmoor Vale* had the spelling of the name changed in April 1950 to *Blackmore Vale*.

One of the results of nationalization was the scheme to provide a common numbering system across the complete British railway system, hence all the Bulleid Pacifics were renumbered in the 34XXX (Light Pacifics) and 35XXX ('Merchant Navy') series. At the time there were forty-eight 'West Country' and twenty-two 'Battle of Britain' Pacifics in service and they were renumbered from No. 34001 to No. 34070 as they passed through the works, with No. 34015 *Exmouth* being the first on 7 April 1948 and No. 34010 *Sidmouth* the last on 27 January 1950. All locomotives built after nationalization entered service with the BR numbering scheme.

Between 1 January 1948 and April 1948 BR had instigated a temporary system in which the Bulleid numbers were prefixed by the letter 'S' to indicate the Southern Region. A significant number of locomotives passed via the works during that period and a total of twenty-two carried the temporary prefix to the running number. The first locomotive to enter traffic with the prefix was No. S21C158 *Sir Frederick Pile*, which left Brighton Works on 14 January 1948. This locomotive is also thought to be the first in the country to carry the British Railways lettering on the tender.

During these changes there were a number of oddities. Nos 34016, 34021 and 34046 were renumbered and fitted with the cast smokebox number plates but still retained the 'S' prefix numbers on the front casing. No. 21C105 became No. S21C105 on 20 February 1948, then No. 21C105 again at Brighton on 24 March 1948 and finally No. 34005 on 28 May 1948. Interestingly, when the 'S' prefix was applied to this locomotive the tender was lettered 'British Railways' and this

No. 21C170 *Manston* shown here in SR malachite green and lined in yellow, but with the original British Railways wording on the tender, 'S' prefix and SR owner's plate on the smokebox.

National Railway Museum, York

was retained even after the prefix had been painted out. The locomotive was therefor running with BR lettering and SR numbering until the substitution of the LMS tender in March 1948, in preparation for the exchange trials. Similarly, No. 21C104 *Yeovil* also ran in traffic with this combination of numbers and lettering, although without the 'S' prefix. Some of the Light Pacifics ran for only a few months with the prefix, for example, Nos S21C105, S21C106 and S21C1036, while other locomotives carried the prefix for a significant time.

The last Light Pacific to be constructed, No. 34110 66 *Squadron*, raises an interesting question. The locomotive appeared out of the erecting shops in January 1951, some 8 months after the penultimate Pacific No. 34109 *Sir Trafford Leigh Mallory*. This was a significant delay in the programmed delivery and at the time it was rumoured that No. 34110 was to be delivered without the Bulleid valve gear but was possibly fitted with Caprotti gear instead. No evidence has been found to substantiate these claims.

Looking back, it is fairly easy to understand that the last Light Pacifics to be built were a continuation of the original orders placed by the SR, before nationalization took place. While the Railway Executive may have been able to cancel them the difficulties caused would probably have outweighed any advantages, and yet it is still hard to justify the construction of the final twenty locomotives during the BR era. The decision to continue raised a considerable degree of controversy about the real need for 140 Pacifics (including the 'Merchant Navy' class) on the lines of the Southern. In the event, the Light Pacifics proved themselves master of the tasks set them and, while they certainly suffered from similar problems to the 'Merchant Navy' class, were able to provide Pacific power with all the advantages to services and passenger traffic on routes where only small engines had previously worked.

CHAPTER SEVEN

IN-SERVICE OPERATIONS

The introduction of the first 'Merchant Navy' Pacific in 1941 obviously caused a lot of speculation and interest and Bulleid was keen to show his design to its best ability. As a result, the locomotive was employed on a number of Western Section semi-fast passenger and goods duties but, unfortunately, a lot of time was also spent at Eastleigh Works ironing out the numerous technical problems that occurred. During this time the larger sandboxes and the improved design of regulator were fitted, but as well as the problems of the engine there were complications with the tender. The leading axleboxes regularly ran hot and the tank welding proved inadequate to deal with water surging when the tanks were partly full. In addition, modifications were required to the draw gear and hand brake mechanism so as a temporary measure the tender was exchanged for No. 3112, which had been built for the second of this batch of locomotives. Consequently, No. 21C1 *Channel Packet* did not enter regular revenue service until June 1941, from Salisbury, some three months after the locomotive was named at Eastleigh Works. This was hardly an auspicious start for a new design.

Channel Packet was joined at Salisbury by No. 21C2 *Union Castle* 12 days later. *Union Castle* was officially named at Victoria on 4 July 1941 and subsequently hauled a four-coach special conveying the guests via the Quarry Hill route to Earlswood. The locomotive journeyed to Redhill for turning and servicing before working the train back to Charing Cross in the early evening. The construction of the rest of the initial batch of locomotives was delayed such that Nos 21C3–21C10 entered service between October 1941 and July 1942. Thus No. 21C3 entered traffic three months after *Union Castle* and it was over a year before No. 21C10 *Blue Star* entered revenue service. During this delay significant efforts were made to overcome the troubles that the first two locomotives suffered and the later members of the batch did achieve a better reliability. All the same, when 21C1–5 were first allocated to Exmouth Junction and 21C6–10 to Salisbury extra fitters had to be allocated to the sheds.

Over this initial period of service, during 1941/2, a number of test trains were run to enable Bulleid to calculate fuel consumption and haulage capacity. Typical of these was No. 21C2 *Union Castle*, which ran on 9 November 1941 with a sixteen-coach special train from Waterloo to Exeter Central. The tare weight was 527 tons – at that time one of the heaviest trains worked out of Waterloo. The train stopped at Woking and Basingstoke, with 72 mph being achieved on the rising grade beyond Fleet, and a real display of power being shown beyond

No. 34065 *Hurricane* at Liverpool Street in May 1951 with the 'Norfolkman' express service.
B.K.B. Green, Initial Photographic

Salisbury where Sherborne was passed at 70 mph and the 1 in 80 bank beyond Crewkerne was breasted at 25.5 mph. On the climb to Honiton Tunnel the speed fell back to 25.5 mph, but reached 57 mph at the summit, and during the following downhill grade the locomotive reached 79 mph before stopping at Sidmouth Junction. The final 12.2 miles to Exeter were covered in 15 minutes 8 seconds, overall a very creditable performance by a new locomotive. Later during the same month No. 21C2 worked 800 ton goods trains between Salisbury and Exeter with equal finesse.

During this period No. 21C4 *Cunard White Star* fell victim to an enemy aircraft attack. Contrary to some esoteric accounts which suggest the train was a freight service travelling on 18 November and that the locomotive was undamaged but vans loaded with bacon were hit and caught fire, the SR report states that the incident occurred on 28 November 1942 at 12.45 between Broadclyst and Whimple in Devon when the locomotive was hauling the 10.10 passenger service from Plymouth to Brighton. The aircraft attacked with cannon and machine-gun fire causing significant damage to the locomotive, putting it out of action, and injuring the crew slightly. The engine firebox and boiler were pierced, as were the smokebox and steampipes, and there were a number of holes in the casing, tender and cab. There were no reports of passenger injuries.

An additional example of the power of the 'Merchant Navy' Pacifics is shown in the log of a further test train involving No. 21C2 between Waterloo and Southampton:

Locomotive: 'Merchant Navy' No. 21C2 *Union Castle*
Load: 517 tons tare, 520 tons gross

Distance miles		Time mins	secs	Speed mph
0.0	Waterloo	0	00	–
1.3	Vauxhall	3	59	38
3.9	Clapham Junction	7	30	42*
5.6	Earlsfield	9	44	56
7.3	Wimbledon	11	44	60
12.0	Surbiton	16	21	66
17.1	Walton	20	29	77
19.1	Weybridge	22	09	72
21.7	Byfleet	4	11	77
		sigs.		
24.4	Woking	27	00	–
28.0	Brookwood	31	29	48
31.0	Milepost 31	35	00	54
33.2	Farnborough	37	16	64
36.7	Fleet	40	18	68
39.7	Winchfield	43	00	69
42.2	Hook	45	00	75
47.8	Basington	49	31	64
50.3	Worting Junction	52	03	46*
58.1	Micheldever	60	00	76
66.6	Winchester	66	45	74
69.7	Shawford	69	31	70
73.6	Eastleigh	72	30	70
75.9	Swaythling	74	43	68
77.3	St Denys	75	44	65
78.1	Northam Junction	77	15	13*
79.2	Southampton Central	†79	31	24*
	Net Running Times	†77	30	–

Notes: *   Speed restriction.
        †   Waterloo start to Southampton pass.

From 1943 the usage of the 'Merchant Navy' class increased although, as a contradiction, availability was never high. When locomotives were available it was not unusual to find them being allocated to main line goods services after completion of the passenger duties, typically the Nine Elms–Exeter partly fitted freight which left London nightly at 23.50. The 'Merchant Navies' allocated to Salisbury, Nos 21C6–10, worked twice the mileage of Salisbury's allocation of the 'King Arthur' class – when they were serviceable.

From mid-October 1943 there were four regular 'Merchant Navy' express services out of Waterloo, leaving at 10.50, 12.50, 14.50 and 17.00. Tuesdays, Wednesdays and Thursdays saw the 10.50 service strengthened to sixteen or seventeen coaches and working through to Exeter. This was the wartime equivalent of the 'Atlantic Coast Express' with a corresponding Up train of eighteen coaches. The Up service presented some problems to the SR as the length of the train could not be handled conveniently at Waterloo. A stop was therefore made at Clapham Junction to detach the six coaches forming the Plymouth section, which was then worked forward to the terminus separately by a convenient M7. The Monday, Friday and Saturday services were provided with reliefs which followed the main trains in both directions, but the loads were smaller. A relief hauled by a 'King Arthur' was also provided for the 17.00 service from Waterloo to Exeter, though, surprisingly the main train was usually lighter than the relief by around four coaches. In the new year of 1944 this situation was reversed and the relief was Pacific-hauled.

When the next batch, Nos 21C11–20, entered into service between December 1944 and June 1945 they were allocated to Nine Elms. Prior to that the locomotives were run in on Southampton to Bournemouth stopping trains, Salisbury goods trains and van trains to London. On allocation to Nine Elms, the early duties included semi-fast services designed to work the locomotives in to the requirements of the operating staff, typically, the 09.54 Waterloo to Basingstoke service.

'West Country' No. 34108 *Wincanton* with a Down Bournemouth line express passing Raynes Park in 1957.

Norman Simmons, Hugh Davies Collection

Eventually the Pacifics graduated to duties such as the 09.30 Waterloo–Bournemouth West express. The arrival of the new Pacifics at Nine Elms left the 'Lord Nelsons' with no duties and they were transferred to Bournemouth, leaving the London shed with a complete stable of Pacifics to work all the Waterloo services. The availability of the first ten 'Merchant Navy' Pacifics was initially poor, seldom exceeding 25 per cent. The later batch proved more reliable, reaching 55 per cent availability, but even this was way below that of the Stanier and Gresley Pacifics.

Between late 1943 and the middle of June 1944 military traffic steadily increased, particularly approaching the D-day invasion of Europe. The SR was in the front line and supplied some 10,000 military trains which moved 5.5 million troops. With the D-day landings on 6 June 1944, this level of support did not stop, and petrol, troop and supply trains continually supported the reinforcement of the invasion forces. During the latter half of 1944 the difficulties of providing these additional and concentrated services were exacerbated by the start of the V-1 bombardment and eventually the V-2 rockets. The situation was further complicated by the British Liberation Army leave trains, which started to operate in January 1945. These ran from Dover on 24 hour notice and, because of the short time allowed for leave, were given priority. It was against this background that the Bulleid Pacifics worked, and while the availability was not exceptional the power to haul long and heavy trains for long distances contributed in no small way to the logistical success of the SR during the war.

No. 21C2 *Union Castle* was used for a series of trials, on the Eastern Section between Victoria and Dover Marine from 14 August to 16 August 1945. Two return journeys were made each day, loaded to ten Pullmans and two bogie vans, operating as far as possible to pre-war schedules. No. 21C1 *Channel Packet* was also used during this period on the 08.35 service from Victoria to Ramsgate as well as for other 'Kent Coast' services. The intention was to give the Battersea crews the opportunity to get acquainted with the class. During the trials the timings of both locomotives were carefully checked to ensure that all permanent way and other restrictions were adhered to. No. 21C1 had been fitted with a speedometer by Eastleigh for these test runs, but to little avail as the device was found to be some 9 mph slow when the locomotive was at 60 mph! However, the results of the trial enabled the Eastern Section Continental express services to recommence and the first train was headed by an immaculate No. 21C17 *Belgian Marine* in malachite green. The load was six coaches, three Pullmans and two vans: this was clearly too light a load for the motive power of the 'Merchant Navies' and subsequently the services were relegated to 'King Arthurs'.

Typical of the power of the 'Merchant Navies' was the run of *Blue Funnel* shown below, whose net times, although spoilt by delays beyond the stop at Yeovil Junction, were still most impressive and compared very well with the pre-war services hauled by 'King Arthurs'. The best of these was that of Salisbury shed's Driver Young in 1934, with No. 768 *Sir Balin*, when the same route was completed in 90 minutes with a thirteen-coach load of 421 tons tare.

One of the routes which always tested locomotives was the steeply graded line between Salisbury and Exeter, particularly when loaded with heavy wartime traffic and also the holiday traffic after the war. Two runs carried out during 1946–7 are worthy of note, the first by No. 21C14 *Nederland Line* with a twelve-coach train and the second by No. 21C13 *Blue Funnel* hauling a lighter ten-coach train. In both cases the power of these locomotives can be clearly seen.

Locomotive:		No. 21C14 *Nederland Line*		No. 21C13 *Blue Funnel*	
Load:		389 tons tare		325 tons tare	
		415 tons gross		345 tons gross	
Distance miles		*Time* mins	secs	*Time* mins	secs
0.0	Exeter Central	0	00	0	00
1.1	Exmouth Junction	3	32	3	25
2.9	Pinhoe	6	02	5	51
4.8	Broadclyst	7	47	7	30
8.5	Whimple	11	12	10	50
12.2	Sidmouth Junction	15	20	14	40
16.8	Honiton	19	38	18	37
18.2	Honiton Tunnel (West)	21	10	20	04
23.8	Seaton Junction	26	04	24	11
27.0	Axminster	28	44	26	35
32.1	Chard Junc	32	58	30	33
37.5	Hewish Crossing	37	50	35	10
			sigs.		
40.1	Crewkerne	42	15	37	15
			sigs.		
46.7	Sutton Bingham	49	33	41	55
48.9	Yeovil Junction	pass		44	14
——					
		51	20	0	00
53.5	Sherborne	55	05	6	32
57.2	Milborne Port	58	35	10	28
59.6	Templecombe	60	45	12	46
				pws	
66.4	Gillingham	66	31	21	13
70.5	Semley	70	25	26	23
75.5	Tisbury	74	55	31	16
79.8	Dinton	78	14	34	52
85.5	Wilton*	82	40	39	53
				pws	
88.0	Salisbury	86	06	44	51
	Net Running Times	81	30	44	30 *
				39	45

Notes: *   Speed restriction.
       pws   Permanent way slack.

'Merchant Navy' No. 35020 *Bibby Line* with the 'Bournemouth Belle' leaving Southampton Central. The crowds have come to see HRH Princess Margaret, who is in the third Pullman car. The locomotive is fitted with a 6,000 gallon tender.

M.H. Walshaw, Hugh Davies Collection

On 15 April 1946 a major milestone in the return to pre-war standards of passenger express services was reached when No. 21C1 *Channel Packet* hauled the 'Golden Arrow' train out of Victoria. The locomotive had been specially prepared by Eastleigh Works earlier that month when a fresh coat of malachite green and gloss varnish had been applied. The smokebox door was fitted with a circular plaque lettered 'Golden Arrow' and crossed diagonally with an arrow, and large wooden arrows were fitted to the sides of the casing, facing forward. The locomotive looked a real treat after the drab wartime grimy black and the shining finish made an interesting comparison with the original matt finish applied to No. 21C1 when new.

Prior to the inaugural trip of the restored 'Golden Arrow', No. 21C1 had worked light engine between Battersea and Ashford on 11 April and following this a trial was carried out with the full train between Victoria and Dover Marine, returning on 13 April 1946. The train was a Pullman car service with the cars themselves having a gold arrow under the windows at each end of the car and the words 'Golden Arrow' or *Flèche d'Or* at opposite ends. On the locomotive a small French Tricolour and a Union Jack were flown on the front above the cast number plate. (Photographic evidence suggests that 'Golden Arrow' services later that month were not fitted with the flags, at least not while running.) When the 'Golden Arrow' service eventually reached its stride, the two flags were brought out of the Stewarts Lane office by Syd Newman, fixed on a V-shaped carrier ready for the buffer beam. If the weather was wet, washed flags were used, if it was dry new ones were used instead.

Having completed the initial start-up and sufficient runs to satisfy the publicity department, No. 21C1 left Battersea shed and returned to the Western Section leaving the 'Golden Arrow' to be worked by members of the 'West Country' class over the following years.

Following the success of the Continental and boat-train services on the Eastern Section it was decided to recommence the Western Section special express trains with the inaugural running of the 'Bournemouth Belle' on 7 October 1946 and the Cunard boat specials to Southampton on 16 October. The 'Bournemouth Belle' was hauled by No. 21C18 *British India Line* and a generous 87 minutes were given for the journey to Southampton so early arrivals were commonplace. The Cunard boat-train was not only the first post-war train of this famous service, but it also headed an all-Pullman train for the RMS *Queen Elizabeth*'s first passenger run to New York. The liner was returning to passenger service after a comprehensive refit following use as a troopship during the Second World War, although it had not worked previously as a civilian passenger ship. As with earlier introductions of the 'Merchant Navy' class to new services, a trial run had been made on 4 October, this being the first occasion that a member of the class had visited the docks.

From the inception of the 'Merchant Navy' class, motive power depots and footplate crews had suggested that fuel and water consumption was high within the class. This had been backed up by the results of the early trials and the shed fuel returns, and with the reversion to normal passenger traffic Bulleid considered it important to gather comparative data under controlled conditions. Consequently, a series of trials took place during the middle of 1946 involving a 'Merchant Navy', a 'Lord Nelson' and a 'King Arthur' locomotive over the West of England main line. The locomotives, Nos 21C14 *Nederland Line*, 861 *Lord Anson* and 789 *Sir Guy*, were based at Exmouth Junction for the period of the trial and manned by two experienced crews, one from Nine Elms and the other from Exmouth Junction. Each of the locomotives in turn worked the 09.00 Waterloo–Salisbury, 12.36 Salisbury–Exeter and 19.30 Exeter–Waterloo services over a five-day period. Following this a number of Salisbury to Exeter trains were worked over a further six-day period, these trains consisting of twelve-, fourteen- and sixteen-coach loads. Both the 'Lord Nelson' and the 'King Arthur' did well in the trials, but No. 861 *Lord Anson* had some difficulty with the sixteen-coach load on 19 September 1946 and as a result No. 789 *Sir Guy* was restricted to fourteen-coach trains. The performance of No. 21C14 was impressive, gaining time with a sixteen-coach train west of Salisbury and having no problems with the normal formations. Unfortunately, the locomotive rather let itself down with a failure on shed and a further failure on arrival at Salisbury. As was predicted, while the power of the Pacifics to do the job was exemplary, the price was paid in high fuel consumption. The details are shown below:

Locomotive No.	Coal burned per train mile lb	Coal burned per dhp mile lb
789	46.60	3.29
861	44.89	3.26
21C14	56.70	3.59

When the trials concluded it was decided that a special eighteen-coach train should be worked to pre-war timings from Woking to Exeter with stops at Salisbury and Sidmouth Junction. The timings were kept with significant ease but the cost in fuel and water consumption was high; coal was consumed at 60.8 lb per train mile. One of the results of the trial was the appreciation that on long runs the tenders fitted may not always be of sufficient capacity. In the short term other problems occupied the minds at Eastleigh, but a larger turntable was installed at Exmouth Junction shed in July 1947 to provide additional space for higher capacity tenders.

With the increasing popularity of the 'Bournemouth Belle' it was decided that another Belle could be introduced to tap the patronage of the 'West Country', and so the 'Devon Belle' service started on 20 June 1947. This express ran 'non-stop' between Waterloo and Sidmouth Junction – at least, that is what the publicity stated. In actual fact, there was a service stop at Wilton in order that locomotives could be changed. The 'Devon Belle' was an all-Pullman car service with an observation car at the rear and ran on Mondays, Fridays, Saturdays and Sundays. At Sidmouth Junction a connection was offered to Sidmouth and at Exeter the train divided, with the first four Pullmans proceeding directly to Plymouth and the eight at the rear, including the observation car, being conveyed on to Ilfracombe.

The inaugural train was worked by No. 21C15 *Rotterdam Lloyd* between Waterloo and Wilton, and from Wilton to Exeter No. 21C3 *Royal Mail* took charge. The Up train to Wilton was worked by No. 21C4 *Cunard White Star*. The locomotives for this service carried a special red headboard with yellow lettering, and side flashes were attached to the smoke deflector plates. Later, for a time, 'West Countries' Nos 21C103 *Plymouth* and 21C117 *Ilfracombe* were rostered for the final portions of the journey, but ultimately this task was given to any available locomotive. The 'Devon Belle' proved to be a popular and successful service and often was strengthened to thirteen or fourteen Pullmans, the extra cars being for Ilfracombe. Timekeeping was good with the Up trains invariably passing Clapham Junction several minutes early. The demand for the service in the winter months was not sufficient to justify the allocation of such luxurious travel and consequently the train stopped running after November of each year. This duty was always a 'Merchant Navy' to the locomotive change at

Wilton and the sheds made a special effort to produce locomotives that were a credit to all concerned.

Typical of the 'Devon Belle' in 1947 is the log of No. 21C4 *Cunard White Star*, from Wilton to Exeter, loaded to fourteen Pullmans:

Locomotive: No. 21C4 *Cunard White Star*
Train: 'Devon Belle', Wilton to Exeter
Load: 14 Pullman coaches, 546 tons tare, 575 tons gross

Distance miles		Time mins	secs	Speed mph
0.0	Wilton	0	00	–
5.7	Dinton	9	19	60/55
10.0	Tisbury	13	53	57
15.0	Semley	19	15	48.5
19.1	Gillingham	22	47	79
21.4	Milepost 107.5	24	39	64
23.7	Milepost 109.75	26	27	83
25.9	Templecombe	28	11	–
27.4	Milepost 113.5	29	40	58
32.0	Sherborne	33	22	87
36.6	Yeovil Junction	36	48	76
39.9	Milepost 126	39	57	58.5
43.9	Milepost 130	43	16	80
45.4	Crewkerne	44	23	–
46.9	Milepost 133	46	02	52
53.4	Chard Junction	51	44	77
		sig. stop		
53.5	Axminster	61	29	15/58
61.7	Seaton Junction	62	58	50
66.4	Milepost 152.5	73	44	27
67.4	Milepost 153.5	75	45	33
68.7	Honiton	77	11	58
71.9	Milepost 158	–		70
73.3	Sidmouth Junction	82	07	–
1.7	Milepost 161.25	3	42	45
3.7	Whimple	5	42	68
7.4	Broad Clyst	8	39	79
11.1	Exmouth Junction	12	06	–
12.2	Exeter	14	55	–

During the summer of 1947 two members of the 'Merchant Navy' class suffered from collision damage, which showed how vulnerable the airsmoothed casing was on these locomotives. On 10 June 1947 No. 21C6 *Peninsular & Oriental S. N. Co.* was involved in a collision with an electric train while running into Waterloo with a West of England express. Luckily, due to the slow impact speeds, no passengers were seriously injured, but while the damage to the electric train was less than excessive severe damage was caused to the Pacific, with the result that the locomotive was under repair from 19 June until 28 August 1947. Following this incident, in July No. 21C14 *Nederland Line* was damaged by a glancing blow from an Adams 0-4-4 tank, No. 204. The tank received only scratches and scrapes, but the Pacific lost most of the cab and firebox sheeting. The locomotive was repaired and the new panels repainted at Nine Elms shed.

It was becoming the practice for the larger motive power depots to carry out light and intermediate repairs on the 'Merchant Navy' locomotives, possibly because the initial quantity of failures caused delays at the works, making it difficult to provide top link services if the locomotives were there for protracted periods. This was partly the cause of some of the delays to the change of numbering after nationalization, for example, No. 21C2 *Union Castle* had a heavy intermediate repair at 67,254 miles in January 1949 while at Exmouth Junction shed. Consequently, the locomotive did not visit Eastleigh Works until January 1950 when it had a general overhaul and only then was the numbering changed to the 35XXX series. No. 21C1 *Channel Packet* was also delayed in the same manner in November 1948.

On 1 January 1948 the SR disappeared as a separate company and the nationalized British Railways came into existence. The Bulleid Light Pacifics had by this time had nearly three years of service experience and complimented the work of the 'Merchant Navy' Pacifics, ultimately across the whole system.

On 7 May 1945 No. 21C101, the first of the new Light Pacifics, as yet unnamed, stood in all its glory in brilliant malachite green outside Brighton Works for official photographs and inspection by the company directors. The plan had been for a special train to run after the inspection, to Worthing and back, but this had to be postponed and No. 21C101 returned to the erecting shop with a boiler defect. The problem turned out to be more serious than was originally understood with the result that the boiler, No. 1261 was replaced with a new boiler, No. 1266, which had been at hand for No. 21C106. While in the works the cylinders were inspected and found to be cracked around the area of the ports; they were also replaced with a set originally destined for a later locomotive. Eventually, No. 21C101 was available for initial tests on the road and by 5 June 1945 they were successfully completed. Over the next two days No. 21C101 ran light engine to Tunbridge Wells West, turning on the Groombridge triangle and returning to Brighton.

Evidently the steaming and running tests were successful as on 14 June 1945 No. 21C101, again shown in exemplary malachite green, was positioned outside in the works yard at Brighton for official photographs. This time the locomotive had the name 'Exeter', the city's coat of arms and the class scroll painted on the side of the casing over the centre coupled wheels. Unfortunately, because of the vast expanse of malachite green the name was all but lost and did not stand out clearly. However, this was a temporary measure and when *Exeter* entered revenue earning service on 21 June 1945 the cast name-plates, scrolls and shields, complete with an enamelled coat of arms, had been fitted.

No. 21C101 worked the 08.00 Brighton to Victoria, via Uckfield and Eridge, on the inaugural service that day. This was followed by the return service at 12.03

'West Country' No. 34107 *Blandford Forum* at Cowley Junction, Whitsun 1962.
Roger Holmes, Hugh Davies Collection

from Victoria to Brighton, via East Grinstead and Sheffield Park. Both services operated successfully but, although the 'West Country' class locomotives were originally given route clearance comparable with the Maunsell N class 2–6–0s, later when detail restrictions were published, the Bluebell line was prohibited between Horsted Keynes and Culver Junction. It was therefore some eight years before another Pacific was seen at Sheffield Park.

As the new members of the class left the works they were worked around to Eastbourne shed for the official photographs taken in the yard, following which the initial trial runs took place. During the final months of 1945 the trials were normally a run to Worthing and back. However, in the new year the practice was changed to work light engine along the coast to Eastbourne, spend a couple of hours on shed and return tender first to Pevensey, and then forward via Stone Cross and Polegate to Brighton. During the same period it became the standard practice to run the new locomotives in by working the 09.41 van train from Brighton to Redhill, a duty which allowed plenty of latitude in timing. Early on, the return runs were made on the 13.47 van train back to Brighton, but as experience was gathered the duties increased to include the 19.05 goods to Norwood, then light engine to London Bridge for the 22.35 mail train back to Brighton.

At the end of June 1945 the first three 'West Country' class locomotives, Nos 21C101–3, passed via Salisbury en route to Exmouth Junction shed. No. 21C102 loitered at Salisbury overnight so that the locomotive could be named at the city station, joining the other Pacifics at Exmouth the next day. By 2 August a further two Light Pacifics, Nos 21C104–5, left Brighton to join the others in the allocation at Exmouth. The Exmouth stud were used in place of the T9 and N classes currently operating the Ilfracombe services and in October of the same year they reached Plymouth for the first time. The 'West Countries' were also used in place of the M7 class operating the early morning duties between Exeter and Axminister.

October 1945 saw the first of the new class operating over the lines in Kent, albeit for an exhibition at Ashford, when No. 21C111 *Tavistock* appeared with a new Bulleid coach at the town's thanksgiving week. Similarly, No. 21C114 *Budleigh Salterton* was displayed at New Romney in the company of a Romney, Hythe & Dymchurch Pacific. At the end of October No. 21C110 *Sidmouth* was allocated to Redhill and worked a number of Maunsell 2-6-0 duties over the Reading line, normally the 07.35 Redhill–Reading, the 12.17 return, the 17.36 to Reading, and the 21.34 back home. During these workings a constant check of coal and water consumption was made, with water being taken only from metered sources at Redhill and Reading, and the coal from special wagons at Reading. Surprisingly, the results of these tests are difficult to locate.

Eastleigh first saw the new Pacifics in November 1945 when Nos 21C110 and 21C115 both worked troop specials from Hove to Southampton via Netley, later running coupled together for servicing at Eastleigh shed. No. 21C110 then worked the 22.05 goods service to Salisbury, while No. 21C115 took another military train from Southampton to Exeter. Also during November, Exeter–Salisbury expresses were handled by the 'West Country' class, as were the 11.30 Brighton to Plymouth trains in the following month.

The motive power planning for the 'West Country' class had always been that the first twenty members of the class should be allocated to Exmouth Junction shed but in December 1945 the rapidly deteriorating condition of services on the Eastern Section called for a fast reappraisal of the requirements. Thus, no sooner had Nos 21C119–20 reached Exmouth than they were ordered to Ramsgate. At the same time the trials being carried out by No. 21C121 on the Waterloo to Basingstoke and Salisbury slow and semi-fast trains, while based at Nine Elms, were quickly concluded and the locomotive moved to Ramsgate to join the other two. By February 1946 Ramsgate's allocation of 'West Country' locomotives had increased to seven (Nos 21C119–25) with No. 21C117 joining the stud in March of that year. All the locomotives were operating the Ramsgate–London expresses. A further incursion into the depths of the Eastern Section was made on 4 April 1946 when No. 21C122 took a directors' special from Brighton to Victoria via Steyning and Dorking, and this was followed by No. 21C129 having charge of the royal train from Victoria to Tattenham Corner on Derby Day.

Following the return of the 'Golden Arrow' service and after the initial publicity the train became the responsibility of the 'West Country' Pacifics and four of the locomotives at Ramsgate, Nos 21C117, 21C119–20 and 21C125, were transferred to Battersea for the purpose. These locomotives also appeared on the other Continental services, as well as on some of the more mundane Chatham line commuter trains. Nos 21C126–30 were sent brand new from Brighton to Ramsgate as replacements.

With the entry into service of the last of this batch, a further order for fifteen additional locomotives (No. 2885) was commenced at Brighton, and these entered

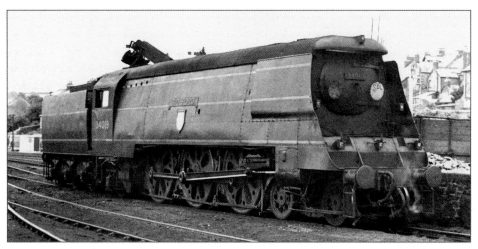

No. 34019 *Bideford* in Southern livery, with British Railways numbers and smokebox door plate but without owner's details on the tender, alongside the coaling stage at Wadebridge on 9 June 1949.

R.J. Buckley, Initial Photographic

service between June and October 1946. This allowed the transfer of Nos 21C117, and 21C119–20 back to the Western Section. Nos 21C117 and 21C120 were allocated to Exmouth Junction and No. 21C119 was loaned to Salisbury for use in the same link as the 'Merchant Navy' Pacifics, working the London expresses. The stiff eastwards start from Salisbury caused some difficulties for local crews during the early workings and they needed assistance from the station pilot, but as the crews began to understand the shortcomings, the performances of the Light Pacifics proved successful.

The allocation of the 'West Country' class at 1 January 1947 was:

Exmouth Junction	Ramsgate	Battersea
21C101–20	21C121–32	21C133–40
21C141–5		

The 'Golden Arrow' service was normally worked by No. 21C135 out of Battersea with No. 21C133 being the relief during periods of service or repair. On the 'Kent Coast' trains the 'West Countries' worked significant services to Margate, Ramsgate and Dover out of Charing Cross, Victoria and Cannon Street. Interestingly, the 09.40 service from Margate to Charing Cross via Dover, when hauled by a 'West Country' class, took over the train at Ramsgate from a Faversham-based D1 or D class 4–4–0. The workings in the West of England involved Nos 21C105–6 being outstationed at Barnstaple, to take over the duties of the two N class Nos 1836 and 1842, and for use on the express services west of Exeter. This created one oddity of over-abundant power when, for several months, a balanced turn consisted of the 11.05 Plymouth Friary to Exeter slow service being doubled-headed – the train normally only consisted of three coaches!

During November 1946 the first three locomotives of the next order (No. 3213) entered service, Nos 21C146–8. They were in the 'West Country' class, although the remainder of the locomotives from that order were classified separately as 'Battle of Britains'. The first 'Battle of Britain' locomotives were Nos 21C149 *Anti-Aircraft Command*, 21C150 *Royal Observer Corps*, 21C151 *Winston Churchill* and 21C152 *Lord Dowding*, and they entered service in December 1946. Nos 21C149–50 were originally intended to have been named *Holsworthy* and *Lapford*, in the 'West Country' class. A total of forty-four 'Battle of Britain' class Light Pacifics were built, with the last two, Nos 34109 *Sir Trafford Leigh Mallory* and 34110 *66 Squadron* being completed in May 1950 and January 1951 respectively. No. 34109 was to be rebuilt in March 1961 and was then withdrawn in September 1964, just over three years later!

As the new batch of Light Pacifics entered service it allowed the 'West Country' class to be moved to the West of England depots and the 'Battle of Britain' class to work on the Eastern Section. The Light Pacifics were rostered on the top link services working out of Nine Elms shed, which included the 'Bournemouth Belle' and the 'Atlantic Coast Express'. Some of the increased number of Light Pacifics were still available, so consideration was given to allocating them to the boat express services. Consequently, in early 1947 gauging tests were carried out in the Old Docks at Southampton and in July of that year No. 21C159 *Sir Archibald Sinclair* successfully headed the Jersey boat-train. Unfortunately, on 25 July the 21.00 Channel Islands boat-train, headed by No. 21C158 *Sir Frederick Pile* came to grief when the locomotive was derailed inside the docks and all passenger traffic was brought to a halt for a number of hours. The boat-trains subsequently reverted to 4–6–0 locomotives, including the 'Lord Nelsons'. It was not until the end of September 1947 after permanent way work to ease two curves and replace a set of points was completed that Light Pacifics were used again within the Old Docks. The first to operate were Nos 21C158 *Sir Frederick Pile* and 21C161 *73 Squadron* on 4 October 1947, hauling two *Queen Mary* boat-trains.

The shed at Dorchester suffered similar problems and restrictions were enforced until the first road could be changed into a loop. Consequently, it was not until 18 August 1947 that the first Light Pacific, No. 21C105 *Barnstaple*, was able to work through to Weymouth on the 13.30 Waterloo to Weymouth service. The locomotive returned with the 18.30 train to London piloted by a T9, No. 719, as far as Bournemouth.

Padstow and Okehampton had by now been provided with new and larger turntables to allow the Light Pacifics access to the lines west of Exeter. This allowed workings over the North Cornwall line including such curiosities as the 05.31 service from Exeter to Launceston, which commonly included a couple of coaches, a few vans, twelve or more goods trucks and a brake van, and the 08.25 'Atlantic Coast Express' from Padstow as far as Exeter. The latter service caused the locomotive to work a stopping goods the day before to Wadebridge, staying on shed overnight and then running empty fish vans to Padstow where the locomotive was turned and serviced ready for the ACE. Fridays saw a modification of this when the locomotive ran light to Padstow immediately after reaching Wadebridge, was stabled at Padstow overnight and then took the 08.05 relief train as far as Exeter.

'Battle of Britain' No. 34081 *92 Squadron* entering Halwill with the 'Atlantic Coast Express'. No. 34081 is now preserved on the Nene Valley Railway, Peterborough.
David Lawrence, Hugh Davies Collection

During 1947 these services were normally shared by four 'West Country' class locomotives, two aptly being Nos 21C107 *Wadebridge* and 21C108 *Padstow*, while typical of the others were Nos 21C111 *Tavistock* and 21C120 *Seaton*. *Tavistock* caused much consternation when it first appeared at Padstow shed, as it caught fire and the local fire service had to be called for assistance.

The 'Atlantic Coast Express' became well known for the number of different destinations served by the train, as well as the number of reliefs during summer weekends. It was not unusual for up to nine different final destinations to be indicated on the train, all having either separate coaches or groups of coaches. The station work at each change was exemplary as only the SR could achieve, and woe betide anyone getting into the wrong coach! One of the nicknames for the ACE was the 'Portmanteau Express', for very obvious reasons.

On 15 December 1947 the 'Night Ferry' services recommenced, with the first Down train being worked by No. 21C156 *Croydon* and L1 4–4–0 No. 1757. The two-year wait for the start of these services after the end of the Second World War was a result of the delay in recovering the Channel ferries, which had been used by the Royal Navy during the war, and refitting them for civilian use. The 'Night Ferry' service became a Dover duty with Nos 21C156–7 being transferred from Battersea to Dover. These two Light Pacifics had inordinate amounts of cleaning work carried out on them to keep them in an immaculate condition, with the motion, buffers, wheels and piping all gleaming and the paintwork shining, so much so that they surpassed even the condition of the locomotives working the 'Golden Arrow' services.

The train for the 'Night Ferry' became the heaviest running in Britain when in the early 1960s the dark blue Wagons-Lit cars were augmented by an additional two cars for Brussels, bringing the total load to nineteen vehicles and over 800 tons gross. It was a very popular service in its day, allowing passengers to travel in luxury between Victoria and Paris's Gare du Nord using the Dover–Dunkerque train ferries – a totally seamless service!

A further extension of Light Pacific duties was the through service from Brighton to Bournemouth, Cardiff and Plymouth, and this became a regular Salisbury duty in April 1947. The locomotive was normally stabled overnight at Brighton, working through to Plymouth the next day and then returning with the Up train on the following day. Once the duties had reached their stride these trains provided some good timekeeping and smart running.

That the Light Pacifics were fully capable of undertaking a number of the high profile top link tasks is evidenced by the number of records taken of the performance of these locomotives. Typical of this is that of the 'Golden Arrow' service in the autumn of 1946, shown below:

'GOLDEN ARROW', VICTORIA TO DOVER

Locomotive: No. 21C135 *Shaftesbury*
Load: 368 tons tare, 390 tons gross

Distance miles		Scheduled mins	Actual mins	secs	Speed mph
0.0	Victoria	0	0	00	–
1.9	Wandsworth Road	–	5	02	–
				sigs.	
3.2	Brixton	7	7	24	–
4.0	Herne Hill	8.5	9	07	28*
			pws		5*
5.7	Sydenham Hill	–	12	50	–
7.2	Penge	–	15	58	49
8.7	Beckenham Junction	17	17	50	38
10.9	Bromley South	–	20	07	51
12.6	Bickley Junction	23	22	45	35*
13.4	Petts Wood Junction	25	24	04	33*
14.9	Orpington	28	25	54	–
16.4	Chelsfield	–	27	56	46
17.7	Knockholt	–	29	39	39.5
21.7	Dunton Green	–	34	07	66
23.2	Sevenoaks	39	35	42	45*
23.8	North End Sevenoaks Tunnel	–	36	27	45
28.1	Hildenborough	–	41	11	70.5
30.6	Tonbridge	47	44	15	35*
			pws		15*
35.9	Paddock Wood	53.5	52	45	–
40.5	Marden	–	57	42	66
43.0	Staplehurst	–	59	54	–
46.3	Headcorn	–	62	32	77.5/75
51.5	Pluckley	–	66	46	79/75
55.0	Chart Siding	–	69	36	72.5
57.2	Ashford	74	71	13	77.5
61.5	Smeeth	–	74	55	67
65.3	Westernhanger	–	78	32	60
66.5	Sandling Junction	84	80	02	50*
69.2	Cheriton Junction	–	83	18	60
71.0	Folkestone Central	–	85	13	50*
72.0	Folkestone Junction	90	86	22	–
			pws		20*
78.0	Dover Marine	100	96	38	–

Notes: * Speed restriction.
        pws Permanent way slack.

This same locomotive, but now renumbered with the British Railways scheme and having been transferred to the Western Region, was recorded again in the latter part of 1948 on the 07.30 Exeter to Waterloo service. The log shows the progress of the locomotive from Andover, and the just under one mile a minute for the 66.4 miles from Andover gives a clear indication of the power of the Light Pacifics.

ANDOVER JUNCTION TO WATERLOO

Locomotive: No. 34035 *Shaftesbury*
Load: 366 tons tare, 385 tons gross

Distance miles		Actual mins	secs	Speed mph
0.0	Andover Junction	0	00	–
3.8	Milepost 62.5	7	11	45
7.2	Whitchurch	10	48	–
10.8	Overton	14	24	–
16.1	Worting Junction	19	34	67
18.6	Basingstoke	21	39	–
24.2	Hook	25	58	80/76
33.2	Farnborough	32	52	80
35.4	Milepost 31	34	39	73
38.4	Brookwood	37	02	81.5
42.0	Woking	39	45	81
47.3	Weybridge	43	41	eased
53.1	Hampton Court Junction	48	26	–
54.4	Surbiton	49	36	–
		sigs.		
59.1	Wimbledon	55	56	–
62.5	Clapham Junction	60	35	–
66.4	Waterloo	66	23	–

With the arrival of the nationalized railways in January 1948 a number of changes took place, not least the plans for new and improved standardized motive power to be common across the system. As part of this goal British Railways decided that comparative trials should be run with the major locomotive designs of each of the original railway companies. These trials were, in the interests of fairness, run over all the main lines of the various railways. Whether these trials actually provided any significant data for future designs is debatable, as the new standard designs were at this time being drawn up using the expertise and experience of designers already fully versed with the various problems of locomotive design. However, it has to be said that the eventual designs produced had 'safe' written all over them and they did not advance the 'science' of locomotive engineering even a single step forward, possibly with the exception of the Class 8 Pacific, No. 71000 *Duke of Gloucester*. This could be argued to have been a good thing but, compared to the advances that Bulleid attempted on his designs, albeit that they made the locomotives difficult and cantankerous at times, the standard classes were still no different from the original Stephenson ideas.

The idea of exchange trials was not new on Britain's railways, as trials between Joseph Beattie's LSWR and J. Cudworth's SER locomotives took place during May and June 1870 on the SER's lines. E.L. Ahrons wrote a lot of truth about these trials, albeit in jest, but nevertheless it is very applicable to all trials, not least the exchange trials in 1948.

> Now it is to some extent an axiom in locomotive circles that when an engine designed and built by Mr L.H. Crosshead, of X Railway, is lent with the consent of the Board for competitive trials against another locomotive designed and constructed by Mr R.H. Crank, of Y Railway, on the road of the latter, Crank's engine almost invariably comes out best. And if it also comes to pass that a return match is played on the metals of X Railway, then Crosshead's always plays a fine innings, being 'not out' at the end of it, whilst Crank's engine is either completely stumped or else 'improved out'. Pursuing the investigation further, three profound conclusions of great scientific value are almost invariably reached as a result of the trials, to wit
>
> 1. that the air of Crank's railway does not agree with Crosshead's engine,
> 2. that on Crosshead's railway the scenery and surroundings do not suit the taste of Crank's locomotive,
> 3. that both engines might just as well have stayed at home.
>
> The trials on Y Railway are carefully conducted by Mr Crank's chief assistant, Mr Boiler, who duly sends in a detailed and exhaustive report dealing with the defective points of Crosshead's, and the superlative merits of Crank's engine; while Mr Ashpan, the outdoor running superintendent of X Railway, compiles a neat essay on somewhat similar lines, but with the roles of the principle characters reversed. And, finally, a few years afterwards, when Mr Crank and Mr Crosshead retire for a well earned rest, and Messrs Boiler and Ashpan reign in their respective steads, the latter gentlemen promptly scrap most of Crank's apparatus and Crosshead's patent appliances and start on a few little things of their own. Thus the inexorable law of locomotive progress!

The fact that the data from the 1948 trials can be made to mean all things to all men possibly confirms E.L. Ahrons' thoughts.

The exchange trials instituted comparative road tests between the principal express, mixed traffic and freight locomotives of all the four major companies that existed before nationalization. The 'Merchant Navy' class worked against the express locomotives, clearly a meeting of equals, but in the mixed traffic category the Light Pacifics were significantly more powerful than the competing LMS 'Black Fives', LNER B1s and GWR 'Hall' 4–6–0 locomotives. The crews allocated for the away performance, handling both the 'Merchant Navy' and 'West Country' locomotives on the other regions, were Driver J. Swain and his mate Fireman A. Hooker, Driver G. James and his mate Fireman G. Reynolds, all of

No. 35017 *Belgian Marine* at King's Cross during the 1948 exchange trials, fitted with the LMS tender in unlined black and with the LNER dynamometer car directly behind the tender.
National Railway Museum, York

Nine Elms shed, and Inspector Dan Knight of the SR Western Section. Three locomotives of each class were selected for the away trials and were coupled to LMS-type tenders fitted with water pick-up apparatus. This, in itself, must have given the firemen some 'interesting' times as of course there was no water pick-up on the SR, so experience of this skill was limited. However, to all intents and purposes this was learnt very quickly by the Southern crews, who became very adept at 'dipping' at speed. The locomotives used were as follows:

'Merchant Navy' Class	'West Country' Class
35017 *Belgian Marine*	34004 *Yeovil*
35018 *British India Line**	34005 *Barnstaple*
35019 *French line C.G.T.*	34006 *Bude*‡
35020 *Bibby Line*†	

Notes: * Used on the home ground between Waterloo and Exeter.
† Prepared but not used in the trials.
‡ Fitted at Perth with tablet-catching apparatus for the single track sections of the Highland Line between Perth and Inverness.

All the Bulleid Pacifics allocated for the trials were returned to the works for careful preparation, either to Eastleigh or Brighton. All were fitted with V-fronted cabs and Flaman speed recorders. The 'Merchant Navy' locomotives had heat-resistant steel firebars and Aiton bellow-joint exhaust steam pipes added, with No. 35020 being fitted with the extra-length smoke deflector plates. The 'West Country' class locomotives were similarly attended to, being fitted with inside ashpan dampers, modified mechanical lubricators and the longer-style smoke deflector plates. No. 34004 also had an opening cut in the left-hand cabside sheets to allow the tablet-exchange apparatus to be fitted in Scotland. The valve gear on the 'West Country' locomotives was adjusted to give 80 per cent maximum cut-off and both classes had the dragboxes and footplates modified to cater for the LMS 4,000 gallon tenders. When the locomotives exited the works they appeared in immaculate condition with the malachite green paintwork absolutely gleaming, which made the black-painted LMS tenders even more incongruous and out of place. It is understood that some of the original LMS management prevented the paint scheme of their tenders from being changed.

Even before the trials started a considerable feat was achieved by Driver Swain and Fireman Hooker when they took the 'West Country' class *Yeovil* from Nine Elms to Scotland to work the Highland Line during the Perth–Inverness trials. In driving and firing the complete route from Euston to Inverness, it is probable that they achieved something that no other engine men have done before or since. On the Down direction they piloted express trains from Euston to Crewe and then from Crewe to Perth so as to avoid light running. On the return they worked a heavy express from Perth to Carlisle over Beattock Summit without any assistance.

No. 34006 *Bude* in Southern livery but with British Railways numbers and a Stanier tender, coupled to the LNER dynamometer car arriving at Marylebone with a train from Manchester on 9 June 1948.

B.W.L. Brooksbank, Initial Photographic

Prior to the trials it was pretty certain that a number of 'knowledgeable' pieces of advice were given to the footplate crews by everyone they talked to: Druimuachdar Summit would be under snow, the Down journey included Shap which was guaranteed to cause stalling because of dirty fires and, of course, Highland men always used sanding continuously, from passing Stanley Junction to Slochd Summit. (Though, interestingly, the sand supply on Bulleid's Pacifics was considered to last a maximum of 15 minutes!)

The timings of the test trains were well within the ability of the Bulleid Pacifics, but the loadings made the tasks set exacting, to say the least. The details shown below give the limits for each trial, although some trains were not made up to the full agreed loadings.

Region	Journey	Load tons tare	Locomotive No.
	Express Passenger Locomotives		
London Midland	10.00 Euston–Carlisle	500	35017
	12.55 Carlisle–Euston	500*	35017
Eastern	13.10 King's Cross–Leeds	512	35017
	07.50 Leeds–King's Cross	512	35017
Western	13.30 Paddington–Plymouth	485†	35019
	08.30 Plymouth–Paddington	500†	35019
Southern	10.50 Waterloo–Exeter	470	35018
	12.37 Exeter–Waterloo	470	35018
	Mixed Traffic Locomotives		
Eastern	10.00 Marylebone–Manchester	373	34006
	08.25 Manchester–Marylebone	373	34006
London Midland	10.15 St Pancras–Manchester	310	34005
	13.50 Manchester–St Pancras	310	34005
Western	13.45 Bristol–Plymouth	420‡	34006
	13.35 Plymouth–Bristol	420‡	34006
Scottish	16.00 Perth–Inverness	350#	34004
	08.20 Inverness–Perth	350#	34004

Notes: * 474 tons from Crewe to Euston.
     † 360 tons between Newton Abbot and Plymouth.
     ‡ 275 tons between Newton Abbot and Plymouth.
     # 255 tons between Aviemore and Inverness.

During the exchange trials the Bulleid Pacifics demonstrated their ability to produce very large amounts of power and to be able to sustain this output over a lengthy period. Typical of this were the efforts of No. 35017 *Belgian Marine*, operating a southbound service on the Penrith to Shap section. The train was

On 27 May 1948 'Merchant Navy' No. 35017 *Belgian Marine* makes a gusty departure from King's Cross with the sanders working. Behind the black Stanier tender is the LNER dynamometer car. Note the cables from the dynamometer to the footplate along the sides of the tender.

B.W.L. Brooksbank, Initial Photographic

525 tons gross and 503 tons tare and had been delayed at Penrith by signals. On the level start the speed was up to 46 mph and this speed settled to 41 mph on the initial 1 in 125 gradient, rising to 46 mph on the 1 in 142 pull before Shap station and reaching 51 mph on the ¾ mile level section through the station. The final minimum speed at Shap Summit, having climbed the last 1¼ miles of 1 in 106–130, was 46 mph. The result was a reduction in the scheduled time from Penrith by 6½ minutes. The report on this section of the trials stated that the actual drawbar horsepower on the 1 in 125 and 1 in 106 gradients was 1,540 and 1,629 respectively.

This Pacific gave a further indication of the 'Merchant Navy' power when, on the south side of Shap with the Down 'Royal Scot' loaded to 530 tons, it was checked by permanent way work at Tebay. As a result, the climb to the final 1 in 75 ascent was started at 57.5 mph and on reaching Scout Green the speed had fallen to 26.5 mph. At this point Driver Swain opened the regulator fully with 43 per cent cut-off; the steam pressure in the chest rose to 255 psi compared with 263 psi in the boiler and the drawbar pull rose from 6.18 tons to 8.6 tons. This was the equivalent drawbar horsepower of 1,710 to 1,835.

The 'West Country' Pacifics also performed with panache and exuberance, in particular, No. 34006 *Bude* put up an especially good performance on the Great Central lines out of London, being the only one of the mixed traffic locomotives to gain time with the test loads on this route. *Bude* developed some tremendous amounts of power during the work on this route, producing 1,960 equivalent drawbar horsepower on the continuous 1 in 132 climb to Annesley, 1,639 on the climb to Amersham up the Chalfont Bank and, on the 1 in 117 climb from Aylesbury to Dutchlands Summit, no less than 1,777 equivalent drawbar horsepower.

Bert Hooker, who was firing for Jack Swain, noted during these times that on a run south from Manchester to Marylebone the pilot driver called and told Jack to shut off, or 'we will be in Rugby a week before time. We have to knock hell out of our B1s to do this section in 24 minutes!' *Bude* did this in 22 minutes and had coasted for some considerable time before reaching Rugby. During that particular run *Bude* achieved a recorded drawbar horsepower of 1,667 or an equivalent drawbar horsepower of 2,110. This was with the locomotive at 260 psi boiler pressure, 240 psi steam chest pressure, a 27 per cent cut off and at a speed of 67.8 mph.

A typical log of No. 34006 while on the Great Central is shown below:

Locomotive: No. 34006 *Bude*
Load: 360 tons tare, 380 tons gross

Distance miles		Actual mins	secs	Speed mph
0.0	Aylesbury	0	00	–
6.2	Quainton Road	7	57	69/76.5
8.9	Grendon Underwood Junction	10	18	67*
10.9	Calvert	12	04	65/71.5
16.6	Finmere	17	18	59/75
21.4	Brackley	21	42	68
24.6	Helmdon	24	46	64/69
28.2	Culworth	28	01	65
29.4	Culworth Junction	29	07	69
31.2	Woodford Halse	31	24	–
0.0	Rugby	0	00	–
3.6	Shawell	5	03	60/61
6.8	Lutterworth	8	04	70.5/61
10.7	Ashby Magna	11	22	75
15.2	Whetstone	15	13	eased
18.9	Leicester Goods Junction South	18	30	62*
19.9	Leicester	20	07	–

Note: * Speed restriction.

Overall, the Bulleid Pacifics performed well in terms of loads hauled and timekeeping, but the high fuel and water consumption haunted the otherwise sparkling performances of these locomotives. The trials also showed up the quantity of lubricating oil used. The report estimated that for every gallon supplied to the LMS 'Black Five' 4-6-0s, 7.4 gallons were needed by the 'West Country' class! The average consumptions related to power of all the locomotives on the trials are tabulated overleaf:

COAL		WATER	
Locomotive	*lb/dhp/hr*	*Locomotive*	*lb/dhp/hr*
ER A4 4–6–2	3.06	ER A4 4–6–2	24.32
LMR 'Duchess' 4–6–2	3.12	LMR 'Royal Scot' 4–6–0	25.81
LMR 'Royal Scot' 4–6–0	3.38	LMR 'Duchess' 4–6–2	27.08
LMR Class 5 4–6–0	3.54	ER B1 4–6–0	27.64
WR 'King' 4–6–0	3.59	LMR Class 5 4–6–0	27.99
ER B1 4–6–0	3.57	WR 'King' 4–6–0	28.58
SR 'Merchant Navy' 4–6–2	3.60	WR 'Hall' 4–6–0	29.97
WR 'Hall' 4–6–0	3.94	SR 'Merchant Navy' 4–6–2	30.43
SR 'West Country' 4–6–2	4.11	SR 'West Country' 4–6–2	32.64

The average boiler evaporation rates, in which the Bulleid Pacifics did exceptionally well, are shown below:

Locomotive	*lb of water per lb of coal*
LMR 'Duchess' 4–6–2	8.67
SR 'Merchant Navy' 4–6–2	8.45
WR 'King' 4–6–0	8.07
SR 'West Country' 4–6–2	7.94
ER A4 4–6–2	7.92
LMR Class 5 4–6–0	7.92
LMR 'Royal Scot'	7.70
WR 'Hall' 4–6–0	7.69
ER B1 4–6–0	7.68

While the real value of the exchange trials is debatable, the results did show that the Bulleid Pacifics had a superb boiler, giving steam freely under any conditions. However, in both classes the inefficiencies of the front end, causing erratic performance and incomplete combustion, provided independent verification of the high costs involved in running these locomotives. Consequently, regardless of what the Southern Region or Bulleid and his successors did, the trials added weight to the need to make fundamental changes in the design of the Pacifics. Ultimately, this resulted in the rebuilding of all of the 'Merchant Navy' class and a significant number of the Light Pacifics.

In May 1948 a second Pullman car express service between Victoria and Ramsgate commenced on the Eastern Section, the 'Thanet Belle', consisting of eight third class cars and two first class. The first train, both Up and Down, was worked by No. S21C170 *Manston*. This new service had a varied amount of patronage over the years and sometimes ran nearly empty. In summer 1951 a title of the train was changed to the 'Kentish Belle' and it probably had a greater variety of motive power than any other Pullman train. It was not uncommon for 'King Arthurs', 'Schools', Maunsell 2–6–0s and BR Class 5s to put in an appearance, as well as all three classes of Bulleid Pacifics.

Early 1949 saw the transfer of No. 34059 *Sir Archibald Sinclair*, on loan to the Great Eastern section of BR Eastern Region. The idea was based on the premise

A 'Battle of Britain' at Cambridge. No. 34057 *Biggin Hill* passes No. 62603 while travelling light engine on 14 July 1951.

B.W.L. Brooksbank, Initial Photographic

that because the Southern Region had more Pacifics than could really be usefully employed, then the possibility of using these in the areas of the Eastern Region where A4s were restricted could help increase traffic. As a way of testing the idea No. 34059 worked specials out of Stratford to Witham, Norwich, Ipswich, Great Yarmouth, Parkstone Quay, Clacton-on-Sea and Cambridge, in all cases with greater loads than the standard for the section. The locomotive made a good showing although, as is common with all 'foreign' locomotives, the local crews had numerous grumbles, particularly about the slipping, insensitive regulator and poor cab lookout. They did, however, appreciate the power, smooth riding, free-steaming boiler and, of all things, the steam reversing gear.

No. 34059 was back on the Waterloo to Bournemouth services on 30 May 1949 and nothing further was heard about any transfers until April 1951. At that time consideration was being given to replacing the Eastern Region B1s on many of the East Anglian secondary express services. No. 34039 *Boscastle* was sent to Stratford on 8 May 1951, and Nos 34057 *Biggin Hill* and 34065 *Hurricane* followed shortly after. These locomotives initially worked the Liverpool Street to Cambridge trains, but ultimately appeared on the 'Norfolkman' and Parkstone Quay 'Continentals'. The Bulleid Pacifics were received with mixed reactions, some crews liking them and others equally hating the sight of them. Parkstone men seemed to do better than most and appreciated the advantages of the locomotives.

Around this time the new BR Standard 'Britannia' Pacifics were travelling further afield and were rostered for the 'Golden Arrow' services out of Victoria. No. 70004 *William Shakespeare* suffered a catastrophic failure at Headcorn while hauling the 'Golden Arrow' which led to a modification programme for the whole class at

Crewe. The Great Eastern section of the Eastern Region had a number of 'Britannia' class Pacifics upon which they were dependent. The modification programme meant that the locomotives were withdrawn from service in batches and it was almost a year before full reliance could be placed on the 'Britannia' Pacifics again. It was totally fortuitous that the Bulleid Pacifics were in place at this time and they were able to partially fill the gaps left by the failed 'Britannias'. This was helped by the additional transfer of Nos 34076 *41 Squadron* and 34089 *602 Squadron*. The Light Pacifics continued to work the 'Continentals', the 'Scandinavian' and the Cambridge services, as well as other boat expresses. Once the 'Britannias' had returned to traffic the Eastern Region expressed no desire to keep the Bulleid Pacifics and they were all back on the Southern Region by May 1952.

With the results of the exchange trials now fully reviewed, there was an increased interest in the use of the Rugby testing plant where tests could be carried out under standard and steady state conditions. The Southern Region provided a 'Merchant Navy' class, No. 35022 *Holland America Line*, and this locomotive commenced the tests in December 1951. The stationary plant tests were carried out at constant rates of evaporation and combustion, and at a constant speed. The coal and water rates were calculated using a summation of the increment method and with use of the Swindon steam flow meter. Typically the speeds covered by the tests ranged from 15 mph to 85 mph using between 10 per cent to 50 per cent nominal cut-off and from 10,000 to 42,000 lb per hour of feed water. The readings were indicated by a modified Farnboro recorder and the tests ran an equivalent of 10,304 miles.

After the stationary tests, a period of controlled road trials took place between Durranhill, Carlisle and Skipton on the Midland main line during October and November 1952. The loads were normally twenty-coach trains of 594 tons gross, which were the heaviest worked over the route given the schedules required and were some 42 per cent higher than those of the LMR Class 7 locomotives. Over the period 3,838 miles were run with no loss of time or serious trouble, except for one instance when the coupling rods were buckled owing to an exceptionally unpleasant bout of slipping at speed. The slipping was evidenced on the test plant as well as on the road, and was mainly caused by the locomotive laying copious amounts of lubricating oil on the wheel tyres and the rollers of the plant. Consequently, despite regular cleaning before and after the tests, a full run to ascertain the maximum power output was never attempted, both for the safety of the locomotive and the plant. The results of the tests indicated that the 'Merchant Navy' class locomotives were capable and effective, but relatively uneconomical.

Despite the free draught provided by the multi-pipe exhaust, the combustion of low grade coal could be very poor. Also, the choke was positioned around 7 in above the effective choke where the vacuum was the highest, and so consideration was given to fitting a single blastpipe and chimney. No. 35019 *French Line C.G.T.* was thus fitted in June 1951 and trials were run from Eastleigh shed. Early on it was found that the initial design was far from satisfactory, with steaming proving to be very poor. The blastpipe was modified by reducing the diameter from 17¼ in to 15½ in, but although the steaming was somewhat improved, the performance was still erratic. The blastpipe was further modified to include a liner with a 16 in

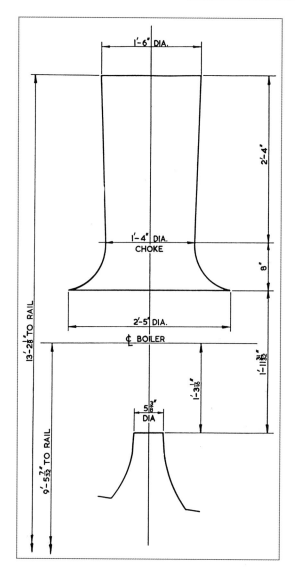

Single blastpipe fitted to No. 35019 in June 1951 and to No. 35022 in 1953. The results on both locomotives were inconclusive.
National Railway Museum, York

diameter, which produced a significant improvement, although crews complained that the steaming was still less than with the original arrangement and that sectional timings could not be maintained with loads of eleven coaches or more. No. 35019 entered regular traffic in February 1952 and had the original blastpipe refitted in September 1954.

A further trial was carried out between March and May 1953 at the Rugby testing plant when No. 35022 *Holland America Line* was fitted with a similar single blastpipe but, after running an equivalent of 2,463 miles, the conclusions were the same as those reached for No. 35019. The major problem with the single blastpipe was the lack of sufficient height to allow efficient operation, because it was limited by the loading gauge. However, even if a longer blastpipe could have been fitted, it has been suggested that the maximum boiler output would still have been reduced.

During 1953 a major problem faced the total 'Merchant Navy' class when No. 35020 *Bibby Line* came close to a disaster at Crewkerne while working the 16.30 Exeter–Waterloo express service. The locomotive driving axle fractured while the locomotive was at speed and No. 35020 became partly derailed. It was only the skill of the footplate crew which stopped a major catastrophe, although significant damage was done to the canopy of Crewkerne station. The failure was identified as having been caused by fretting corrosion fatigue under the sprocket-wheel seats and to flaws in the axle pieces under the crank web seats. The report on the incident also concluded that 'The underlying reason for the failures however must be attributed to the high stresses in the existing design of crank axle and the method adopted for attaching the sprocket to the axle.' Consequently, on 11 May 1953 orders were received for all members of the class to be withdrawn from service to allow the axles to be ultrasonically tested and have magnetic flaw detection tests. To cover the duties of the 'Merchant Navy' locomotives 'Britannias', V2s, 'Black Fives' and B1s were transferred from the other regions. Considering how close they were based, it is surprising that no Western Region locomotives were used. The first 'foreign' workings recorded were on 13 May 1953 when the 'Britannias' No. 70029 *Shooting Star* worked the 'Bournemouth Belle', No. 70023 *Venus* the 15.54 Waterloo to Basingstoke service and No. 70024 *Vulcan* the 21.00 Nine Elms to the West of England fitted freight. A number of the 'Britannias' arrived on shed dirty and grimy, and in some cases without tools, but within a couple of days all the visiting locomotives were transformed into gleaming examples of Southern Region pride and expertise.

All the suspect driving axles were given magnetic flaw detector tests at Eastleigh Works, although Nos 35005, 35010, 35012–14, 35017, 35027 and 35029 were dismantled at Ashford, either in the shed or the works, and the axles were taken to Eastleigh by road. The tests on twenty-eight members of the class were completed by 18 May and flaws were found on fourteen locomotives, the rest being returned to traffic. However, on further examination flaws were also found in the axle pieces under the web seats and so further testing was carried out at the motive power depots. An additional five locomotives had these flaws, and so a total of nineteen crank axles were withdrawn from service.

With the completion of the inspection and the programme of axle changes going ahead, it meant that the class could return to traffic. The first 'Merchant Navy' class locomotives returned on 16 May 1953, when No. 35018 *British India Line* hauled the 09.00 Waterloo to Exeter service, No. 35006 *Peninsular & Oriental S. N. Co.* the 18.48 perishables from Templecombe and No. 35026 *Lamport & Holt Line* the 10.00 Victoria to Dover Marine. The following day Nos 35001–4, 35010–12, 35027, 35029–30 were also available for traffic and by the end of May only Nos 35020, 35022 and 35028 were still out of service. The major motive power crisis had been overcome and similar checks were subsequently programmed for the Light Pacifics.

By this time the use of ultrasonic testing equipment was more widespread, and was now positioned at Nine Elms, Battersea, Bricklayers' Arms and Exmouth Junction motive power depots as well as at Eastleigh and Ashford Works. As a result, the

'Merchant Navy' class No. 35029 *Ellerman Lines*, in immaculate condition heading the French president's train on 8 May 1951, made up of Pullman stock and showing the royal train discs.
National Railway Museum, York

Light Pacifics began to have tests carried out on 15 May and they were completed on 23 May. Twelve crank axles were flawed and had to be replaced, five had flaws in the sprocket seating, one had flaws in the crank web seats and six had flaws in both.

Eastern Region B1 locomotives were loaned during the inspection repair period, but because of the limited number of the Light Pacifics withdrawn each day not all the B1s were used, in fact some were returned home within a week. By the third week in June all the B1s had returned and the Light Pacifics had returned to traffic. Following these problems a new design of crank axle was produced, having balanced crank webs with increased diameter axle pieces, and the sprocket was changed so that it was fitted to the crank web as opposed to clamping it to the axle.

At the same time as the new design axle was fitted a number of locomotives received new steel axleboxes and manganese liners. Those with modified axleboxes are shown below:

Locomotive	Date fitted
35010 *Blue Star*	06/55
35011 *General Steam Navigation*	02/55
35019 *French Line C.G.T.*	04/55
35023 *Holland–Afrika Line*	10/55
35026 *Lamport & Holt Line*	01/55
35027 *Port Line*	11/54

Around the time of the failure of the driving axles and prior to being rebuilt the Bulleid Pacifics were involved in a number of incidents, some more unpleasant than others. One incident, which would be funny were it not for the injury to the driver, occurred when the whistle on No. 34012 *Launceston* failed in the on position. The train was the 'Bournemouth Belle' on 13 January 1953. The driver used his whistle while approaching Woking and it stayed on from Woking to Basingstoke, where he stopped for a change of locomotive. On being offered U class No. 31798 the driver decided to fix the offending whistle himself but, in doing so, he fell from the casing and broke his leg. Consequently, a spare driver as well as a locomotive was needed, and in the event No. 31798 reduced the deficit time to 17 minutes by the time Southampton was reached.

On a more serious note No. 34050 *Royal Observer Corps* was in collision with Z class No. 30954 on 4 April 1955, while entering the yards at Exmouth Junction with the 19.45 freight from Yeovil. The yard shunter was running slowly along the same line and both locomotives collided. Serious damage was caused to both locomotive's cylinders and valve gear, and the casing of the Pacific was badly crumpled. Re-railing of both locomotives was not completed until the next day when they were finally pulled apart and in the meantime freight traffic was seriously disrupted, with Up trains being dealt with at Exeter Central and Down trains at Exmouth Junction Down sidings. The track was also badly damaged and temporary lengths had to be laid to enable the wagons for the 00.01 Exmouth Junction to Launceston goods train to be released.

November 1956 saw the 13.55 Meldon Quarry–Salisbury stone train also involved in an accident. The locomotive was No. 34049 *Anti-Aircraft Command* which had stalled inside Blackboy Tunnel on the 1 in 100 climb out of Exeter Central. The train consisted of ten bogie hoppers and a brake van which were vacuum-fitted throughout. When the locomotive stalled the trucks ran back and the last three derailed at the catch points. Single line working was in operation until 09.00 the next day. The driver of the train stated in his report that slipping commenced part-way up the bank and became so violent that he lost control of the train, only regaining it as the catch points were reached. Ineffective sanding was blamed, although later inspection showed that three out of four sandboxes were empty after the incident.

During 1957 'Battle of Britain' locomotives were involved in two accidents both resulting in casualties to passengers. On 30 June No. 34088 *213 Squadron* was heading the eleven-vehicle, 08.55 Victoria to Dover Marine 'Continental Express', when approaching Herne Hill the driver did not slow down to a stop at the home signal and collided with 'Schools' No. 30921 *Shewsbury* at the country end of the station. The 'Schools' was pushed forward 300 yd and had its tender badly damaged, but luckily no derailment occurred. The 'Battle of Britain' received a crushed front end and some minor damage to seven coaches, and the driver of the 'Schools' and two passengers were injured in the accident.

On Wednesday 4 December 1957 another 'Battle of Britain' was involved in a horrific accident at St Johns Wood when in fog No. 34066 *Spitfire*, working the delayed 16.56 Cannon Street to Dover business express, ran into the rear of the 17.18 Charing Cross to Hayes electric service at 30 mph. The electric had been waiting for the Parks Bridge Junction signals to the south of St Johns to clear when the Dover train crashed into the rear. The cab and guard's compartment were crushed and the next coach was driven forward into its neighbour, telescoping the carriage, breaking windows and ripping away some bodywork. The guard was killed instantly. Up to this point the accident would have been less serious, but the Pacific's tender and following coach hit the girders supporting the bridge which carried the electrified lines of the Nunhead to Lewisham line. The bridge immediately collapsed across the tender and first two coaches of the Dover train, flattening them to rail level as well as removing half the roof of the third coach and causing some damage to the fourth. A third train, the 17.52 Holborn Viaduct to Dartford service electric, was en route to pass over the bridge, but stopped in time and avoided plunging onto the wreckage. Over 2,000 passengers were on the two trains, 770 on the Dover train and 1,480 on the electric. In all, 90 people died in the accident and 108 received serious injuries, most of the casualties being in the two crushed coaches.

Rescue operations took all night and the line was not fully cleared until 00.30 on 7 December. The subsequent enquiry found that the driver of No. 34066 had passed a double yellow signal and then a single yellow before starting to break at the danger signal, but because of his speed he was unable to stop in time. It was considered that the fog, the driver's concern about water consumption and the fact that he was driving a left hand equipped locomotive on track designed with right-hand signalling were all contributory to the accident, but the driver was held fully responsible and was tried for manslaughter at the Old Bailey. The jury failed to agree, and at the subsequent retrial the prosecution was dropped after a petition from the driver's home town and after considering his failing mental and physical health.

The 'Merchant Navy' class was not without mishap and during 1954 No. 35023 *Holland–Afrika Line* broke a tender axle near Broad Clyst while heading the 'Atlantic Coast Express'. The train was hauled to Pinhoe by a following locomotive, No. 82017, working the 12.35 Exeter to Broad Clyst, and No. 35009 *Shaw Savill* was able to take the ACE on to Waterloo, albeit delayed. A more serious incident occurred later that year when on 10 December No. 35025 *Brocklebank Line* broke a coupling rod while passing Honiton with the 09.00 Waterloo–Exeter express. The locomotive casing suffered severe damage, several train windows were broken and about 200 yd of track were damaged, but fortunately there was no derailment and injuries were slight. However, while the locomotive was standing for a number of minutes the oil leaking from the locomotive caught fire and the boiler lagging was consumed in flame, with the result that the local fire service was required to assist!

On Christmas Eve 1954 No. 35030 *Elder-Dempster Lines* with the relief 'Continental Express' service suffered a broken tender tyre at Paddock Wood. The train was ultimately worked on to London by a U1 class, which was following with a van train at Paddock Wood but, having to work wrong line, passed the failed Pacific.

By this time serious consideration was being given to implementing a modification programme for the Bulleid Pacifics, beginning with the 'Merchant Navy' class. The idea was to improve reliability and availability without losing the advantages of the power and versatility of Bulleid's designs. A number of Light Pacifics were also destined to be modified following the work on the 'Merchant Navy' class. Thus ended a period of radical design devoted to the needs of express locomotives.

CHAPTER EIGHT

THE BRITISH RAILWAYS REBUILDS

The problems caused by the failure of the crank axle on No. 35020 *Bibby Line* focused minds on the problems surrounding the 'Merchant Navy' class. The Pacifics had experienced over 200 design modifications, with varying degrees of success, but in reality they were only stopgap measures. For some time, after Bulleid had left the SR in 1949, a number of Southern managers had started a move to rebuild the Bulleid Pacifics. Bulleid's successor, H.H. Swift, was an electrical engineer but it was his deputy, W.G. Burrows, who set the scene for changes to overcome the difficulties of Bulleid's design, and correspondence between the Eastleigh locomotive works manager and the locomotive accountant at Brighton laid out the proposals for the rebuilds. To compound the problems with the Bulleid Pacifics, a number of coupling rod incidents had occurred over the years, with serious failures on No. 35025 *Brocklebank Line* in 1954 and No. 35016 *Elders Fyffes* in 1955. In addition, the tests at Rugby had been interrupted in order to straighten rods and stories of rods being straightened in the running sheds with a jack against the wall abounded.

The unhappy reports mounted up as the idea of rebuilding developed, whether this was natural progression of information or a deliberate justification of the desire to rebuild is unclear. A memo from Swift at the CME's office in Brighton to J.W.J. Webb at the regional accounts office in Dorking in January 1955 reports that the oil usage of the 'Merchant Navy' and 'West Country' class due to leakage was 2 gallons per 100 miles, or approximately 120,000 gallons for all 140 locomotives per year. On top of this 15 pints of engine and cylinder oil were allocated to the engine men and artisan staff. For comparison, the total required by a 'Lord Nelson' class locomotive was 9.5 pints per 100 miles.

Another report stated that during 1953 thirty-eight cases of fire were reported, and in some cases the fire had not only gained hold under the casing and scorched the paintwork, but had also severely damaged the pipework, melting the Yorkshire joints on the lubricator pipes. Furthermore, a total of 5,501 days were lost for the 140 locomotives from all causes during 1953, which represents 39.3 days per locomotive, of which over 18 per cent were because of the valve gear. Clearly, some changes needed to be undertaken.

On 1 April 1955 a meeting was held in the locomotive works manager's office at Eastleigh where the decision to rebuild thirty Pacifics was made. A

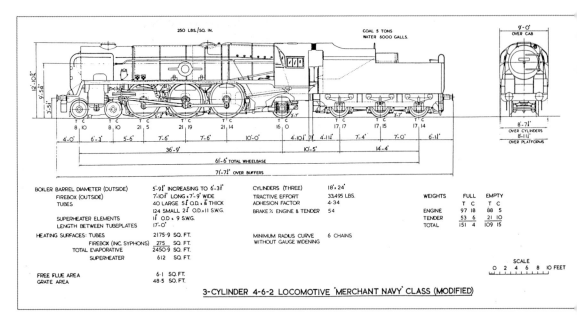

Schematic of the rebuilt 'Merchant Navy' class locomotives.

National Railway Museum, York

memorandum of the meeting informed those present 'that the possibility of re-building the "Merchant Navy" and "West Country" Classes of locomotives with a view to economies in repair and running costs had been examined for some considerable time; recommendations had been made to rebuild these locomotives as a more orthodox design. Information had now been received that the British Transport Commission had authorised the conversion of thirty of these locomotives to locomotives of a more orthodox design.'

The Chief Technical Assistant (Locomotives) on the Southern Region was a Mr R.G. Jarvis, based at Brighton, and he was tasked with preparing the designs for the rebuilds. His designs focused on the features which gave most trouble in service, typically the valve gear, mechanical lubricators, the steam reversing gear, the intermediate drawbar gear and the airsmoothed casing. During this design review stage M. Lockhart in the Brighton drawing office proposed modifying the Bulleid Pacifics to a two-cylinder design, based very much on the 'Britannia' Standard Pacifics. However, this idea never left the drawing board.

In the event, the proposed design retained the original boiler, frames, outside cylinders, wheels and axleboxes and either replaced or removed the following existing components: the valve gear and rocker shafts; inside cylinder; smokebox, superheater header and steampipes, etc.; reversing gear; piston heads and rods; oil bath; airsmoothed casing; mechanical lubricators; regulator; cylinder cocks; sandboxes; and the tender raves, tank sieves, water level gauge and intermediate draw gear.

Prior to the full agreement to the go-ahead for these changes, Jarvis instigated a number of modifications which were carried out on three of the 'Merchant Navy' class: Nos 35012 *United States Lines*; 35013 *Blue Funnel*; and 35021 *New Zealand Line*.

This was an experiment to determine if fewer changes could be carried out to improve the class service and cost record and also, one suspects, to provide further justification for the full rebuild. These modifications included strengthening the 3:8 valve operating levers and bearings, strengthening the mechanical lubricator drives, fitting LNER cylinder cocks and LMS automatic steam chest drains and adding strength to the frame stretchers. A further change was to the drawbar which had at times suffered from bending, particularly when the locomotive was traversing tight radius turns. The drawbar was pin-jointed at the engine drag box, but at the tender end had a spherical bearing surface which was designed to transmit the load to the tender underframe. The curved bearing surface rubbed against the flat block of the engine drag beam and thus very high loadings were produced on the drawbar, causing the bending. The modification changed the flat block at the engine to a curved rubbing surface faced with manganese steel to reduce wear and the pin-jointed plunger was cushioned by rubber springs. Safety links were also fitted between the engine and tender. This design was a definite improvement and became standard on all the rebuilt members of the class.

Order No. HO 7998 provided for the rebuilding of fifteen members of the 'Merchant Navy' class and the first, No. 35018 *British India Line* was moved into Eastleigh Works on 16 November 1955. The original intention, as outlined in the memorandum of 1 April 1955, was 'to carry out the re-building in line with the repairs of those classes of locomotives, and provided every detail was ready, there appeared no reason why the modifications should not take place in the course of normal repairs. It is anticipated that it would be necessary to repair about two locomotives per month and it is hoped to carry through the alterations at this rate.' In fact, the rebuilding programme never achieved this aim, even after the Light Pacifics were also involved.

The rebuilding changes also included modifications brought on by the failures of the coupling rods under bending forces caused by the driving wheels slipping, particularly at speed when the wheels could be slightly out of phase. The original design of coupling rod was constructed out of I-section class C steel with a tensile strength of 32–8 tsi. The replacement rods were plain section and constructed of 50 tsi fine grain steel, and were thus able to absorb much more energy under bending moments. This new design was subsequently used on all of the rebuilds and on some of the unrebuilt locomotives.

The outside cylinders were retained, but the original design was completely renewed, using an inside cylinder fitted with a cast-steel liner, and the steam chest was moved to the right to be in line with the valve gear and was arranged for inside admission. By using a steel casting, significant weight savings were achieved. In the original design the piston rods were forged with the cross-heads and the pistons were attached with locknuts, however, the pistons had a habit of working loose and breaking through the cylinder covers with disastrous results. On the rebuilt locomotives the design was changed so that the pistons were riveted onto the rods and the latter were cottered onto separate cross-heads. The design also incorporated a means of transmitting the actuation from the plane of

Detail of the springing and
wheel arrangement for the
rear truck on a rebuilt
'Merchant Navy'.
Author's Collection

the valve gear to the steam chest centre line. The new rods were fitted with cast-iron packing pieces, which were also used on the valve spindles of the outside cylinders.

The chain-driven valve gear and oil bath were removed and replaced by three sets of Walschaerts valve gear. The original outside admission valves were retained on the outside gear and a new cylinder and valve gear for the inside valves was fitted. The outside gear was driven by return cranks on the driving crankpins and by arms attached to the cross-heads; the motion was transmitted by a 9:8 rocker to the valve spindle from the top of the combination lever. Because of the difference between the centre line of the valve gear and the axis of the steam chest, a suspension link carried the weight of the valve gear. A short link connected the suspension link to the valve spindle cross-head. The valves had a maximum travel of 6¾ in with the return crank rod attached to the return crank through an SKF self-aligning roller bearing. The inside valve gear was driven by an eccentric mounted on the right-hand crank web of the driving axle and was attached by a spigot and five studs to the drive sprocket of the crank axle. This was a design directly resulting from the failure of the crank axle at Crewkerne in 1953.

On the original coupling rods an ingenious design of securing cap was produced by R.G. Curl, a senior locomotive draughtsman. The design was brought about by Bulleid's dislike of the standard split-ended taper pin and consequently the fastening was a hexagonal–pentagonal securing cap. This design caused many a problem at the running sheds, even in some cases leading to the judicious use of a welding torch to remove the rods! During the early days of British Railways it was replaced by the conventional plate washer and large nut with a split taper pin. In 1954 No. 35003 *Royal Mail* was fitted with four studs and nuts securing a large washer, following the style used on the LMS. This design was later used on the rebuilds and it had the significant advantage of providing a convenient method of securing the return crank of the Walschaerts valve gear.

One of the constant complaints of the footplate crews concerned the lack of sensitivity on the steam reversing gear. While it is an exaggeration to say that it gave all or nothing, the reality was probably not that different. The various modifications applied to the reverser, including a new locking cylinder, had not proved to be totally successful and so on the rebuilt locomotives it was replaced by a BR pattern screw reverser, based very much on those fitted to the later LMR 'Duchesses'. The reversing handle faced the driver and the cut-off was notated on a drum-type indicator. Movement was transmitted by the use of a tube fitted with universal joints, connected to a screw located on a bracket and attached to the outsides of the mainframes. A short bridle rod connected the reversing screw to the reversing rod. Unlike other locomotives with three or more cylinders where an auxiliary shaft is required, it was possible to use one shaft for all three sets of valve gear on the rebuilt Pacifics. The radius rods were lifted by an arrangement in which a slide block worked in a slot in the rod itself, with the slide block being attached directly to the reversing shaft arm.

Sensibly, the one major success of Bulleid's design, the boiler, was retained without any changes, although the airsmoothed casing was removed. The boiler on the rebuilt Pacifics was clad in the conventional manner and supported on crinolines, giving easier access to the pipework, and insulation was provided by fibreglass mattresses, although asbestos was sometimes used. With the now-cylindrical boiler it was possible to fit running plates along the sides and these were supported by brackets on the mainframes. The excellence of the Bulleid boiler was continued when the design was copied almost exactly on the BR Class 8 Pacific No. 71000 *Duke of Gloucester*, which was built in 1954 at Crewe.

The irregular-shaped smokebox was replaced by a cylindrical design which was supported by the saddle formed by the upper part of the new inside cylinder and the new fabricated stretcher. In spite of this, the original oval smokebox door of the Bulleid design was retained, which gave the locomotives a 'happy' look when viewed from the front. The saddle stretcher was bolted to the front of the cylinder casting and to the mainframes, increasing the rigidity of the front of the locomotive. The saddle itself gave access to the front cover of the inside cylinder to allow the removal of the piston and rod. The Bulleid chimney was replaced by a new cast-iron pattern of the same diameter, 2 ft 5 in, similar to that fitted to the 'Lord Nelson' No. 30852 *Sir Walter Raleigh* in 1956, and fitted with a petticoat

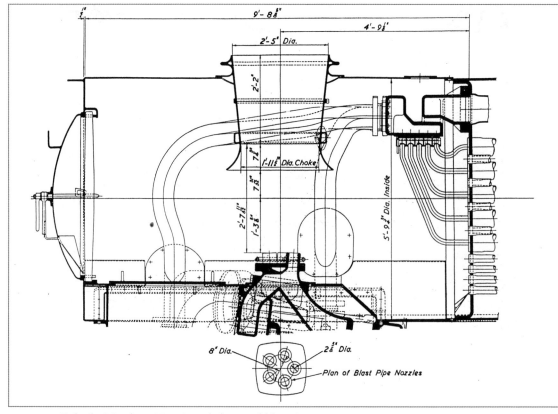

Rebuilt 'Merchant Navy' smokebox and blastpipe arrangements.

Railway Gazette

and exhaust ejector ring. The Lemaître multi-jet blastpipe was retained, but the height of the chimney choke was reduced by 7 in and the choke diameter by 1½ in. The boiler was also fitted with a new superheater, having direct supply to each of the three cylinders; the right-hand pipe fed the middle cylinder, the inside pipe the right-hand cylinder and the left-hand pipe the left-hand cylinder. All the steampipes passed outside the smokebox via stuffing boxes on the smokebox wrapper and the new superheater reduced the surface area from 655 sq. ft to 612 sq. ft. The original smoke deflectors were replaced by more conventional ones, mounted on the front of the side running plates.

The ashpans were also redesigned: the central of the three sections was fitted with two hoppers, each with bottom doors, and the outer two were fitted with a single hopper and door. The doors on the ashpans were operated by a linkage common to all doors, from ground level, making disposal a little easier. The firebox grate consisted of cast-iron rocking grate sections of the BR standard/Hudson grate design, divided into two groups which could be moved separately from the footplate. The grate design allowed for a small movement to provide some fire cleaning while running and a larger movement for dumping the fire when on shed.

The smoke deflectors and revised sandbox fitted to the rebuilt 'Merchant Navy' class. Note the lubricators on the running plate.

Author's Collection

How successful this design was when running is unclear as it raised a number of adverse comments from footplate crews. Front and rear dampers were incorporated on each of the three sections of the ashpan on the rebuilds and could be controlled by the crews from the footplate by two screw controls. The controls either opened the rear or the front dampers on all three ashpans. The design was so arranged that if the ashpans were deformed for any reason then the damper control linkage would still operate successfully.

The Wakefield lubricators supplying the cylinders and steam chests were moved to a position on the running plates, two on the left side and one on the right. After the first of the rebuilds went into service the left-hand lubricators were moved further back on the running plate. An additional lubricator, a ten-feed, was also positioned on the right-hand running plate to supply oil to the slide bars, the inside valve spindle cross-head guides and the coupled axleboxes. All the lubricators were driven by small levers attached to the expansion links of the outside valve motion. The lubrication to the steam chest of the outside cylinders was atomized and the atomized feeds to the inside cylinder was introduced into the steampipe because of the position of the steam chest under the smokebox. The cylinder barrels were lubricated by non-atomized feeds into the tops and bottom while the remaining non-atomized feeds went to the piston rod packing and the valve spindle rear bush. Swab boxes on the piston rod and axlebox guides were lubricated by trimming feeds, while the connecting and coupling rods were oil lubricated. A significant difference on the rebuilds was the

The Wakefield lubricators on a rebuilt 'Merchant Navy' locomotive, which were positioned on the running plate just to the rear of the smokebox.

Author's Collection

wide use of grease lubrication, which was applied to the valve gear, the rubbing blocks and the spring and hanger pins as well as the springing to the leading and trailing trucks.

Sanding on the Bulleid Pacifics had always been a bit of a lottery and had been changed a number of times since the first locomotive was constructed, including sanding on the tender for tender-first running. On the rebuilds the sanding was returned to the front driving wheels, with the sandbox being mounted just to the rear of the smoke deflectors. Initially this was fitted with a high swan-neck filler, but in use it was found to be impractical and it was not continued on the later rebuilds. The sand pipes which originally had provided sand to the front of the trailing coupled wheels were turned so that they now supplied sand to the rear of the centre coupled wheels for tender-first running. The sandboxes for the centre coupled wheels were placed between the frames with a twin box at the front supplying sand for forward running and a twin box at the rear supplying sand for tender-first running. This was still not the perfect solution but it gave better results than the original design. The BFB wheels and the clasp brakes were retained, but the coupled axleboxes were changed to steel with manganese liners, in line with modern practices.

The cab layout stayed very much the same as the final versions of the unrebuilt Pacifics, with the V-shaped front and the side sheets following the same contours as Nos 35021–30, and it included the hole cut in the lower part of the panel to give access to the boiler mud hole doors. The original pattern sliding ventilator was replaced with one supported on brackets designed to improve the ventilation and be easier to use. The firedoor was modified to be controlled by a hand-operated lever, as opposed to a foot pedal, positioned on the right-hand side of the door. The removal of the enclosed valve gear and oil sump resulted in 'stink bombs' being fitted to the centre big ends. The centre crank pin was fitted with a metal container with a glass bulb inside which was designed to burst at 160°F. The bulb contained either garlic or aniseed fluid and the cab had a notice which stated that a garlic or aniseed odour indicated an overheating big end; the design was based on an idea from the LNER. Upon hearing about this, Bulleid suggested in a letter to R.C. Bond that the big end should be enclosed in an oil bath. The driving and firing controls, except for the firedoor and the reversing screw handle, were similar to the original locomotives although the driver's seat was placed further back because of the new pattern of reverser.

The tenders of the Bulleid Pacifics were always problematical and fundamentally the design was not strong enough to deal with the knocks and buffeting received during everyday service. Various modifications had been carried out during the lifetime of the original Pacifics, some with more success than others, and so it was decided that as part of the rebuilding of the Bulleid Pacifics the design of the tenders should also be reviewed and the opportunity taken to improve matters. The most obvious of the changes was the cutting-down of the side and rear raves

Ellerman Lines showing the wedge-shaped cab front and the reversing shaft on the rebuilt locomotives.

Author's Collection

on the tender body and the addition of a curved rear to the coal bunker. With the removal of the raves, a sloping cover to the fire-iron trough was added thus making it a fire-iron tunnel, and a brass-framed spectacle was added at the cab end for tender-first running. The modified tenders were all eventually fitted with the standard BR ladders with square section outer stiles and by the 1960s the water filler lids were fitted with foot-operated catches as opposed to the Bulleid design. The tender axleboxes were ultimately all fitted with the modified covers which included a grease nipple below the lettering.

As part of the design review for the rebuild process six locomotives were designated for having work carried out to test the feasibility of various options. These included three 'Merchant Navy', two 'West Country' and one 'Battle of Britain' class locomotives:

'Merchant Navy' class	'West Country' class	'Battle of Britain' class
35012 *United States Lines*	34011 *Tavistock*	34065 *Hurricane*
35013 *Blue Funnel*	34043 *Combe Martin*	
35021 *New Zealand Line*		

All these locomotives were fitted with the early modified tenders, resulting in the less than pleasing appearance of a locomotive complete with an airsmoothed casing running with a cut-down tender.

The first tender to be modified was No. 3342, a third series 6,000 gallon tender coupled to No. 35021; this tender is today found running with No. 35028 *Clan Line*. The other modified tenders, second series 5,100 gallon patterns Nos 3122 and 3124, were coupled to Nos 35012 and 35013 respectively. A further 6,000 gallon tender, No. 3347, was modified and attached to No. 35020 *Bibby Line* in 1953. The modified tenders included the original lockers, hand brake, coal-space door and shovelling plate, however, the sandboxes were removed. The fireman's side of the tender included a water gauge which was operated from a float and pivot arm in the tender water tank. One improvement for the crew was the addition of a light above the coal-space door to help the fireman when pulling coal forward at night. Further improvements included covering the vacuum cylinders, a new design of water strainer to help lessen the ingress of coal particles to the feed water and the addition of shut-off valves to enable the sieves to be removed for cleaning without the need to empty the tank. These changes had proved effective in reducing injector troubles caused either by clogged sieves or by choked injector orifices.

The original 5,000 gallon tender modifications commenced during June 1956 and appropriately the first tender was No. 3111, which was the original tender attached to No. 35001 *Channel Packet*. This tender was unusual for the modified series in that the vacuum cylinders were not covered but were secured by banding similar to the SR method. This series of tenders had the long spring hangers removed and the rear lower tender steps moved from the buffer to the corner of the tender tank if these had not been previously dealt with. The TIA water treatment was fitted, with the TIA tank positioned on the right-hand rear of the tender. When the BR water treatment was installed, because of the additional space created, the vacuum cylinders were repositioned behind the coal bunker and were offset to the left.

The second series tenders of 5,100 gallon capacity displayed a different profile when cut down, having a bunker which curved inwards at the top and a front which curved up to the cab, although on some tenders this was missing. The cab had the water fillers removed and a water gauge added on the fireman's side. The vacuum cylinders were unusually completely enclosed and this type of tender had two different sizes of cover. Interestingly, the later BR rebodied tenders also had totally enclosed vacuum cylinders. The tenders were originally sent to traffic with the original SR-style rear ladders, but these were later changed to the BR type.

The changes to the size of the vacuum cylinder covers were related to the type of water treatment method fitted. With the TIA water treatment, the TIA system was placed on the left-hand side with the cylinders on the right. A cover the width of the bunker enclosed the cylinders and on the lower left of the cover the TIA system protruded to allow filling. With the BR water treatment, the small vacuum cover appeared which in essence was the same as that on the BR rebodied 5,250 gallon tenders. The briquette holder for the water treatment was positioned beside the water filler on the right-hand side at the rear of the tank.

The 6,000 gallon tenders were the first to be modified and, like the 5,100 gallon tenders, removal of the side raves left the bunker sides curving in at the top and the front curved to the cab roof. The TIA treatment was situated at the rear of the tank top on the right-hand side, which enabled the change to the BR water treatment to be carried out in a reasonably straightforward manner with the filler being placed in basically the same position. Initially the early modified tenders kept the TIA water treatment and the SR ladders at the rear, but ultimately both of these were changed to the BR pattern.

A fourth style of tender was also coupled behind the rebuilt Pacifics: the BR rebodied version. A number of the original tenders fitted to the Bulleid Pacifics suffered from serious corrosion, with the result that new wash plates and strengthening were required during 1944/5, and from 1945 to 1947 more strengthening work was undertaken and extra plating was added. Because of the history of these difficulties, BR decided to build a new tender tank body of a nominal 5,250 gallons, which could fit the frames of both the 'Merchant Navy' class and the Light Pacific tenders. The body was designed and built at Ashford and a total of ten tanks were produced; six were fitted to 'Merchant Navy' tender frames, one was modified to 6,000 gallons and three were used on 'West Country'/'Battle of Britain' tenders. The remaining tank was kept at Ashford as a stationary storage tank and was never used with a locomotive. Even though they had an increased capacity, because of their design these tanks could be used on the first series of 'Merchant Navy' frames. The first 'Merchant Navy' tender to be rebodied was No. 3115 in May 1959; this tender was attached to No. 35005 *Canadian Pacific*.

'Merchant Navy' No. 35022 *Holland America Line* with a Southampton Central to Bournemouth service at Beaulieu on 26 June 1956. The locomotive is in immaculate condition and this is likely to have been a running-in turn following rebuild that month.
M.H. Walshaw, Hugh Davies Collection

The tenders still retained the 5 ton coal capacity but, because of the water capacity, the sides were higher than on the other Pacific tenders. Consequently, the fire-iron tunnel was sunk into the top of the tender which gave a continuous line from front to rear. The two vacuum cylinders were covered and in each corner of the tank top were rectangular filler holes, hinged to open at the front. In between the fillers was the BR water treatment cover. The tenders were fitted with only one rear ladder which was offset to the left and had raised grab handles on both stiles, the left handle being of SR design and the right of BR square pattern. Because of the position of the rear ladder extra handrails were provided, two vertical rails on either side of the tender rear corner and a third horizontal rail on the right-hand side, a little over halfway up. The cab end of the tender was also provided with handrails and a small grab handle below them.

A design was put forward in 1963 to modify this pattern of tender by changing the water filler. Service operation had found that having a filler on both sides of the tender was of no practical use and consideration was given to a single central filler, to the rear of the tank. Also, two ladders were to replace the single central one. In the event these modifications did not proceed as by this time money spent on steam locomotive modifications was considered to be ill-advised.

A further tender was modified in December 1961 when the self-weighing tender, No. 3343, was condemned. It was decided to rebuild the tank but because of the longer 2 ft frame of the 6,000 gallon tender, the tank had to be lengthened. The rear ladders were also changed to two of the SR style, with semi-circular tops.

After the reintroduction of the tenders consideration was given to how the liveries should be arranged on these hybrid locomotives: rebuilt tenders coupled behind original Pacifics. Initially, it was decided that the locomotive should have a new overall paint scheme which, while remaining Brunswick green, should include rectangular

The name-plate of the rebuilt 'Merchant Navy' No. 35029 *Ellerman Lines*.
Author's Collection

lining on the cab and tender sides, with the same style of lining on the engine casing. No. 35012 *United States Lines* was known to have been in this livery in 1952 but this colour scheme had a limited duration. Following a rethink on the style for these locomotives, the final scheme treated the tender and cab side sheets as a conventional locomotive and the front, airsmoothed casing, etc., as a Bulleid Pacific. The tender and cab were painted with rectangular orange and black lining, with the Brunswick green visible between and with the small BR lion and wheel symbol. The tender rear was green, as were the bunker sides, but the rear of the bunker and vacuum covers were black. The engine followed the convention of previous Pacifics, having the top and front of the casing and the splash skirt black, with the buffer beam red.

When the first of the modified Pacifics, No. 35018 *British India Line*, emerged from Eastleigh Works as a conventional locomotive in February 1956 the livery was based on the BR 'Britannia' class Pacifics. The colours were still Brunswick green on the boiler, dome, cab front and sides, and the tender sides and rear, with orange and black lining. However, now the lining was vertical around the boiler bands from the front of the firebox to the rear of the smokebox, and the cylinders had two vertical orange and black bands at each end. The running plate valance was also lined with a single orange line along the top and bottom of the plate. The tender and cab sides retained the rectangular lining and the tender still carried the small BR emblem. Ultimately, all the modified Pacifics carried the new BR crest, which appeared in 1956. Even those Pacifics with the rebuilt tenders had the large-sized crest, which at 21¾ in high was still smaller than the largest size of the original emblem. The smokebox, chimney, smoke deflectors, cylinders and the frames of the tender and engine, including the wheel and springs, were all painted black, as was the top of the running plate. The buffer beam was painted red and a new frame for the name-plate was required to take account of the boiler curvature.

One further addition to the livery of the Bulleid Pacifics of all the different classes, both rebuilt and original, was a yellow triangle on the cab sides below the number to indicate the fitting of BR water treatment.

No. 35018 *British India Line* left the erecting shops on 9 February 1956 for the formal photographs, at which stage the locomotive was complete except for the handrails on the smoke deflectors. Trial runs took place over the next eight days until No. 35018 was rostered for traffic on 17 February 1956. During that period runs were carried out to Botley, Brockenhurst and Basingstoke, with some success apart from the occasional overheating of bearings and adjustments to piston valve clearances. The locomotive was given official approval during the formal inspection by the chairman of the British Transport Commission, the general manager, divisional officers and the press on 13 February 1956.

On 15 February 1956 a letter was sent to Mr K.H. Morris, the Locomotive Works Manager at Eastleigh, from the Chief Mechanical and Electrical Engineer at Brighton. The letter expressed the general manager's pleasure and offered congratulations on the excellent results that the mechanical side of the department had achieved. It also went on to say: 'Many complimentary remarks were made about the design and workmanship of the locomotive, and surprise was expressed that it had been possible to carry out the modifications which were required and, at the same time, give the locomotive such pleasing lines which would normally only be expected from a new design.'

The locomotive was allocated to Nine Elms for regular duties. The rebuilt locomotives were significantly heavier than the original locomotives, which in working order weighed between 96 tons 1 cwt and 97 tons 16 cwt. This compares with 99 tons 12 cwt for No. 21C1 when it was first built, although after the weight reduction programme the later members of the class weighed approximately 94 tons. The full details of the modified 'Merchant Navy' locomotives are shown below:

PRINCIPAL DIMENSIONS OF THE MODIFIED 'MERCHANT NAVY' CLASS

Cylinders × 3 diameter × stroke	18 × 24 in
Bogie wheel diameter.	3 ft 1 in
Coupled wheel diameter	6 ft 2 in
Trailing wheel diameter	3 ft 7 in
Wheelbase	36 ft 9 in
Heating surfaces	
Tubes	2,176 sq. ft
Firebox and syphons	275 sq. ft
Superheater	612 sq. ft
Grate area	48.5 sq. ft
Tractive effort	33,495 lb
Boiler pressure	250 psi
Adhesion weight	64.90 tons
Engine weight	97.90 tons
Tender weight	47.25 tons

April 1956 saw the second member of the class, No. 35020 *Bibby Line*, leaving the works and this locomotive was used for a number of trials to ascertain the performance of the rebuilds. A series of controlled road tests, under the auspices

Rebuilt 'Merchant Navy' No. 35002 *Union Castle* with the Up 'Royal Wessex' between Fleet and Farnborough in September 1958. The train is at speed with a significant load and this shows how well the smoke deflectors worked.

M.H. Walshaw, Hugh Davies Collection

of Mr S.O. Ell of the Swindon testing section, took place over the West of England route between Salisbury and Exeter using the Swindon dynamometer car. A number of normal service trains were also worked under revenue-earning conditions, including the 'Atlantic Coast Express', and the results were compared with the exchange trials of 1948. More details are given in chapter nine.

In August 1957 No. 35025 *Brocklebank Line* ran on the Swindon stationary testing plant to investigate a knock which had developed after approximately 35,000 miles. The results showed that the inside and outside valve head settings needed to be modified. In some cases it was found that the pressures at the front and rear of the cylinders differed by as much as 100 lb. The valve events were set up when the locomotive was cold and the allowances for heat expansion were incorrect, consequently the setting for the inside valves needed to be set back by $\frac{1}{16}$ in, and those of the outside set forward by $\frac{3}{8}$ in. Accurate setting of the valve events was critical for efficient performance of the rebuilt locomotives and this was regularly checked at intermediate repair. Who said that steam engineering did not need precision?

The first fifteen 'Merchant Navy' class locomotives were completed by May 1957. Order No. HO 9199 rapidly followed for the rebuilding of the final fifteen locomotives, with the first of this batch, No. 35030 *Elder-Dempster Lines*, being completed in April 1958. The last of the 'Merchant Navy' class to be rebuilt, Nos 35006 *Peninsular & Oriental S.N. Co.* and 35028 *Clan Line* left Eastleigh Works in October 1959. No. 35001 *Channel Packet*, the pioneer of the class, left the works in the rebuilt form in August 1959 having had the longest period in the original condition, nearly 18½ years, and having run 807,318 miles.

At the time of the decision to move ahead with the 'Merchant Navy' rebuilds it was agreed that the Light Pacifics should also be included in the programme and provisional authorization for fifteen rebuilds was granted in November 1956. This was subsequently confirmed in February 1957 when the number for rebuilding was increased to thirty in two separate orders, No. HO 8428 in 1957 for fifteen and No. HO 9361 in 1958 for a further fifteen. The first rebuilt locomotive was intended to be No. 34040 *Crewkerne*, which entered Eastleigh Works at the end of April 1957 in preparation for commencing the modification programme. In the event, prior to work starting on No. 34040, information was received that No. 34005 *Barnstaple* was stopped at Nine Elms depot with badly fracture frames and a damaged centre cylinder. Consequently, this locomotive was towed to Eastleigh and substituted for No. 34040, becoming the first Light Pacific rebuild. *Crewkerne* returned to traffic in the original condition and was not rebuilt until October 1960. Out of the total number of 110 Light Pacifics only 60 were rebuilt.

Work started on No. 34005 on 14 May 1957, but it was soon found that the frames were badly wasted below the firebox as well as being cracked ahead of the leading coupled wheels, so a spare set of frames was used to replace the damaged ones. The spare frames had been constructed at Ashford in September 1950 as part of the front end vibration tests carried out on No. 34041 *Wilton*. By the end of May the new frames had been set up and the new centre cylinder been fitted and on 26 June 1957 No. 34005 *Barnstaple* was brought out of the erecting shops and steamed in the works yard. At this point the locomotive had no name-plates, but on the following day the brackets were attched to the running plate and boiler barrel and the name-plates were fitted.

The position of the name-plates on the rebuilt Light Pacifics differed from that on the original designs. On both the rebuilt 'West Country' and the 'Battle of Britain' class the name-plate was reversed, being sited at running plate level below the associated shield or crest, which itself was mounted approximately halfway up the boiler barrel. The separate 'West Country' class scroll was positioned below the name-plate in a similar manner to the 'Battle of Britain' class plate. All of the plates were fixed to brackets shaped to accommodate the various sizes of name-plate details. 'West Country' No. 34023 *Blackmore Vale* was involved in a tribute to the Southern Railway's CME when the then assistant works manager at Eastleigh, Mr J.G. Click, arranged for a wooden name-plate with the name *O.V. Bulleid* to be temporarily fitted to the side of the locomotive's airsmoothed casing. This locomotive was part of a further tribute on 19 September 1982 when special shields were fitted to the casing incorporating Bulleid's name. They were unveiled by his son Mr H.A.V. Bulleid at the Bluebell Railway, Sheffield Park.

A small modification had to be made to the fixing of the name-plates on the modified Pacifics as rainwater was prone to collect on the spacing plate of the name-plate mounting. This eventually dripped from the back of the plate onto the top of the driving axleboxes, tending to wash away the lubricating oil from the guide faces. As a result two ¼ in holes were drilled into the space plates and these allowed the water to drip onto the running plates.

Barnstaple was allocated to Eastleigh shed on 28 June 1957 and worked the Up Winchester and return on that day. Subsequently, it worked a number of local revenue service trains from Bournemouth and Southampton as well as Netley line cross-country workings and trips from Portsmouth and Reading. On 3 August No. 34005 worked the 11.40 service from Weymouth to Bradford and on the following week was transferred to Battersea, working the Eastern Section 'Continental Express' from 9 August 1957.

The changes to the Light Pacifics were very similar to those carried out on the 'Merchant Navy' class with, naturally, all the same problem areas addressed by the rebuilding. One alteration which was completed at the same time as the rebuilding was the widening of the cabs on locomotives that had been constructed with the 8 ft 6 in wide cab designed for the Hastings route. This was increased to 9 ft in line with the rest of the Light Pacifics. The changes increased the locomotive's weight, in working order, from approximately 86 tons for the original design to 90 tons 1 cwt. This had the effect of reducing the route availability of the rebuilds and, in particular, they were never allowed to Barnstaple, Padstow or Ilfracombe. The details of the rebuilt Light Pacifics are shown below:

PRINCIPAL DIMENSIONS OF THE 'WEST COUNTRY' AND 'BATTLE OF BRITAIN' CLASSES

Cylinders × 3 diam × stroke	16.375 × 24 in
Bogie wheel diameter	3 ft 1 in
Coupled wheel diameter	6 ft 2 in
Trailing wheel diameter	3 ft 1 in
Wheelbase	36 ft 6 in
Heating surfaces	
Tubes	1,869 sq. ft
Firebox and syphons	253 sq. ft
Superheater	488 sq. ft
Grate area	38.25 sq. ft
Tractive effort	27,720 lb
Boiler pressure	250 psi
Adhesion weight	58.30 tons
Engine weight	90.05 tons
Tender weight	42.12 tons

The tenders fitted to the Light Pacifics were all cut down and were intended to be 5,500 gallon capacity to cope with the heavier express duties that the rebuilt Pacifics were destined for; in addition, these tenders would also match the increased width of the cabs. The tender coupled to No. 34005 was No. 3358, originally from No. 34094 *Mortehoe*. The tender changes included the same modifications that were applied to the 'Merchant Navy' class. However, on the second batch of Light Pacific rebuilds the tenders were not all of 5,500 gallon capacity and No. 34062 *17 Squadron* was running with a 4,500 gallon tender, albeit with the modifications of the other tenders. This locomotive was the first to be coupled to a narrow 4,500 gallon tender and the effect of a standard width cab coupled to a narrow tender marred the overall appeal of the rebuilds. Three tenders were completely rebuilt, the frames and new tanks made at Ashford and the tenders assembled at Eastleigh. These could be identified by the increased height of the side plates, so that the water tank was completely masked except for the sloping tops. The three tenders concerned are shown overleaf:

Tender No.	Original capacity (gall.)	Original locomotive No.	Final capacity (gall.)	Coupled to rebuilt locomotive No.
3361	4,500	21C119	5,250	34046
3313	4,500	21C162	5,250	34039
3354	5,500	34100	5,250	34031

Barnstaple proved a great success on the Victoria–Dover/Folkestone express services and when it was later joined by No. 34027 *Taw Valley* a significant improvement in the 'Continental Expresses' was noted. Ultimately, *Taw Valley* was transferred to Bricklayers' Arms for the 'Kent Coast' and business services. The subsequent thirteen locomotives were also allocated to the Eastern Section so that by the spring of 1958 seven of the fifteen locomotives were assigned to Bricklayers' Arms and eight to Ramsgate.

At Ramsgate a number of comparative trials took place during the middle of 1958 between Nos 34026 *Yes Tor* (rebuilt) and 34078 *222 Squadron* (unrebuilt) on the Cannon Street business services over the Tonbridge and Chatham routes. Unfortunately the 'Battle of Britain' caught fire at Chestfield and Swalecliffe Halt and also failed on one occasion with a jammed whistle, but otherwise the results were reasonable. The trials confirmed the hoped-for economies and fully justified the principle behind the rebuilds. The results can be seen below:

Locomotive No.	Type	Coal (lb/mile)	Coal (lb/dhp/hr)
34026	Rebuilt	41.42	3.38
34078	Original	50.64	3.51

Following the completion of the last of the first fifteen Light Pacifics Eastleigh returned to the orders for the 'Merchant Navy' class, but it was soon considered that better advantage could be gained by rebuilding another batch of Light Pacifics. Consequently, the last batch of 'Merchant Navy' locomotives was postponed and a further fifteen Light Pacifics were rebuilt instead under order No. HO 9361. They were constructed at two-weekly periods between August 1958 and April 1959, and were allocated to the Western Section, frequently working express services that had previously been the province of the larger 'Merchant Navy' Pacifics. Six were stationed at Bournemouth, five at Nine Elms, three at Salisbury and one at Exmouth Junction; four were 'Battle of Britain' class locomotives.

Once No. 34062 *17 Squadron* was well on the way to completion the balance of the 'Merchant Navy' rebuilds commenced, with No. 35024 *East Asiatic Company* being brought into the works at Eastleigh. Consequently, it was another 10 months before further work could be carried out on the Light Pacific rebuilds.

The third batch of Light Pacifics, a further fifteen, was started in March 1960, with No. 34059 *Sir Archibald Sinclair* being the first to enter Eastleigh. This batch was completed by October of the same year with an average of nearly two leaving the works every month. By this time it was not possible for all the rebuilt locomotives to have 5,500 gallon tenders and as a result the tender that went with the locomotive into the works was the tender delivered after rebuilding. All these tenders had the modifications and cut down raves. One exception was No. 34059, which received a 5,250 gallon reconstructed tender. Of this batch none was allocated to particular duties and most returned to the sheds they had come from.

Originally, in 1959, it had been considered that seventy-five Light Pacifics would be rebuilt, but by the middle of 1960 the Kent electrification programme was progressing rapidly and a complete reappraisal of the steam motive power requirements for the region indicated that only sixty Light Pacific rebuilds would now be required. Consequently, a final fifteen were commenced, on order No. HO 9903, in October 1960. Again the final locomotives did not have any tender capacity changes and no specific attempt was made to match the locomotives with specific services.

Up until April 1959, and No. 34062, all the Bulleid Pacific rebuilds were fitted with outside valve spindles and blind guides which did not require piercing the running plate ahead of the smokebox. This generated a number of failures and a modified layout was produced which included extended valve spindles with open-ended guides. The problem arose as a result of the uneven balance of the valve caused by a greater area being under pressure at the front end of the valve, which in turn gave rise to excessive wear of the die blocks and motion pins. The problem also contributed indirectly to the knocking on the coupled wheels. The modified spindles pierced through the running plate and were housed initially in open-ended pockets fitted to the base of the smoke deflector plates. However, they were damaged by ash and grit and so the pockets were changed to a closed type. These

The drive for the Smith-Stone speed recording system which is taken from the rear driving wheel via a crank on the coupling rod.
Author's Collection

were later altered again and they became progressively larger. The final design, which was retrofitted to the other rebuilt locomotives, was fitted to both the inside and the outside of the smoke deflectors. The pocket supported a step on the inside, while the outside step was repositioned some 4 in higher on top of the pocket.

By the late 1950s all the Bulleid Pacifics were fitted with Smith-Stone speedometers which were driven from the left-hand rear coupled wheel via a flexible drive to the driver's side of the cab. The large indicator dial gave a very clear reading of the speed but, unlike the Flaman speed recorders fitted on some of the original 'Merchant Navy' Pacifics, there was no facility for recording the speed. The speedometer system was calibrated to a maximum speed of 100 mph.

One of the persistent problem areas with the 'Merchant Navy' class following rebuild was a succession of failures in traffic due to the eccentric straps. These caused some 65 per cent of failures during 1957–8 at Nine Elms, and Bournemouth suffered similarly. Commencing with No. 35030 *Elder-Dempster Lines* in April 1958, stronger, modified eccentric straps were fitted and from that point the failures were reduced significantly.

Following the disastrous accident at Harrow & Wealdstone on 8 October 1952 when 112 people died in the worst railway accident on British Railways during peacetime, BR was forced to increase the route miles with Automatic Train Control (renamed Automatic Warning System or AWS in 1960). By 1959 the Southern Region locomotives were being fitted with this system which consisted of an electromagnetic receiver under the front buffer beam complete with a steel protection plate to stop damage caused by the screw coupling. Nife cells placed in a battery box sited over the buffer beam between the frames provided the power and the cab was equipped with an indicator, bell, horn and cancelling button for the driver. In 1962 the battery box was moved closer to the buffer beam because the motive power depot staff were having difficulty in accessing the centre cylinder and also excessive heat was causing damage to the batteries. The first section of track to be completed with AWS was that from Salisbury to Exeter Central in March 1960, which was part of a five-year plan to cover the routes from Exeter Central to Bournemouth West.

A further modification was the addition of a Giesl oblong ejector which was fitted to No. 34064 *Fighter Command* in April 1962. The scheme was intended to finally solve the lack of forward visibility on the original Light Pacifics, and in addition it helped control the continual problems of spark-throwing which the Bulleid Pacifics were reputed to suffer from, something that lineside dwellers and farmers were not very impressed with. The ejector consisted of seven nozzles situated below a narrow chimney, through which the exhaust was ejected with great velocity pushing it high above the casing and cab. The system was designed to reduce the shock losses which occurred during the mixing of the exhaust steam and gas, and consequently to draught the locomotive more effectively with less back pressure. The modification was a complete success and later No. 34064 was regarded as one of the best Pacifics. The original intention was that the rest of the unmodified Light Pacifics should be altered, but by this time additional expenditure on steam traction was severely limited and no further work was carried out.

The completion of the final Light Pacifics and all of the 'Merchant Navy' class ended the last major engineering event in the lives of the Bulleid Pacifics and it is worth considering if the costs of the rebuilding work really represented value for money. As a part of the initial review of the rebuilding programme, a clear comparison of building a new locomotive and rebuilding the existing class had been made, using examples based on the 'Merchant Navy' class. It was estimated that the cost of thirty Crewe-built 'Britannia' class Pacifics minus the scrap value of the 'Merchant Navy' locomotives would come to £586,000, while the estimated cost of rebuilding all the 'Merchant Navy' class, less the value of the possible scrap material discarded would come to around £222,500. Clearly, on the initial review, a case was made for the rebuilding programme, but of course this would very much depend on how good the existing boilers and fireboxes were. The Eastleigh boilersmith reported on the life expectancy of the 'Merchant Navy' boilers and other items and when the report came back with positive results then the decision was made to rebuild rather than scrap.

The case for a new design, either a rebuild or a new locomotive, was a very strong one which concerned not only running costs but also mechanical reliability and repairs. In 1952 the 'Merchant Navy' class had on average 62 days per locomotive out of traffic for running repairs and examinations. This was some 20 per cent higher than the 'Lord Nelson' class at 39 days, and cost £650 for each 'Merchant Navy' locomotive. The Southern Region believed that the gross cost of rebuilding the Bulleid Pacifics could be recouped from operational and staff savings and from the increased availability; the saving from coal, water and oil alone was estimated at £11,700 per annum. The final estimated gross cost of rebuilding was £168,450 for the class, or £5,615 per locomotive. Consequently, after deleting the cost of staff and repairs, which came to £16,350, and the cost of materials recovered during rebuilding at

In 1958 rebuilt 'West Country' No. 34014 *Budleigh Salterton* approaches Paddock Wood with an Up express.

Norman Simmons, Hugh Davies Collection

£5,500 (not considered in the original first estimate of £222,500), the outlay was £4,887 per locomotive. This was a total of £146,600 for the class and was considered recoverable if the locomotives remained in service until 1962 recouping £148,648. In the event, the first 'Merchant Navy' class locomotive rebuild cost £5,997 19s 3d. The estimates were rarely scientific. The statement 'not included in estimate' appeared regularly on the final cost summary; typically, this was a price of £12 4s 6d. A further underestimate was '£36 3s 0d for special packing not included in the estimate'.

However, in 1962 when the final sums for the 'Merchant Navy' class were completed the general manager of the Southern Region reported that more than £194,000 had been saved per annum over the equivalent use of the original locomotives. A saving of some 25 per cent could be attributed to the rebuilding programme, twice what had been expected, and this was notwithstanding the fact that the final cost per rebuild was £8,188 per locomotive, an increase of 46 per cent over the 1955 cost. Clearly, the 'Merchant Navy' Pacifics were able to repay the rebuild cost and furthermore were able to provide the motive power depots with greater availability, probably because this class had a long payback period.

Moving to the Light Pacifics the final cost of the rebuilding programme was £670,000, against an initial estimate of £541,250 for all 110 locomotives. On the early figures, the recovery could have been achieved if the locomotives had run until 1966 (recouping £592,907). In the event, less than 50 per cent were still working in 1966 or later (the remaining thirty-four were withdrawn in 1967) and of these not all were rebuilt. The average cost per locomotive was approximately £9,000, £10,900, £12,800 and £13,400 for each of the four batches respectively. Despite the 60 per cent reduction in repair costs, an 8.4 per cent decline in coal used and a decrease in oil consumed to 6.25 gallons per 100 miles, plus the increased mileage between intermediate and general repairs, it is doubtful that the Light Pacifics ever truly paid for the cost of the rebuilding. However, the overall running costs for the Light Pacifics were estimated to have been reduced by as much as 17.5 per cent and the good performance of the original designs had still been retained, so even without a full payback of the rebuild costs, the changes must be considered successful.

Not everybody was happy with the changes to the Southern Pacifics. Mr B.J. Wilson of Bishopstoke, Eastleigh, wrote to the CME complaining bitterly about the changes: 'I wish to lodge a very strong protest against the entirely unnecessary interference with the Merchant Navy engines . . .'. His letter continued for four pages and the Locomotive Works Manager at Eastleigh was instructed by Brighton to reply:

> I acknowledge receipt of your letter of 15 April which sets out your views on the modifications to the Merchant Navy Class Locomotives.
>
> Yours Sincerely

So much for customer relations!

However, regardless of the differing views, the increased availability and reliability contributed greatly to the final ten years or so of steam traction on the Southern Region and both the 'Merchant Navy' class and the Light Pacifics gave excellent service, finally showing what a great locomotive Bulleid had built.

CHAPTER NINE

THE FINAL YEARS

Following the rebuilding of the first 'Merchant Navy' Pacifics it was considered appropriate that a series of controlled trials should take place to produce comparative data between the rebuilds and original Pacifics. No. 35020 *Bibby Line* was taken into the works at Eastleigh on 25 May 1956 to have the tender exchanged. The original cut-down tender was changed for one still retaining the high side sheeting, thus allowing easy fitting of the cables from the dynamometer car, as well as giving better protection to the coal space where trials staff occasionally travelled. The tender fitted was a 6,000 gallon design, No. 3345. This was repainted with the panelling and the emblem lowered to match the engine cab side sheets, and a broad band of black was painted on the top of the side sheeting. This difference in livery caused an interesting comparison after the trials when the tender was fitted behind unrebuilt No. 35028 *Clan Line*. The engine retained the lining bands while the tender was panelled and so the emblems did not line up with the engine cab numerals.

The initial trials using the dynamometer car took place over the West of England main line between Salisbury and Exeter as it was considered that the interference from other traffic or signal checks would be minimal. The trials consisted of a number of fast and integrated trains, and the runs were completed without any incident or time debited against the locomotive. The rate of working was controlled by a gauge in the blastpipe which measured the rate of steaming and the maximum rate of working was recorded at over 32,000 lb of steam per hour, with a coal rate of 4,780 lb/hr. Apparently, the only limiting factor was the capacity of the tender. With a load of 436–500 tons behind the locomotive, the average coal consumption was 3.44 lb/dhp/hr and as little as 3.24 lb/dhp/hr, significantly better than the original Pacifics. Following the dynamometer trials a number of service trains were worked, typically the ACE, 'Royal Wessex' and the 'Bournemouth Belle'. On these trains again no time was lost to the locomotive, although a tender box was found to be hot at Exeter after one run and this was dealt with satisfactorily before the return journey.

Overall, the results showed that the rebuild performed very well. Slipping was significantly less during starting and could not be detected from the footplate during running. The valve gear operated without trouble and the boiler steamed freely with good coal consumption. The details of the coal consumption are shown overleaf:

Date	Journey	Coal burnt (lb/mile)	Load (tons)
25/06/56	12.30 Exeter–Salisbury	45.52	400
25/06/56	14.15 Salisbury–Waterloo	37.14	471
26/06/56	15.00 Waterloo–Salisbury	48.49	500
26/06/56	16.47 Salisbury–Exeter	50.26	395

During this time the Western Section was experiencing larger loads and more intense schedules than those on the Continental services. Consequently, the initial rebuilt 'Merchant Navy' locomotives were allocated to Bournemouth, with the original locomotives being based at Battersea. Once the rebuilt locomotives were available a new 2-hour schedule, inclusive of a stop at Southampton, was introduced between Bournemouth and London, giving a long overdue acceleration over the Bournemouth line. On Monday to Fridays seven express services were operated, three from Waterloo and four from Bournemouth Central. In addition, the Exeter to Waterloo services were also improved, typically cutting 19 minutes from the 16.30 Exeter service, giving a start-to-stop timing of 54 minutes for the 49 miles between Exeter and Yeovil Junction.

During the summer of 1958 the Western Section found itself with a serious lack of powerful motive power at weekends. However, towards the autumn the 'West Country' rebuilds started to appear on this section and as the demand decreased the traffic managers were able to match demand with locomotive power. In particular, No. 34045 *Ottery St. Mary*, a Bournemouth locomotive, was a regular

Hildenborough in 1957 with 'Battle of Britain' No. 34080 *74 Squadron* hauling 'The Man of Kent'.

Norman Simmons, Hugh Davies Collection

with the 'Royal Wessex' and No. 34047 *Callington* was rostered by Nine Elms for the 09.30 express service from Waterloo to Bournemouth. However, the mainstay of major express power remained the twenty-seven 'Merchant Navies' based at Nine Elms, Bournemouth, Exmouth Junction and Salisbury.

The final stage of the electrification programme to Ramsgate was completed on 31 May 1959 and the first through train was the 08.00 Victoria to Ramsgate on 2 June 1959, which was operated by an electric locomotive, No. E5004, hauling nine steam stock coaches. Some steam services continued to operate until the night of 14/15 June when the service changed over totally to electric. The last Up steam train from Ramsgate was the 20.52 with No. 34001 *Exeter* in charge. The locomotive was decorated with a small wreath on the smokebox door and left to the sound of whistles from other locomotives in the vicinity. Stream traction was now redundant on this line, if only on paper, and a number of transfers of locomotives were therefore made. Eight Light Pacifics were moved to Bricklayers' Arms from Ramsgate to join the seven already working from that shed and these locomotives worked the business services via Tonbridge.

LIGHT PACIFICS AT BRICKLAYERS' ARMS

Ex-Ramsgate locomotives		*Original Bricklayers'* *Arms allocation*	
34016 *Bodmin*	34025 *Whimple*	34001 *Exeter*	34012 *Launceston*
34017 *Ilfracombe*	34026 *Yes Tor*	34003 *Plymouth*	34013 *Okehampton*
34021 *Dartmoor*	34027 *Taw Valley*	34004 *Yeovil*	34014 *Budleigh Salterton*
34022 *Exmoor*	34037 *Clovelly*	34005 *Barnstaple*	

A number of the original locomotives saw service until the end of steam in the unrebuilt state and some ran into the early 1960s in their original condition. The quantity of Pacifics now available allowed the Southern Region to enhance some services or introduce new trains, one of which was the Glasgow to Eastbourne sleeper train which commenced on 30 May 1958. No. 34066 *Spitfire* was rostered to work this train and it became a regular Battersea Pacific duty.

Another new duty for the Pacifics was the 18.10 service from Victoria to Uckfield, a train with a long history of 'time lost by engine' which was a source of numerous complaints. The rostering of a Light Pacific produced a complete transformation, so much so that the preceding train, the 17.49 ex-Victoria which was habitually late leaving Oxted, was now the limiting factor for the Pacific. This was eventually solved by the allocation of two BR Class 4 4–6–0s which took over from the 2–6–4 tanks rostered for the 17.49 train.

Towards the latter part of the 1950s the Light Pacific rebuilds became more numerous on the Western Section. While No. 34053 *Sir Keith Park* was the only regular visitor to Exeter before April 1959, as the numbers increased the Light Pacifics were seen more often, with No. 34031 *Torrington* making a number of appearances and No. 34062 *17 Squadron* returning to Exmouth Junction shed. During the summer of 1959 a number of rebuilds visited from Nine Elms with the

'Battle of Britain' No. 34084 *253 Squadron* at Eastleigh after having rolled over during the Hither Green accident.

National Railway Museum, York

holiday express services, often replacing 'Merchant Navies' on these duties. By this time all the Light Pacifics were allowed to work to Okehampton and Plymouth and on 28 July 1959 *17 Squadron* was the first rebuilt Light Pacific to cross the Meldon Viaduct. Although it was some time before further examples travelled so far, No. 34026 *Yes Tor* was the next to cross in April 1960. However, by 1961 most of the Exeter–Plymouth expresses were being rostered to Light Pacifics.

As the 1950s came to a close two 'Merchant Navy' locomotives had lucky escapes. No. 35004 *Cunard White Star*, working the 17.15 Salisbury–Waterloo service on 6 January 1959, was approaching Porton station when a sudden landslip of hundreds of tons of waterlogged soil fell across the track. It was only the quick thinking of a ganger who warned the signalman that avoided a very serious accident. The track at this point was not completely cleared until around two days later. Later in the same month, No. 35024 *East Asiatic Company* was in charge of the 22.30 Waterloo–Weymouth service when, in dense and freezing fog, the train overran the slowly moving 22.15 Nine Elms fitted goods, being hauled by No. 35008 *Orient Line* on the same track. The driver of the passenger train had misread the signals near Esher. The impact was light and, after a detailed inspection and with improving visibility, both trains were able to continue.

During the same time period, on 29 October 1959, the Light Pacifics did not escape from incident. No. 34020 *Seaton* overran the Up slow, home signal at St

Denys while in charge of the 18.30 Weymouth to Waterloo express, embedding itself in the ramp of the Up platform, having previously derailed itself after hitting the sand drag. The damage was not serious, but major problems were caused to the local signalling cables and point rodding which led to difficulties for other services for a number of hours after the incident. The locomotive was not completely rerailed until 1 November 1959. Interestingly No. 34022 *Exmoor*, which was rebuilt in December 1957, was involved in a similar incident on 12 December 1960, when yet again the driver misread the signals and the same penalty was paid.

In a similar vein, No. 34084 *253 Squadron* also came to grief when the locomotive passed a red signal at Hither Green while in charge of the 02.10 vans train from Dover Marine to Bricklayers' Arms. The locomotive drove through the buffer stops and rolled down the embankment on its side. The vans were quickly removed and the locomotive was not blocking the lines, but the signalling cables were damaged causing delays for several days.

A further accident, which was more serious and caused the death of a driver and a number of injuries to passengers, involved No. 34040 *Crewkerne* on 11 April 1961 at Waterloo. The locomotive had worked the 13.25 service from Weymouth and was returning light engine to Nine Elms when it was struck on the west crossing by the 16.38 electric service from Effingham Junction. The speeds were relatively low but the impact crushed the first coach of the electric, leading to the serious casualties. Waterloo was in chaos and suburban services were not back to normal until the following morning. The steam express trains were erratic for a while longer because the incident was further complicated by No. 34095 *Brentor* becoming derailed at the exit to Nine Elms shed. One suspects that the shed master at Nine Elms must have been less than happy!

The year 1959 also saw the addition of some minor changes to the 'Merchant Navy' Pacifics, including the coupled wheel springs being changed to the 'Britannia' type on No. 35016 *Elders Fyffes* in November. This change was not welcomed by the crews who considered the ride to be much harsher than with the Bulleid design. Ultimately, a further seven, Nos 35002, 35007, 35010, 35016, 35020, 35027 and 35030, were modified from 1960 to 1961. Another modification concerned No. 35023 *Holland–Afrika Line*, when nylon tubing sections were fitted to the coupled axlebox guide face oil pipes in February 1959. The intention was to eliminate the problem of pipe fractures, but initially the nylon piping was not strong enough for the task and it was only when ICI produced a special piping that the change became common across all the Pacifics. A further change, which was applied to all of the rebuilt Pacifics, originated in April 1959 from a staff suggestion. A U-shaped retainer was secured to the smokebox door to hold the lower handle of the smokebox door catch or dart, allowing the upper handle to lock the dart without the lower handle moving. The cost for this change was *5s 8d* each (approximately 28.5p).

On 5 December 1960 a landslide occurred on the Somerset & Dorset line and the 'Pines Express' was re-routed via Fordingbridge, Salisbury, Bristol and Westerleigh Junction, with the result that No. 34102 *Lapford* worked throughout from Bournemouth West to Birmingham New Street. The locomotive was stabled overnight at Saltley and returned the next day with the southbound 'Pines' over the same route but it had to come off at Bournemouth Central as the last coal had been fired at Highcliffe. The suggestion was that the LMR crew, not being familiar with the Bulleid boiler, had overfired on the first stage of the journey.

In July 1961 No. 34050 *Royal Observer Corps* was presented with a long service medal at Waterloo station before leaving with a Royal Observer Corps (ROC) special to Bournemouth. The locomotive had been in traffic for 12 years and under the rules of the ROC 'serving' members were entitled to a medal for long service at this stage. The medal took the form of appropriately colour plaques mounted below the numerals on the cabside.

Sadly, by the close of 1962 the end of steam traction on Britain's railways was rapidly approaching and across the various regions of British Railways wholesale withdrawals of locomotives were occurring. The Bulleid Pacifics and Class 5 4–6–0s became virtually the only locomotives working out of Waterloo by December of that year, with S15s and Maunsell 2–6–0s appearing occasionally and Class 4 4–6–0s rarely being seen. During this time the 'Atlantic Coast Express' with its mile-a-minute bookings in each direction between Salisbury and Sidmouth Junction was probably the most difficult steam duty in the country. The crews had to work the train very hard, particularly on the Up service, as marshalling at Exeter always lost at least 2 minutes and the locomotive had to be pushed to make up lost time. Typical of the actions of the 'Merchant Navies' in the twilight of steam was No. 35013 *Blue Funnel* which, on 30 March 1963, departed 2¾ minutes late from Exeter but arrived at Salisbury right time despite a permanent way slack near Axminster and signal delays at Wilton. The speed exceeded 84 m.p.h. on three occasions and Honiton Bank was climbed with panache. Similar hard work was carried out when 2-hour 'Bournemouth Belle' services were introduced on Saturdays during the summer of 1963. The Bulleid Pacifics excelled themselves with all these services.

At the end of 1963 the Southern Region's responsibilities for the West of England services passed across to the Western Region of British Railways. Some 150 locomotives were transferred, including 7 'Merchant Navy' and 27 Light Pacifics, and also the motive power depots at Exmouth Junction, Yeovil Town, Barnstaple and Wadebridge. However, the responsibility for the locomotive repairs remained with Eastleigh, which was probably logical. Having gained control of the Southern Region western routes, the old GWR had been able to exact final revenge for the competition prior to nationalization in 1948. In the early 1960s a gradual running down of services took place in the Southern Region, which in turn helped to precipitate the rundown and eventual withdrawal of Southern steam.

The FA Cup provided a number of occasions when the Bulleid Pacifics wandered away from their home ground. This was particularly notable with the semi-final match between Birmingham City and Southampton on 27 April 1963 when twelve Light Pacifics were rostered to take specials to Birmingham Snow Hill, a virtual convoy of trains! The locomotives involved were Nos 34009,

34028, 34039–40, 34042, 34045–6, 34050, 34052, 34088, 34094 and 34098. In addition, the schoolboys' international was taking place at Wembley, entailing another special behind No. 34102 *Lapford*, which ran from Poole and was turned at Watford Junction. A further excursion on the same day, albeit on a smaller scale, was a more modest football meeting when No. 34017 *Ilfracombe* took supporters from Christchurch to Swindon. This was a very busy day for the Southern Region and for the Light Pacifics, but it was a successful one, as all the fans arrived on time and left the various grounds on schedule.

September 1963 saw the closure of Battersea as a steam depot and with the simultaneous rundown of Brighton shed the nine Light Pacifics were all transferred to Salisbury. This resulted in Exmouth becoming responsible for the last remaining Plymouth through services. Officially, 6 January 1964 marked the formal end to steam on the Central Section, although for a number of months steam specials were rostered with Nine Elms Pacifics. By the middle of the year the Pacifics had all but vanished from the Central Section and what steam power there was came from inter-region specials, normally the LMR, and these were hauled by motive power from that region.

In August 1964, as part of the move towards full electrification and the provision of main line diesel locomotives, the last general repair of a 'Merchant Navy' was completed, which was to No. 35007 *Aberdeen Commonwealth*. As the others of the class came up for repair they were run as long as possible without risk and were then withdrawn from traffic. Nos 35002 *Union Castle* and 35015 *Rotterdam Lloyd* were withdrawn, following this policy, in February 1964. By November 1964 a further five 'Merchant Navy' locomotives had been withdrawn: Nos 35001, 35006, 35009, 35018 and 35025.

At the end of 1962 Eastleigh had decided that the original Light Pacifics were not to receive any more general repairs and the dates of final general repairs are: No. 34061 *73 Squadron* – 03/11/62; No. 34092 *City of Wells* – 24/11/62; No. 34007 *Wadebridge* 08/11/62. Similarly, the rebuilt Light Pacifics had no further general repairs after February 1964 and thereafter most of the repairs were casual or light intermediate, although a number of locomotives did receive a repaint as well as an intermediate repair between 1962 and 1964. No. 34019 *Bideford*, in October 1964, was the last of the original built Light Pacifics to receive a repaint. No. 34012 *Launceston* was the last rebuilt Light Pacific to have significant work carried out when in September 1964 the locomotive exited the shops after heavy intermediate repairs and a repaint. As an interesting aside to the Pacifics receiving repairs at Eastleigh, when No. 34044 *Woolacombe* arrived at Eastleigh during June 1963 for a non-classified repair the motion and wheels had been painted red. This had presumably been carried out by the motive power depot, but in any case the Eastleigh Works Manager was not impressed. In a letter dated 20 June 1963 the works manager asked for paint stripper to be applied before the locomotive was out-shopped!

On 17 August 1964 the Exeter–Waterloo line express service was taken over by Western Region 'Warship' class diesels rostered on six services during the day. Early trains suffered a number of failures and steam standby locomotives were

The 'Atlantic Coast Express' approaching Farnborough at speed hauled by No. 35011 *General Steam Navigation*.

Bob Barnard, Hugh Davies Collection

frequently called upon to take over, in fact on one day all six express services were steam hauled! Eventually, as the crews became used to the new motive power and the teething troubles were overcome, the diesels settled down to provide a reliable if somewhat boring service.

As the 'Warships' became established a major shift of steam motive power occurred in Autumn 1964 when the 'Merchant Navies' were shared between Bournemouth, Salisbury and Weymouth sheds. This left Nine Elms with nine Class 5s for express duties although two 'Merchant Navies' and a Light Pacific were stabled there at night. By the latter part of 1964 the reliability of the 'Warships' was such that Salisbury no longer needed to have No. 35007 *Aberdeen Commonwealth* and this locomotive was also transferred to Weymouth.

On 4 September 1964 the last steam-hauled Down 'Atlantic Coast Express' was run. No. 35022 *Holland-America Line* was in charge and was immaculately clean, complete with the train headboard. This locomotive performed in a manner worthy of the occasion by arriving at Salisbury right time after having lost time on the outskirts of London because of a number of signal checks. The rest of the journey to the West Country was a fitting end to this famous steam service. The diesel-operated service commenced on 7 September 1964.

One interesting series of events led to No. 35029 *Ellerman Lines* hauling the York to Bournemouth West train, together with the locomotive and assisting locomotive. The train locomotive, No. 6996 *Blackwell Hall*, failed en route at Sway and requested help from New Milton. A 2-6-0, No. 76012, was despatched from Bournemouth and assisted until Christchurch, but was unable to restart with the dead 'Hall'. The train then had to wait for the arrival of the 'Merchant Navy', which hauled the train plus the two locomotives into Bournemouth Central apparently providing most of the motive power. When the 'Hall' was inspected in the shed, it was found that the smokebox was full of ash up to the blastpipe. Under the circumstances it had done well to travel so far, although one wonders whether the footplate crew might have been able to clear the smokebox, had they tried, before the locomotive totally failed. However, it again shows the power and ability of the 'Merchant Navy' class, even at this late hour.

The unrebuilt Light Pacifics were now being seriously considered for withdrawal and when No. 34055 *Fighter Pilot* failed while hauling the 11.00 Brighton to Cardiff service on 22 April 1963 the locomotive was laid up and finally condemned. During this time Nos 34035, 34043, 34063, 34074 and 34084 were in store at Exmouth Junction shed and it was decided to withdraw them all except Nos 34063 and 34084. By the end of 1963 a further six had also been withdrawn, 34011, 34049, 34067–9 and 34110. In September of the same year the Pacifics based at Brighton were moved to Salisbury. With the end of steam on the West Country services, the Waterloo expresses, Brighton through services and some semi-fast services changed to diesel haulage in September 1964. Consequently, the Western Region withdrew seven Light Pacifics and transferred a further eight to Eastleigh and two to Salisbury. The total number of the original-built locomotives withdrawn by the end of 1964 was twenty-nine, which left a further twenty-one still in service.

The first of the rebuilt Light Pacifics to be withdrawn was No. 34028 *Eddystone*, which was withdrawn in May 1964 having only run 286,962 miles in the 69 months since its reconstruction in August 1958. By the end of the year a further nine rebuilt members of the class had also gone. Added to the agonies of the Bulleid Pacifics at this time was the discovery of a significant number of frame fractures, an ongoing problem which was first discovered in the late 1940s and early '50s and was never successfully cured, despite the improved stiffening and new vertical and horizontal stretchers fitted after the trials with No. 34041 *Wilton* in 1950. These failures put further pressure on the case for withdrawals, particularly in the last years of steam. The repairs required welds as long as 2½ ft in some cases and clearly this did not fit in with the policy of very limited or no remedial work on the Pacifics. The rebuilt Pacifics also suffered a further problem which was to be used to hasten withdrawal – the cracking of the new inside cylinder – and this became the reason for up to 23 per cent of the 1964–6 withdrawals. By the end of 1966 seventy-four Light Pacifics had been withdrawn.

To commemorate the final departure of steam from the main line through Cornwall, No. 34002 *Salisbury* took a special train from Plymouth over the Brunel bridge to Penzance and back. A further rail tour saw the working of the 'East Midlander' hauled by No. 34038 *Lynton*, working from Didcot to Eastleigh. The return service also had *Lynton* in charge and the locomotive journied as far as Swindon via Romsey, Salisbury, Westbury and Chippenham.

With the sad task undertaken by No. 34051 *Winston Churchill* on 30 January 1965, as the great man for whom the locomotive was named took his final journey

No. 34051 *Winston Churchill* at Clapham Junction on 30 January 1965 with the funeral train of Sir Winston Churchill.

B.W.L. Brooksbank, Initial Photographic

to Bladon in Oxfordshire, the interest created in this locomotive was such that it was decided to preserve it. When the locomotive was withdrawn in September 1965 it was set aside, pending display at the National Railway Museum in York. A further five of the original Light Pacifics had been withdrawn in the same year.

In addition, as 1965 progressed further withdrawals took place of the 'Merchant Navy' locomotives when they were stopped for heavy repairs, Nos 35004–5, 35016, 35019–21 and 35024 being taken out of stock that year. No. 35004 *Cunard White Star* was somewhat unfortunate as the locomotive had been into Eastleigh Works between August and October 1965 and had its mileage allowance increased by 10,000 miles. However, the locomotive slipped disastrously near Hook while in charge of the 07.24 Bournemouth Central–Waterloo on 28 October 1965, causing broken and buckled coupling rods. Apart from this the damage was minimal, but the official policy was strict and the locomotive was condemned.

The period from 1965 to 1966 was one of general rundown of the British Railways steam locomotive stock across the country, as famous classes were withdrawn. By now all Stanier's 'Duchesses' had gone and only a limited number of Gresley's A4s were still in service, and diesel or electric motive power was replacing them. On the Southern Region electrification was well in its stride and the disruption was causing lengthy single line workings and diversions on the Bournemouth line, with the result that the daily steam-powered workings became more and more tedious and frustrating for the footplate crews. Very little recovery time was made available during these runs and it was next to impossible to regain the lost times on the latter stages of each journey. To further complicate the situation, maintenance was poor and the quality of the coal supplied was low, so that even the Bulleid boilers were having difficulties. Often as not, the locomotives themselves were very dirty and this did little to encourage any pride in the task. One shining exception was the motive power at Salisbury where, to the end, the locomotives always seemed to be clean.

The official date for the unhappy closure of that very special route, the Somerset & Dorset line, was 2 January 1966, and special steam-hauled farewell journeys were run. These had both Light Pacifics and 'Merchant Navy' class locomotives in charge even though weight restrictions would, in the normal course of things, have restricted the 'Merchant Navies' from operating over these lines. The special trains were hauled by No. 35011 *General Steam Navigation* from Waterloo, with No. 34015 *Exmouth* and 2–6–0 No. 31639 coming on at Broadstone for the journey to Bath where the train was handed over to 8F 2–8–0 No. 48309 for the passage to Weston-super-Mare via Bristol (Temple Meads). A further change of motive power saw two 2–6–2 tanks, Nos 41283 and 41307, take the train back to Templecombe where No. 35011 was again available for the service back to Waterloo via the West of England main line. If only such an itinerary was available today!

The Somerset & Dorset line closure was postponed and the Railway Correspondence & Travel Society ran a further farewell tour on 6 March 1966 using No. 35028 *Clan Line* over the Aldershot and Alton line to Winchester, Southampton Central and Templecombe Junction. The 'Merchant Navy' was replaced by two 2–6–2 tanks, Nos 41249 and 41283, for the run to Highbridge where they in turn were replaced by Light Pacific No. 34013 *Okehampton* for the journey to Mangotsfield North Junction, at which point diesel No. D7014 was added to the rear of the train for the journey to Bath Green Park. For the run over the Somerset & Dorset line and on to Templecombe, the train was hauled by No. 34013 with No. 34057 *Biggin Hill* piloting. Finally, for the return to Waterloo the special was again run behind No. 35028.

Further rail tours were undertaken by Light Pacifics during 1966. No. 34015 *Exmouth*, piloted by a badly steaming U class, No. 31639, met the heavy climb over the Mendip Hills head on and gained 2 minutes on arrival at Bath. No. 34002 *Salisbury* travelled even further afield on a rail tour which took the locomotive from Waterloo to Nottingham via Neasden and the Great Central main line. The locomotive was taken off at Nottingham and was serviced for the return journey into Marylebone, where the class had not been seen since the trials of 1948.

One interesting special was that taken by No. 35026 *Lamport & Holt Line* on 22 October 1966 when the locomotive hauled a rail tour to York, where it shared the spotlight and public interest with a very well-known locomotive, LNER A1 (later BR A3) Pacific No. 4472 *Flying Scotsman*.

The rebuilt Light Pacific No. 34013 *Okehampton* seemed to appear on nearly every 'last steam' special during 1966. On 20 February the locomotive headed a special from Victoria to Brighton via the Uckfield line and thence to Fareham, with the return from Portsmouth via Guildford and Epsom to London. A farewell trip to Portsmouth Harbour (and on to the Isle of Wight) was run by No. 34013 on 31 December 1966 and it had previously been rostered for the last steam 'City Express' from Cannon Street to Ramsgate on 12 June 1959. The locomotive also headed the last steam service on the Weymouth to Waterloo 17.30 express on 7 July 1967. The locomotive had received a general repair in January 1964 plus a repaint and was considered by the crews to be a 'goer', with the firing easy.

As 1966 progressed the inevitable withdrawals continued, with Nos 35010, 35011, 35017, 35022, 35027 and 35029 being sold for scrap during the year leaving ten 'Merchant Navy' class locomotives still in service, Nos 35003, 35007–8, 35012–14, 35023, 35026, 35028 and 35030. Of these Nos 35012, 35014 and 35026 were badly run down and were only available to give assistance until the following spring. The others worked until the end of steam, except for No. 35013 which was withdrawn a week earlier.

In order to keep the locomotives in approaching serviceable condition, an unofficial policy of beg, borrow and steal developed, which lead to events that would not have been tolerated in earlier times. Typically, when No. 35007 had its tyres condemned in August 1966 the previously condemned stock was examined for a decent set. Finally, those on No. 35017 *Belgian Marine* were considered acceptable, although the examiner's comments that the right driving tyre had moved $\frac{9}{16}$ in and the left leading tyre $\frac{11}{16}$ in but they were believed to be sound did not exactly inspire confidence. Thankfully, these tyres successfully carried No. 35007 until its withdrawal. During these times, all kinds of changes took place involving tenders, cylinders, motion and bogie/wheel sets, with little or no record being kept. These procedures did not just affect the 'Merchant Navy' class but, of course, all steam traction left on the Southern.

The electric services to Basingstoke from Waterloo started on 2 January 1967, and with the engineering work all but finished the speed restrictions were lifted. This allowed crews to show that while steam was in the autumn of its life, it was not dead. There were many extremely good runs during this period with No. 35013 *Blue Funnel* completing the journey from Southampton to Bournemouth in 29½ minutes, attaining a speed of 62 mph on the Pokesdown Bank. In a similar

No. 35017 *Belgian Marine* at Eastleigh in May 1966 in a sorrowful state, withdrawn and awaiting disposal. Note that some enterprising soul has chalked 21C17 on the space left by the smokebox door number plate.

B.K.B. Green, Initial Photographic

vein, No. 35028 *Clan Line* achieved 66 mph on the bank through Winchester, finally reaching Waterloo 13¾ minutes early after a net time from Southampton of 75½ minutes. A further example of the power of the 'Merchant Navies' at this time was No. 35013 *Blue Funnel*, when after leaving Waterloo 14 minutes late with a load of twelve bogies and one van, it arrived at Winchester 1 minute early. The speed recorder on this locomotive was jammed solidly at 104 mph!

As 1967 progressed the steam duties were reduced and further unrebuilt Light Pacifics were withdrawn, two in March 1967 and another two in April, while No. 34057 *Biggin Hill* failed with a fractured inside cylinder in May and was similarly withdrawn, followed by three other locomotives later in June. The final two original Light Pacifics left were Nos 34023 *Blackmore Vale* and 34102 *Lapford* which carried on until the final days of steam on the Southern Region.

The West of England express services were now all hauled by 'Warship' diesel locomotives and failures were few and far between. One notable event was the failure of No. D866 at Salisbury with the 10.15 Exeter St David's to Waterloo service. No. 34108 *Wincanton* was summoned from the shed to take the ten-coach train on to London. The departure from Salisbury was some 15½ minutes late but at Porton the speed had risen to 59 mph and after Grately 87 mph was attained. Andover was reached in 19 minutes and Basingstoke 19½ minutes after leaving Andover, with a maximum speed of 88 mph reached at Fleet, and the time lost would have been totally made up but for poor station work at Basingstoke. As it was the Pacific gave a superb example of how a steam locomotive can perform, even in its twilight years. The return service at 17.00 was also hauled by *Wincanton* and the locomotive had no difficulty in meeting the diesel schedule.

The Railway Correspondence & Travel Society ran a 'Farewell to Southern Steam' special on Sunday 18 June 1967 hauled by Nos 73029 and 34023 *Blackmore Vale*, with Nos 34108 *Wincanton* and 34089 *602 Squadron* assisting and, finally, with No. 35013 *Blue Funnel* used for the return run back to Waterloo. On 2 July 1967 the official Southern Region 'Farewell to Steam' specials were run from Waterloo. In the event, only two trains were needed and these were hauled by No. 35008 *Orient Line* with eleven coaches running to Weymouth and No. 35028 *Clan Line* with ten coaches running to Bournemouth. The locomotives were in exceptional condition, sparkling clean and mechanically good, and both were refitted with name-plates as these had been removed from all the Pacifics for security reasons as the time for disposal approached. On the return from Weymouth *Orient Line* was piloted as far as Bournemouth by No. 35007 *Aberdeen Commonwealth*.

Over the next few weeks there were occasional steam workings, in particular on the van or boat-trains from Southampton or with Nos 35007 and 35030 in charge of the 17.30 Weymouth–Waterloo service. One spectacular last fling was that of No. 35007 on 6 July 1967 when, with the 17.30 Weymouth train, it reached 98 mph near Bramshott. The 'Bournemouth Belle' was also steam hauled on a number of occasions, No. 34025 *Whimple* being in charge on 3 July while on 5 July No. 34024 *Tamar Valley* worked the Down train and No. 34036 *Westward Ho* worked the Up. The last steamed-hauled service into Waterloo, the 14.11 from Weymouth, was in the charge of No. 35030 *Elder Dempster Lines* on 9 July 1967 while previous to that Nos 34021 *Dartmoor* and 34052 *Lord Dowding* double-headed with No. 34095 *Brentor* and hauled the 11.00 boat-train from Southampton and a special perishables van train to Westbury, respectively. During the last weeks locomotives were worked in batches to the various motive power depots at Weymouth, Salisbury and Nine Elms, where they then awaited disposal. So it was, almost in a feeling of embarrassment, that an epic period of steam traction on the Southern came to an end. With it also ended a chapter in the life of one of the most controversial locomotive types in this country, although fortunately active preservation measures are preventing its complete demise.

While many still hate them and yet, equally, others will not hear a bad word said about them, there really is no in between. What can be said without fear of contradiction is that the engineering concept, if followed completely and managed from the top with the strength and power of persuasion that Gresley possessed, would have had a fundamental impact on future designs. As it was, the originality of the Bulleid Pacifics did create a catalyst for the future and in the rebuilt state the locomotives gave the Southern Region a locomotive to be proud of, one which could hold its head up high and be fully comparable to the A4s and 'Duchesses'. The sheer difference of these great locomotives drew attention and, after all is said and done, love them or hate them, they cannot be ignored.

CHAPTER TEN

THE PRESERVATION SCENE

The power and attraction of the Bulleid Pacifics is probably best illustrated by the number currently in preservation all around the country – a total of thirty-one are preserved, of which eleven are 'Merchant Navy' class locomotives and twenty are Light Pacifics. This includes both the original Southern Railway-built locomotives and the later British Railways-built designs, and also, of course, the BR rebuilds. The number of Bulleid Pacifics in preservation far exceeds any other class of locomotive, including the Stanier 'Black Fives', GWR 'Halls' and the BR 4MT 2–6–4 tanks.

With so many locomotives in preservation and the popularity of both types of Pacifics, it would take a separate book just to describe their individual attributes, history and where they currently reside. Consequently, this book gives broad details of the locomotives in preservation and some specific details on a small selection of the class. The selection of locomotives included has been completely arbitrary and based purely on personal choice. I make no apologies for this and hope that the reader does not feel too frustrated if their favourite locomotive is not included.

The list of preserved locomotives and locations at the end of this chapter is produced with the information at hand at the time of writing. These locations are liable to change so readers are advised to confirm with the relevant sites before planning to visit their favourite locomotive.

NO. 34051 *WINSTON CHURCHILL*

Winston Churchill is currently on static display at the National Railway Museum in York, although owing to space constraints at the museum the locomotive is far from obvious, being sited behind No. 563 and almost hidden from view. There are no plans to return the locomotive to steam and the asbestos lagging has been removed from the boiler and firebox. The locomotive is displayed in the final British Railways green paint scheme and lining, and is complete with the airsmoothed casing as modified by BR.

No. 34051 was built at Brighton, being completed during December 1946, and was originally numbered 21C151 under the Bulleid notation. The locomotive was renumbered in October 1948 and was withdrawn from service in September 1965. Preservation was undertaken as a result of the interest shown in this locomotive during the funeral of Sir Winston Churchill when No. 34051 hauled the funeral train to his last resting place on 30 January 1965.

'Battle of Britain' class No. 34051 *Winston Churchill*, in preservation at the National Railway Museum, York.

Author's Collection

Ellerman Lines beautifully sectioned at the National Railway Museum, York.

Author's Collection

NO. 35029 *ELLERMAN LINES*

Ellerman Lines could probably lay claim to being one of the most well-known preserved Bulleid Pacifics, being beautifully sectioned at the National Railway Museum. The locomotive is displayed so that on one side the visitors can view the complete internal workings of a steam locomotive and on the other side it is seen as it would have been when it was in traffic. The concept is a credit to the engineering expertise of the NRM. The locomotive's coupled wheels are turned slowly by electric motors so that the valve gear and events can be seen in action. It is exhibited in the BR rebuilt state and in the final BR green paint scheme and lining.

No. 35029 was completed at Eastleigh in February 1949 and entered traffic as a BR locomotive complete with the then new BR number scheme. It was the penultimate 'Merchant Navy' locomotive to be built and was withdrawn from service in September 1966.

NO. 35010 *BLUE STAR*

Blue Star is currently on static display at the Colne Valley Railway in Essex. The locomotive is painted overall in unlined black with the number painted in white on the cab side plates. The black paint gives some cosmetic appeal, but at the same time reduces further deterioration while funds are gathered to fully restore the locomotive (any support would be gratefully received, contact the Colne Valley Railway). The locomotive is shown without a tender and in the BR rebuilt state.

Blue Star was the tenth 'Merchant Navy' locomotive to be completed at Eastleigh, coming out of the erecting shops in July 1942 with the original Bulleid

No. 35010 *Blue Star* prepares to leave Waterloo with the 'Bournemouth Belle' on 23 November 1952. Note the older style headboard.

T.G. Wassell, Hugh Davies Collection

number 21C10. The locomotive was renumbered in December 1948 and was rebuilt in January 1957. No. 35010 was withdrawn in September 1966 and eventually found its way to the North Woolwich Station Museum before finally arriving at the Colne Valley Railway in 1997.

NO. 34081 *92 SQUADRON*

92 Squadron underwent major work at the Nene Valley Railway to return the locomotive back into steam in 1998. The intention was for No. 34081 to be put back to traffic on the railway in May 1998, although a number of locomotive parts were stolen from the railway early in 1998. In the event, it moved under its own power for the first time in nearly thirty-four years when five 10-mph trips were carried out on 10 March 1998. The locomotive is in the original unrebuilt state and at this time it is intended that the locomotive should be out-shopped in BR Brunswick green livery.

No. 34081 was completed at Brighton in September 1948 carrying the BR number scheme from new. The locomotive was one of the earlier members of the class to be withdrawn, being taken out of service in August 1964. On 28 March 1998 No. 34081 hauled its first train when it took a two-coach empty stock working prior to return to passenger service.

'Battle of Britain' class No. 34081 *92 Squadron* at the Nene Valley Railway in November 1997, being rebuilt for eventual steaming in May 1998.

Author's Collection

A further two locomotives worthy of mention are Nos 35028 *Clan Line* and 34027 *Taw Valley*, both of which have current main line certification and have shown over the years just how well the Bulleid Pacifics can perform, given a little tender loving care. Much has been written and many pictures published of these two well-known locomotives. The seven-year certificate for *Clan Line* expires on 19 July 2001; the Merchant Navy Locomotive Preservation Society is currently committed to continued main line operation and a full main line overhaul is expected at the expiry of the present certification. *Taw Valley*'s certificate runs out on 29 January 2003 and is expected to be renewed by the 34027 Group that owns it.

'Merchant Navy' No. 35028 *Clan Line* with an Up passenger service approaching Hildenborough in 1957.

Norman Simmons, Hugh Davies Collection

No. 34027 *Taw Valley* in immaculate condition, ex-works at Eastleigh on 30 June 1953.

B.K.B. Green, Initial Photographic

PRESERVED LOCOMOTIVES

'Merchant Navy' Class

Locomotive	Build date	Location
35005 *Canadian Pacific*	1941	Mid-Hants Railway
35006 *Peninsular & Oriental S. N. Co.*	1941	Gloucestershire & Warwickshire Railway
35009 *Shaw Savill*	1942	Mid-Hants Railway
35010 *Blue Star*	1942	Colne Valley Railway
35011 *General Steam Navigation*	1944	West Somerset Railway*
35018 *British India Line*	1945	Mid-Hants Railway
35022 *Holland-America Line*	1948	Sellindge, Kent
35025 *Brocklebank Line*	1948	Great Central Railway
35027 *Port Line*	1948	Bluebell Railway
35028 *Clan Line*	1948	Southall†
35029 *Ellerman Lines*	1949	National Railway Museum

Light Pacifics

Locomotive	Build date	Location
34007 *Wadebridge*	1945	Bodmin & Wenford Railway
34010 *Sidmouth*	1945	Sellindge, Kent
34016 *Bodmin*	1945	Mid-Hants Railway
34023 *Blackmore Vale*	1946	Bluebell Railway
34027 *Taw Valley*	1946	Southall†
34028 *Eddystone*	1946	Sellindge, due to move to Great Central Railway
34039 *Boscastle*	1946	Swanage Railway
34046 *Braunton*	1946	West Somerset Railway
34051 *Winston Churchill*	1946	National Railway Museum
34053 *Sir Keith Park*	1947	West Somerset Railway
34058 *Sir Frederick Pile*	1947	Avon Valley Railway
34059 *Sir Archibald Sinclair*	1947	Bluebell Railway
34067 *Tangmere*	1947	Mid-Hants Railway‡
34070 *Manston*	1947	Great Central Railway
34072 *257 Squadron*	1948	Swanage Railway
34073 *249 Squadron*	1948	Mid-Hants Railway
34081 *92 Squadron*	1948	Nene Valley Railway
34092 *City of Wells*	1949	Keighley & Worth Valley Railway
34101 *Hartland*	1950	North Yorkshire Moors Railway
34105 *Swanage*	1950	Mid-Hants Railway

Notes: * Due to move to the West Somerset.
  † With the lease difficulties at Southall the ultimate site for this locomotive is unclear.
  ‡ Currently being rebuilt at the East Lancashire Railway.

APPENDICES

Note: In all appendices the locomotives are identified by the BR running numbers for the sake of standardization.

APPENDIX 1 LOCOMOTIVE SUMMARY: 'MERCHANT NAVY' CLASS

Number	Name	SR Number	Built	Rebuilt	Withdrawn
35001	Channel Packet	21C1	02/41	08/59	11/64
35002	Union Castle	21C2	06/41	05/58	02/64
35003	Royal Mail	21C3	09/41	08/59	07/67
35004	Cunard White Star	21C4	10/41	07/58	10/65
35005	Canadian Pacific	21C5	12/41	05/59	10/65
35006	Peninsular & Oriental S. N. Co.	21C6	12/41	10/59	08/64
35007	Aberdeen Commonwealth	21C7	06/42	05/58	07/67
35008	Orient Line	21C8	06/42	05/57	07/67
35009	Shaw Savill	21C9	06/42	03/57	07/64
35010	Blue Star	21C10	07/42	01/57	09/66
35011	General Steam Navigation	21C11	12/44	07/59	02/66
35012	United States Lines	21C12	01/45	02/57	04/67
35013	Blue Funnel Certum Pete Finem*	21C13	02/45	05/56	07/67
35014	Nederland Line	21C14	02/45	07/56	03/67
35015	Rotterdam Lloyd	21C15	03/45	06/58	02/64
35016	Elders Fyffes	21C16	03/45	04/57	08/65
35017	Belgian Marine	21C17	04/45	03/57	07/66
35018	British India Line	21C18	05/45	02/56	08/64
35019	French Line C.G.T.	21C19	06/45	05/59	09/65
35020	Bibby Line	21C20	06/45	04/56	02/65
35021	New Zealand Line	–	09/48	06/59	08/65
35022	Holland America Line	–	10/48	06/56	05/66
35023	Holland–Afrika Line	–	11/48	02/57	07/67
35024	East Asiatic Company	–	11/48	04/59	01/65
35025	Brocklebank Line	–	11/48	12/56	09/64
35026	Lamport & Holt Line	–	12/48	01/57	03/67
35027	Port Line	–	12/48	05/57	09/66
35028	Clan Line	–	12/48	10/59	07/67
35029	Ellerman Lines	–	02/49	09/59	09/66
35030	Elder-Dempster Lines	–	04/49	04/58	07/67

Note: * Initially named *Blue Funnel Line* but later changed as shown.

APPENDIX 2 LOCOMOTIVE SUMMARY:
'WEST COUNTRY' AND 'BATTLE OF BRITAIN' CLASSES

Number	Name	SR Number	Built	Rebuilt	Withdrawn
34001	Exeter	21C101	05/45	11/57	07/67
34002	Salisbury	21C102	06/45	–	04/67
34003	Plymouth	21C103	06/45	09/57	09/64
34004	Yeovil	21C104	07/45	02/58	07/67
34005	Barnstaple	21C105	07/45	06/57	10/66
34006	Bude	21C106	07/45	–	03/67
34007	Wadebridge	21C107	08/45	–	10/65
34008	Padstow	21C108	09/45	–	06/67
34009	Lyme Regis	21C109	09/45	07/60	01/61
34010	Sidmouth	21C110	09/45	02/59	03/65
34011	Tavistock	21C111	10/45	–	11/63
34012	Launceston	21C112	10/45	01/58	12/66
34013	Okehampton	21C113	10/45	10/57	07/67
34014	Budleigh Salterton	21C114	11/45	03/58	03/65
34015	Exmouth	21C115	11/45	–	04/67
34016	Bodmin	21C116	11/45	04/58	06/64
34017	Ilfracombe	21C117	12/45	11/57	10/66
34018	Axminster	21C118	12/45	10/58	07/67
34019	Bideford	21C119	12/45	–	03/67
34020	Seaton	21C120	12/45	–	09/64
34021	Dartmoor	21C121	01/46	01/58	07/67
34022	Exmoor	21C122	01/46	12/57	04/65
34023	Blackmoor Vale/Blackmoor Vale*	21C123	02/46	–	07/67
34024	Tamar Valley	21C124	02/46	02/61	07/67
34025	Rough Tor/Whimple†	21C125	03/46	11/57	07/67
34026	Yes Tor	21C126	03/46	02/58	09/66
34027	Taw Valley	21C127	04/46	09/57	08/64
34028	Eddystone	21C128	04/46	08/58	05/64
34029	Lundy	21C129	05/46	12/58	09/64
34030	Watersmeet	21C130	05/46	–	09/64
34031	Torrington	21C131	06/46	12/58	02/65
34032	Camelford	21C132	06/46	10/60	10/66
34033	Chard	21C133	07/46	–	12/65
34034	Honiton	21C134	07/46	08/60	07/67
34035	Shaftesbury	21C135	07/46	–	06/63
34036	Westward Ho	21C136	07/46	09/60	07/67
34037	Clovelly	21C137	08/46	03/58	07/67
34038	Lynton	21C138	09/46	–	06/66
34039	Boscastle	21C139	09/46	01/59	05/65
34040	Crewkerne	21C140	09/46	10/60	07/67
34041	Wilton	21C141	10/46	–	01/66
34042	Dorchester	21C142	10/46	01/59	10/65
34043	Combe Martin	21C143	10/46	–	06/63
34044	Woolacombe	21C144	10/46	05/60	05/67
34045	Ottery St. Mary	21C145	10/46	10/58	06/64
34046	Braunton	21C146	11/46	02/59	10/65
34047	Callington	21C147	11/46	10/58	06/67
34048	Crediton	21C148	11/46	03/59	03/66
34049	Anti-Aircraft Command	21C149	12/46	–	12/63

Number	Name	SR Number	Built	Rebuilt	Withdrawn
34050	Royal Observer Corps	21C150	12/46	08/58	08/65
34051	Winston Churchill	21C151	12/46	–	09/65
34052	Lord Dowding	21C152	12/46	09/58	07/67
34053	Sir Keith Park	21C153	01/47	11/58	10/65
34054	Lord Beaverbrook	21C154	01/47	–	09/64
34055	Fighter Pilot	21C155	02/47	–	06/63
34056	Croydon	21C156	02/47	12/60	05/67
34057	Biggin Hill	21C157	03/47	–	05/67
34058	Sir Frederick Pile	21C158	03/47	11/60	10/64
34059	Sir Archibald Sinclair	21C159	04/47	03/60	05/66
34060	25 Squadron	21C160	04/47	11/60	07/67
34061	73 Squadron	21C161	04/47	–	08/64
34062	17 Squadron	21C162	05/47	04/59	06/64
34063	229 Squadron	21C163	05/47	–	08/65
34064	Fighter Command	21C164	07/47	–	05/66
34065	Hurricane	21C165	07/47	–	04/64
34066	Spitfire	21C166	09/47	–	09/66
34067	Tangmere	21C167	09/47	–	11/63
34068	Kenley	21C168	10/47	–	12/63
34069	Hawkinge	21C169	10/47	–	11/63
34070	Manston	21C170	11/47	–	08/64
34071	615 Squadron/601 Squadron‡	–	04/48	05/60	04/67
34072	257 Squadron	–	04/48	–	10/64
34073	249 Squadron	–	05/48	–	06/64
34074	46 Squadron	–	05/48	–	06/63
34075	264 Squadron	–	06/48	–	04/64
34076	41 Squadron	–	06/48	–	01/66
34077	603 Squadron	–	07/48	07/60	03/67
34078	222 Squadron	–	07/48	–	09/64
34079	141 Squadron	–	07/48	–	02/66
34080	74 Squadron	–	08/48	–	09/64
34081	92 Squadron	–	09/48	–	08/64
34082	615 Squadron	–	09/48	04/60	04/66
34083	605 Squadron	–	10/48	–	06/64
34084	253 Squadron	–	11/48	–	10/65
34085	501 Squadron	–	11/48	06/60	09/65
34086	219 Squadron	–	12/48	–	06/66
34087	145 Squadron	–	12/48	12/60	07/67
34088	213 Squadron	–	12/48	04/60	03/67
34089	602 Squadron	–	12/48	11/60	07/67
34090	Sir Eustace Missenden Southern Railway	–	02/49	08/60	07/67
34091	Weymouth	–	09/49	–	09/64
34092	Wells/City of Wells#	–	09/49	–	11/64
34093	Saunton	–	10/49	05/60	07/67
34094	Mortehoe	–	10/49	–	08/64
34095	Brentor	–	10/49	01/61	07/67
34096	Trevone	–	11/49	04/61	09/64
34097	Holsworthy	–	11/49	03/61	04/67
34098	Templecombe	–	12/49	02/61	06/67
34099	Lynmouth	–	12/49	–	11/64
34100	Appledore	–	12/49	09/60	07/67

Number	Name	SR Number	Built	Rebuilt	Withdrawn
34101	*Hartland*	–	02/50	09/60	07/66
34102	*Lapford*	–	03/50	–	07/67
34103	*Calstock*	–	02/50	–	09/65
34104	*Bere Alston*	–	04/50	05/61	06/67
34105	*Swanage*	–	03/50	–	10/64
34106	*Lydford*	–	03/50	–	09/64
34107	*Blandford/Blandford Forum* $	–	04/50	–	09/64
34108	*Wincanton*	–	04/50	05/61	06/67
34109	*Sir Trafford Leigh Mallory*	–	05/50	03/61	09/64
34110	*66 Squadron*	–	01/51	–	11/63

Notes: *   Name changed in 1950 to correct spelling.
      †   *Whimple* was named *Rough Tor* for only a few days.
      ‡   Carried the name *615 Squadron* for a short period in 1948.
      #   Originally named *Wells* until November 1949.
      §   Named *Blandford* until October 1952.

APPENDIX 3 LIVERIES:
'MERCHANT NAVY' CLASS

All locomotives were finished in malachite green from new except those that went straight
to wartime black, shown below. February 1949 No. 35024 *East Asiatic Company* left
Eastleigh in dark blue, with horizontal red bands. Likewise No. 35026 *Lamport & Holt
Line* went straight into service in BR blue.

Number/Name		Wartime black	Date to blue	Date to Brunswick green
35001	*Channel Packet*	12/43	10/49	05/52
35002	*Union Castle*	06/44	01/50	06/51
35003	*Royal Mail*	06/42	06/50	08/53
35004	*Cunard White Star*	07/43	10/50	07/54
35005	*Canadian Pacific*	03/42	02/50	02/54
35006	*Peninsular & Oriental S. N. Co.*	05/42	03/51	09/53
35007	*Aberdeen Commonwealth*	06/42	03/50	12/52
35008	*Orient Line*	06/42	07/49	05/52
35009	*Shaw Savill*	06/42	08/49	02/53
35010	*Blue Star*	07/42	11/49	11/52
35011	*General Steam Navigation*	12/44	–	11/51
35012	*United States Lines*	01/45	02/51	07/52
35013	*Blue Funnel*	02/45	08/50	12/52
35014	*Nederland Line*	02/45	–	08/51
35015	*Rotterdam Lloyd*	03/45	02/51	06/53
35016	*Elders Fyffes*	03/45	05/50	03/53
35017	*Belgian Marine*	04/45	07/49	04/53
35018	*British India Line*	05/45	09/49	07/51
35019	*French Line C.G.T.*	06/45	01/50	06/51
35020	*Bibby Line*	06/45	05/50	06/52
35021	*New Zealand Line*		11/50	02/52
35022	*Holland America Line*		07/50	02/52
35023	*Holland–Afrika Line*		–	03/52
35024	*East Asiatic Company*		10/50	06/51
35025	*Brocklebank Line*		09/49	06/52
35026	*Lamport & Holt Line*		07/49	06/52
35027	*Port Line*		04/50	11/53
35028	*Clan Line*		01/51	06/53
35029	*Ellerman Lines*		02/51	07/52
35030	*Elder-Dempster Lines*		05/50	05/53

Note: Nos 35011, 35014 and 35023 were never painted blue.

APPENDIX 4 LIVERIES:
'WEST COUNTRY' AND 'BATTLE OF BRITAIN' CLASSES

Number	Name	Date to Brunswick green	Experimental livery
34001	Exeter	12/49	
34002	Salisbury	10/49	
34003	Plymouth	03/52	
34004	Yeovil	04/50	
34005	Barnstaple	05/50	
34006	Bude	07/50	
34007	Wadebridge	05/51	
34008	Padstow	06/50	
34009	Lyme Regis	12/50	
34010	Sidmouth	01/50	
34011	Tavistock	09/50	26/05/48
34012	Launceston	02/51	
34013	Okehampton	04/50	
34014	Budleigh Salterton	11/49	
34015	Exmouth	01/50	
34016	Bodmin	01/50	
34017	Ilfracombe	01/51	
34018	Axminster	10/50	
34019	Bideford	11/50	
34020	Seaton	07/50	
34021	Dartmoor	06/50	
34022	Exmoor	09/50	
34023	Blackmoor Vale/Blackmore Vale	04/50	
34024	Tamar Valley	12/51	
34025	Rough Tor/Whimple	03/50	
34026	Yes Tor	12/50	
34027	Taw Valley	12/51	
34028	Eddystone	02/51	
34029	Lundy	02/50	
34030	Watersmeet	03/50	
34031	Torrington	11/49	
34032	Camelford	01/51	
34033	Chard	12/51	
34034	Honiton	05/50	
34035	Shaftesbury	02/52	
34036	Westward Ho	02/52	
34037	Clovelly	10/50	
34038	Lynton	05/52	
34039	Boscastle	08/49	
34040	Crewkerne	08/50	
34041	Wilton	06/51	
34042	Dorchester	11/51	
34043	Combe Martin	09/50	
34044	Woolacombe	12/50	
34045	Ottery St. Mary	05/50	
34046	Braunton	08/50	
34047	Callington	12/51	
34048	Crediton	08/52	

Number	Name	Date to Brunswick green	Experimental livery
34049	Anti-Aircraft Command	06/51	
34050	Royal Observer Corps	04/52	
34051	Winston Churchill	12/50	
34052	Lord Dowding	08/52	
34053	Sir Keith Park	01/51	
34054	Lord Beaverbrook	04/51	
34055	Fighter Pilot	05/51	
34056	Croydon	01/50	03/06/48
34057	Biggin Hill	04/51	
34058	Sir Frederick Pile	02/51	
34059	Sir Archibald Sinclair	04/51	
34060	25 Squadron	11/51	
34061	73 Squadron	10/49	
34062	17 Squadron	12/49	
34063	229 Squadron	07/51	
34064	Fighter Command	06/50	11/06/48
34065	Hurricane	03/51	12/06/48
34066	Spitfire	05/50	
34067	Tangmere	04/51	
34068	Kenley	09/50	
34069	Hawkinge	10/52	
34070	Manston	03/53	
34071	615 Squadron/601 Squadron	02/52	
34072	257 Squadron	04/52	
34073	249 Squadron	12/50	
34074	46 Squadron	06/50	
34075	264 Squadron	09/52	
34076	41 Squadron	09/50	
34077	603 Squadron	08/51	
34078	222 Squadron	08/51	
34079	141 Squadron	05/51	
34080	74 Squadron	08/51	
34081	92 Squadron	04/50	
34082	615 Squadron	09/50	
34083	605 Squadron	09/52	
34084	253 Squadron	03/50	
34085	501 Squadron	03/50	
34086	219 Squadron	10/50	02/12/48
34087	145 Squadron	10/50	17/12/48
34088	213 Squadron	12/50	22/12/48
34089	602 Squadron	06/50	
34090	Sir Eustace Missenden, Southern Railway	03/52	
34091	Weymouth	new	
34092	Wells/City of Wells	new	
34093	Saunton	new	
34094	Mortehoe	new	
34095	Brentor	new	
34096	Trevone	new	
34097	Holsworthy	new	
34098	Templecombe	new	
34099	Lynmouth	new	

Number	Name	Date to Brunswick green	Experimental livery
34100	*Appledore*	new	
34101	*Hartland*	new	
34102	*Lapford*	new	
34103	*Calstock*	new	
34104	*Bere Alston*	new	
34105	*Swanage*	new	
34106	*Lydford*	new	
34107	*Blandford/Blandford Forum*	new	
34108	*Wincanton*	new	
34109	*Sir Trafford Leigh Mallory*	new	
34110	*66 Squadron*	new	

Note: All of the Light Pacifics up to 09/49 first appeared in malachite green livery. The experimental livery was apple green with two widely spaced cream bands edged in red and grey.

APPENDIX 5 TENDERS AND MILEAGES: 'MERCHANT NAVY' CLASS

Number	Name	First tender	Final mileage
35001	Channel Packet	3111	1,095,884
35002	Union Castle	3112	1,101,914
35003	Royal Mail	3113	1,131,793
35004	Cunard White Star	3114	1,129,417
35005	Canadian Pacific	3115	976,806
35006	Peninsular & Oriental S. N. Co	3116	1,134,319
35007	Aberdeen Commonwealth	3117	1,318,765
35008	Orient Line	3118	1,286,418
35009	Shaw Savill	3119	1,127,452
35010	Blue Star	3120	1,241,929
35011	General Steam Navigation	3121	1,069,128
35012	United States Lines	3122	1,134,836
35013	Blue Funnel	3123	1,114,658
35014	Nederland Line	3124	1,062,394
35015	Rotterdam Lloyd	3126	813,950
35016	Elders Fyffes	3125	900,637
35017	Belgian Marine	3127	1,017,754
35018	British India Line	3129	956,544
35019	French Line C.G.T.	3128	947,344
35020	Bibby Line	3130	981,479
35021	New Zealand Line	3333 (BB)	859,661
35022	Holland America Line	3335 (BB)	903,542
35023	Holland–Afrika Line	3341	941,326
35024	East Asiatic Company	3333 (BB)	839,415
35025	Brocklebank Line	3343	884,081
35026	Lamport & Holt Line	3260 (WC)	858,784
35027	Port Line	3288 (WC)	872,290
35028	Clan Line	3344	794,391
35029	Ellerman Lines	3347	748,343
35030	Elder-Dempster Lines	3348	850,876

Notes: The mileages are taken from the locomotive cards, which ceased in 1964. Thereafter, the repair sheets were consulted and finally the motive power depot records. Consequently, the figures for locomotives withdrawn in 1967 may be lower than the acutal mileages.

BB   'Battle of Britain' class
WC   'West Country' class

APPENDIX 6 TENDERS AND MILEAGES: 'WEST COUNTRY' AND 'BATTLE OF BRITAIN' CLASSES

Number	Name	First tender	Final mileage
34001	Exeter	3251	1,079,957
34002	Salisbury	3252	1,003,613
34003	Plymouth	3253	811,674
34004	Yeovil	3254	920,972
34005	Barnstaple	3255	837,332
34006	Bude	3256	1,099,338
34007	Wadebridge	3257	823,193
34008	Padstow	3258	961,734
34009	Lyme Regis	3259	959,762
34010	Sidmouth	3260	922,906
34011	Tavistock	3261	800,455
34012	Launceston	3262	847,523
34013	Okehampton	3263	944,928
34014	Budleigh Salterto	3264	837,477
34015	Exmouth	3265	903,245
34016	Bodmin	3266	811,674
34017	Ilfracombe	3267	856,641
34018	Axminster	3268	974,317
34019	Bideford	3269	701,316
34020	Seaton	3270	789,688
34021	Dartmoor	3271	950,142
34022	Exmoor	3272	793,647
34023	Blackmoor Vale/Blackmore Vale	3273	921,268
34024	Tamar Valley	3274	839,964
34025	Rough Tor/Whimple	3275	872,938
34026	Yes Tor	3276	916,244
34027	Taw Valley	3277	764,316
34028	Eddystone	3278	851,549
34029	Lundy	3279	828,489
34030	Watersmeet	3280	744,279
34031	Torrington	3281	841,182
34032	Camelford	3282	853,398
34033	Chard	3283	884,916
34034	Honiton	3284	942,133
34035	Shaftesbury	3285	764,306
34036	Westward Ho	3286	894,546
34037	Clovelly	3287	810,658
34038	Lynton	3288	819,984
34039	Boscastle	3289	745,508
34040	Crewkerne	3290	769,624
34041	Wilton	3291	626,417
34042	Dorchester	3292	726,761
34043	Combe Martin	3293	749,112
34044	Woolacombe	3294	894,998
34045	Ottery St. Mary	3295	761,465
34046	Braunton	3296	779,210
34047	Callington	3297	845,991
34048	Crediton	3298	847,615
34049	Anti-Aircraft Command	3299	723,947

Number	Name	First tender	Final mileage
34050	*Royal Observer Corps*	3300	796,814
34051	*Winston Churchill*	3301	807,496
34052	*Lord Dowding*	3302	936,502
34053	*Sir Keith Park*	3303	825,317
34054	*Lord Beaverbrook*	3304	737,443
34055	*Fighter Pilot*	3305	706,607
34056	*Croydon*	3306	957,081
34057	*Biggin Hill*	3307	939,597
34058	*Sir Frederick Pile*	3308	812,586
34059	*Sir Archibald Sinclai*	3309	877,107
34060	*25 Squadron*	3310	934,417
34061	*73 Squadron*	3311	701,443
34062	*17 Squadron*	3312	836,576
34063	*229 Squadron*	3313	736,984
34064	*Fighter Command*	3314	759,666
34065	*Hurricane*	3315	730,489
34066	*Spitfire*	3316	652,908
34067	*Tangmere*	3317	688,269
34068	*Kenley*	3318	700,417
34069	*Hawkinge*	3319	673,643
34070	*Manston*	3320	702,614
34071	*615 Squadron/601 Squadron*	3321	782,028
34072	*257 Squadron*	3322	698,843
34073	*249 Squadron*	3323	684,325
34074	*46 Squadron*	3324	639,592
34075	*264 Squadron*	3325	643,241
34076	*41 Squadron*	3326	803,425
34077	*603 Squadron*	3327	745,642
34078	*222 Squadron*	3328	779,643
34079	*141 Squadron*	3329	765,302
34080	*74 Squadron*	3330	749,863
34081	*92 Squadron*	3331	741,511
34082	*615 Squadron*	3332	697,386
34083	*605 Squadron*	3333	737,467
34084	*253 Squadron*	3334	663,249
34085	*501 Squadron*	3335	661,415
34086	*219 Squadron*	3336	700,982
34087	*145 Squadron*	3337	704,638
34088	*213 Squadron*	3338	656,583
34089	*602 Squadron*	3339	661,252
34090	*Sir Eustace Missenden, Southern Railway*	3340	743,948
34091	*Weymouth*	3351	469,073
34092	*Wells/City of Wells*	3352	502,864
34093	*Saunton*	3353	888,004
34094	*Mortehoe*	3354	672,346
34095	*Brentor*	3355	796,614
34096	*Trevone*	3356	722,326
34097	*Holsworthy*	3357	743,659
34098	*Templecombe*	3358	819,105
34099	*Lynmouth*	3359	628,771
34100	*Appledore*	3360	712,916
34101	*Hartland*	3361	568,479

Number	Name	First tender	Final mileage
34102	*Lapford*	3362	593,438
34103	*Calstock*	3363	629,172
34104	*Bere Alston*	3364	678,853
34105	*Swanage*	3365	623,405
34106	*Lydford*	3366	691,443
34107	*Blandford/Blandford Forum*	3367	665,103
34108	*Wincanton*	3368	808,361
34109	*Sir Trafford Leigh Mallory*	3369	719,818
34110	*66 Squadron*	3370	609,147

Note: The mileages are taken from the locomotive record cards, which ceased in 1964. Thereafter, the repair sheets were consulted and finally the motive power depot records. Consequently, the figures for locomotives withdrawn in 1967 may be lower than the actual mileages.

APPENDIX 7 DISPOSAL: 'MERCHANT NAVY' CLASS

Disposal site	Numbers
J. Buttigieg, Newport, Monmouthshire	35007, 35008, 35013, 35017, 35023, 35030
John Cashmore Ltd, Newport, Monmouthshire	35003, 35012, 35014, 35019, 35026
Birds (Swansea) Ltd, Bridgend, Glamorgan	35016, 35021
Slag Reduction Co. Ltd, Rotherham, West Riding of Yorkshire	35002, 35015
Eastleigh Works, Hampshire	35020
Birds (Swansea) Ltd, Morriston, Swansea, Glamorgan	35001
Cohen's (cut up on site at Eastleigh)	35004
Ivor C. Woodfield & Sons, Town Dock, Newport, Monmouthshire	35024
Preserved	35005, 35006, 35009, 35010, 35011, 35018, 35022, 35025, 35027, 35028, 35029

APPENDIX 8 DISPOSAL:
'WEST COUNTRY' AND 'BATTLE OF BRITAIN' CLASSES

John Cashmore Ltd, Newport, Monmouthshire

34001, 34002, 34004, 34006, 34012, 34013, 34015, 34018, 34019, 34021, 34024, 34025, 34031, 34034, 34036, 34037, 34038, 34040, 34041, 34044, 34048, 34052, 34056, 34057, 34060, 34071, 34076, 34077, 34079, 34082, 34087, 34088, 34089, 34090, 34093, 34095, 34097, 34100

J. Buttigieg, Newport, Monmouthshire

34005, 34008, 34009, 34017, 34026, 34032, 34033, 34042, 34047, 34066, 34084, 34085, 34086, 34098, 34102, 34103, 34104, 34108

Eastleigh Works, Hampshire

34011, 34035, 34043, 34049, 34055, 34068, 34069, 34074, 34110

Birds (Swansea) Ltd, Bynea, Llanelli, Carmarthenshire

34020, 34030, 34054, 34065, 34078, 34080, 34096, 34106, 34107

Birds (Swansea) Ltd, Bridgend, Glamorgan

34014, 34062, 34063, 34064, 34075, 34083

Woods, Queenborough, Kent

34003, 34029, 34061, 34091

Birds (Swansea) Ltd, Morriston, Swansea, Glamorgan

34050, 34099, 34109

Woodham Bros, Barry, Glamorgan

34045, 34094

Ivor C. Woodfield & Sons, Town Dock, Newport, Monmouthshire

34022

Preserved

34007, 34010, 34016, 34023, 34027, 34028, 34039, 34046, 34051, 34053, 34058, 34059, 34067, 34070, 34072, 34073, 34081, 34092, 34101, 34105

BIBLIOGRAPHY

Allen, C.J., and Townroe, S.C. *Bulleid Pacifics of the Southern Region*, Ian Allan, 1951

Bradley, D.L. *Locomotives of the Southern Railway*, part 2, The Railway Correspondence and Travel Society, 1976

Creer, S., and Morrison, B. *The Power of the Bulleid Pacifics*, Oxford Publishing Company, 1983

Day-Lewis, S. *Bulleid, Last Giant of Steam*, George Allen & Unwin, 1964

Earnshaw, Dr A. *Steam for Scrap, The Complete Story*, Atlantic Transport Publishers, 1992

Fairclough, A., and Wills, A. *Southern Steam Locomotive Survey, The Bulleid Light Pacifics*, Bradford Barton

Fry, A.J. *Bulleid Power, The 'Merchant Navy' Class*, Alan Sutton Publishing, 1990

Haresnape, B. *Bulleid Locomotives*, Ian Allan, 1993

Madgin, H. *Preserved Stock*, Full Blast Publishing, 1996

Mannion, R.J. *The Duchess, Stanier's Masterpiece*, Sutton Publishing, 1996

——. *The Streaks, Gresley's A4s*, Sutton Publishing, 1997

Rogers, H.C.B. *Steam from Waterloo*, David & Charles, 1985

Turner, R.C. *Black Clouds and White Feathers* Oxford Publishing Company, 1990

Whitehouse, P., and Thomas St John, D. *The Great Days of the Southern Railway*, David St John Thomas, 1992

National Railway Museum records:
Spec/SR/8
Test/BR/11
Test/SR/1
Test/SR/2
Tech/SR/1
Locomotive Test Reports, SR 4–6–2 classes
  Southern Railway Report, No. 88, Jan. 1947
  Southern Railway Report, No. 89, Mar. 1947
British Transport Commission Bulletin, No. 10, Jan. 1954
British Transport Commission Bulletin, No. 20, 1958
Railways South East 1991–93
Locomotive/Rolling Stock Records, SR/BR 4–6–2 classes
  Engine History Cards, Hist/SR/4
  Loco Boiler History Cards, Boil/SR/13
  Correspondent Files, Corr/SR/1, Corr/SR/2, Corr/SR/3

INDEX